DON TROIANI'S

BLACK SOLDIERS IN AMERICA'S WARS
1754–1865

DON TROIANI'S
BLACK SOLDIERS IN AMERICA'S WARS
1754–1865

Don Troiani and John U. Rees
with James L. Kochan

STACKPOLE
BOOKS

Essex, Connecticut
Blue Ridge Summit, Pennsylvania

STACKPOLE BOOKS

An imprint of The Globe Pequot Publishing Group, Inc.
64 South Main Street
Essex, CT 06426
www.globepequot.com

Distributed by NATIONAL BOOK NETWORK

Paintings by Don Troiani

British Library Cataloguing in Publication Information available

Library of Congress Cataloging-in-Publication Data
Names: Troiani, Don, author, illustrator. | Rees, John U., author. |
  Kochan, James L., 1958– author.
Title: Don Troiani's Black soldiers in America's wars, 1754–1865 / Don
  Troiani and John U. Rees, with James Kochan.
Other titles: Black soldiers in America's wars, 1754–1865
Description: Essex, Connecticut : Stackpole Books, [2025] | Includes
  bibliographical references. | Summary: "Nationally renowned military
  artist Don Troiani teams with historian John Rees to highlight the role
  of under-recognized African American soldiers in America's early wars"—
  Provided by publisher.
Identifiers: LCCN 2024021770 (print) | LCCN 2024021771 (ebook) | ISBN
  9780811773713 (cloth) | ISBN 9780811773720 (epub)
Subjects: LCSH: African American soldiers—History. | United States—Armed
  Forces—African American troops. | United States—Armed Forces—African
  Americans. | African American soldiers—History—Pictorial works. |
  United States—Armed Forces—African American troops—Pictorial works. |
  United States—Armed Forces—African Americans—Pictorial works. | War
  in art.
Classification: LCC E185.63 .T76 2025 (print) | LCC E185.63 (ebook) | DDC
  355.0089/96073—dc23/eng/20240516
LC record available at https://lccn.loc.gov/2024021770
LC ebook record available at https://lccn.loc.gov/2024021771

Printed in India

This work is, first of all, dedicated to Linda, without whose support my avocation/ obsession/life's-work would not have been possible. To Marcus Rediker, who provided inspiration; to Don Troiani and Andrew Bamford, who gave me invaluable opportunities. And to Matthew C. White, close friend and cousin, without whose insights this work would have been a very different tome.
John Rees

To those who fought for this country past and present.
Don

Contents

Preface. *"Many of our Fathers fought and died . . ."* ix

CHAPTER 1.   *"Brought to this country and sold as a slave"*:
From Africa to the Americas. 1

CHAPTER 2.   *"The thundering of the great guns"*:
French and Indian War (1754–1763). 4

CHAPTER 3.   *"Life, Liberty, and the Pursuit of Happiness"*:
The War of the American Revolution (1775–1783) 14

CHAPTER 4.   *"If we mean to be what we ought to be"*:
Interwar Years through the War of 1812 (1791–1815) 72

CHAPTER 5.   *"Our Lives for Liberty"*: American Civil War Era
(1842–1865) 98

Afterword 139

Acknowledgments. 141

Notes. 142

Suggested Further Reading. 150

Preface

"Many of our Fathers fought and died . . ."[1]

In February 1831 Philadelphia Black businessman, abolitionist, and Revolutionary veteran James Forten wrote William Lloyd Garrison, editor of the newly founded antislavery newspaper the *Liberator*. In essence Forten spoke against the American Colonization Society, an organization founded in 1816 to purchase and free American slaves, then send them to resettle on Africa's west coast. He ended his missive with this note:

> According to a statement made by [ACS member] Mr. [Francis Scott] Key they have removed in 14 years, about as many hundred Emigrants. I will venture to say that at least a half Million [Black Americans] have been born during the same period. We ask not their compassion and aid, in assisting us to emigrate to Africa, we are contented in this land that gave us birth, and which many of us fought for, and many of our Fathers fought and died, during the war which established our Independence.[2]

Forten recalls the soldiers and seamen of African descent who served in integrated Continental Army and militia units, as well as on naval vessels, for the cause of American independence. He continued,

> I well remember that when the New England Regiment marched through this city [on September 2, 1781], on their way to attack the English Army under the command of Lord Cornwallis, there was several Companies of Coloured People, as brave Men as ever fought and I saw those brave soldiers who fought at the Battle of Red Bank, under Col. Green, where Count Donop the Commander was killed, and the Hessians defeated—all this appears to be forgotten now—and the descendants of these Men, to whom we are indebted for the part they took in the struggle for Independence, are intended to be removed to a distant and inhospitable Country, while the Emigrants from every other Country, are permitted to seek an asylum here from oppression, and to enjoy the Blessings of both Civil and Religious Liberty, equally with those who are entitled to it by Birth Right—[3]

The "New England Regiment" he tells of was the Rhode Island Regiment, reintegrated in early 1781, having two companies of African and Native American soldiers, and seven white companies. On October 22, 1777, just over three months before the 1st Rhode Island Regiment was reorganized to contain only Black and Indian private soldiers, it was a fully integrated unit fighting, with its brother Second Regiment, in the Battle of Fort Mercer at Red Bank, New Jersey. That event, as James Forten rightfully recalls, was a small but seminal victory for the American cause, and further proof that, alongside their white and Native comrades, men of African descent could stand steadfastly against an overwhelming force of well-trained European troops and win. It was also, as he notes, ample evidence that Black Americans deserved the rights enjoyed by their white-skinned brethren.[4]

James Forten's claim of civil rights for Black men and women would have resonated with the concerns of most, if not all, soldiers of African descent fighting in North America, from 1754 to 1865. Whether they entered military service as persons long-free, newly emancipated, or yet-enslaved, these Black men had some connection to, and care for, the enslavement of African people by white inhabitants of North America and the Caribbean Islands. Add to that, by default the mere color of their skin transformed them into an underclass, and, in some locales, liable to possible re-enslavement.[5]

While the subject of this work is Black men (mostly free or freedmen) serving as soldiers from the mid-eighteenth century to the second third of the nineteenth century, early on they had much in common with some compatriots in the white, non-propertied, lower classes. In seventeenth-century Britain, landless, jobless, rootless, impoverished, imprisoned, and rebellious people (men, women, and children) were sometimes sent overseas, essentially non-free. As Peter Linebaugh and Marcus Rediker note, prior to the mid-seventeenth century, before the influx of large numbers of kidnapped Africans, "whether waged or unwaged, the hewers of wood and drawers of water were slaves, though the difference was not yet racialized." The disparity in their circumstances was, if white bonds-people survived, they or their descendants eventually gained their freedom and could become landholders; the color of their skin did not keep them in perpetual slavery or denigration. By contrast, in 1621 "Antonio, a Negro," possibly from Angola, arrived in bondage at the Jamestown colony. By 1625 he was listed as a "servant," and at some point before 1641 he was known as Anthony Johnson, a landowner. Having married "Mary a Negro woman," Johnson raised livestock, and even acquired his own Black servant. By 1650 Anthony Johnson had 250 acres of land along the Pungoteague Creek on Virginia's eastern shore, plus five servants. In early 1670, Anthony Johnson died, passing on his property to his descendants. That August a white jury decided that Anthony's landholdings could be seized by the colony "because he was a Negroe and by consequence an alien." Johnson had gifted his son Richard fifty acres, where he had lived five years with his wife and family; as a result of the jury decision, that land was acquired by George Parker, a white neighbor. Like Anthony Johnson's family, the Africans who followed him (free and unfree, civilians, soldiers, and sailors) learned that in a white-ruled realm, people of color could take nothing for granted.[6]

1. *"Brought to this country and sold as a slave"*[1]

From Africa to the Americas

Any wide study of soldiers of African descent during this period must address the elephant in the room: How did large numbers of people from Africa arrive during the seventeenth, eighteenth, and nineteenth centuries on the North American continent and in the Caribbean?

While some people of African descent had been present in Europe since at least the Middle Ages, the advent of the European slave trade resulted in a vast diaspora of Black peoples. The trafficking began in the mid-fifteenth century when Portuguese vessels began to raid the West African coast; among the captured "goods" were human beings. From that point into the first half of the seventeenth century, Portugal was the leading mover of enslaved Africans, the largest proportion of which were shipped to the Spanish colonies. In the eighteenth century, England dominated the trade in enslaved Africans to North America and the English Caribbean islands. The bulk of the ships sailed from Liverpool, London, and Bristol in England, and Newport in Rhode Island, and the greatest number of slaves were destined for the Caribbean. There, enslaved workers' lives and abilities were cut short by hard labor, poor provisions, and disease, so much so, that there was a constant need for new imports to account for attrition.[2]

Between 1628 and 1860, some 390,000 Africans were imported to mainland North America, while from 1606 to 1807 approximately 2.3 million disembarked in the British Caribbean islands, with almost half of those going to Jamaica. On the mainland, the Northern town of Newport handled the majority of incoming slave ships for New England, while Charleston, South Carolina, was the main Southern slave port. (Most human chattel slated for the mainland arrived directly from Africa, but a portion was shipped from Caribbean ports.)[3] Kenneth Morgan notes,

> most slaves [were] clustered south of the Delaware [River] Valley. In 1750, for instance, 210,400 (86.9 percent) of the 242,100 slaves in North America lived in the Chesapeake and Lower South. On the eve of the American War of Independence less than 3 per cent of the New England population and less than 8 per cent of the Middle Colonies' population was black. . . . By 1780 the black share of the Chesapeake population [was] . . . 39 per cent, while the African-American element in the Carolinas and Georgia [was] . . . 41 per cent.[4]

These ratios can be compared to the British Caribbean islands, which had a populace "more than five-sixths [83.3 percent] slave." In French Saint-Domingue in 1789, on the eve of the unrest there, the enslaved formed almost 90 percent of the island's inhabitants, and in Spanish Florida, "the slave population rose from 29 percent of the total in 1784 to 53 percent in 1814." To these must be added small numbers of free Blacks and maroons (escaped slaves who formed their own permanent enclaves in mountainous or wilderness areas).[5]

While the British Africa trade waned in the 1780s and 1790s, other nations continued and even increased importation. Between 1775 and 1807 fifteen thousand enslaved Africans landed on Puerto Rico, Jamaica, and Cuba. Still, slavery came under attack in unprecedented ways. Debate and activism within the British world, but especially in the colonies (then states) to the north of Maryland, manifested in Pennsylvania's 1780 "Act for the Gradual Abolition of Slavery"—an unprecedented piece of legislation that pioneered similar legislation or judicial rulings in other Northern states. After two-and-a-half years of Black revolution in Saint-Domingue, in February 1794 the French National Assembly abolished slavery in their colonial possessions (it was already banned in the homeland). On March 25, 1807, George III signed "An Act for the Abolition of the Slave Trade," the legislation taking effect May 1. That same year the U.S. Congress passed the "Act Prohibiting the Importation of Slaves," which went into effect on January 1, 1808. Despite those bans, slave smuggling continued into the mid-to-late nineteenth century. In July 1860, the schooner *Clotilda* carried into Alabama's Mobile Bay the last load of imported slaves to reach the United States, consisting of 109 men, women, and children.[6]

Though the Africa trade was now unlawful, enslavement of Africans continued. On July 31, 1833, the British Parliament passed the Emancipation Act, to take effect on the same date in 1834. Relying on a six-year apprenticeship, enslaved inhabitants were not to be released until 1840, but circumstances advanced British Caribbean emancipation to July 31, 1838. During the American Civil War (1861–1865), following the September 1862 Antietam battle, President Abraham Lincoln issued the Emancipation Proclamation; taking effect on January 1, 1863, that proclamation freed slaves only in the rebelling states. In January 1865, three months before the war's end, the House of Representatives passed the Thirteenth Amendment to the Constitution, abolishing slavery in the United States. President Lincoln approved it in February, and by December 6, 1865, it was ratified by the needed three-fourths of the states.[7]

From 1754 to 1783 substantial numbers of men and women of African descent, free and enslaved, worked or fought in North America's wars for the belligerent powers. Some portion of those were among the first of their generation to come directly from Africa. Five men have been found who told of their origin in nineteenth-century pension applications; many others likely had the same background, but the facts went unrecorded or have yet to be discovered.[8] One man's account will stand in for all; Massachusetts veteran Prince Dunsick testified in his 1819 deposition:

When I was about eight years of age, I was stolen from Africa, my native country, and brought to America; my native name was Prince Dunsick—but on my arrival I was called by my master's name which was Bailey. By this name of Prince Bailey, I enlisted and served in the Revolutionary War . . . and was discharged by the same name. I never lived with my old master Bailey afterwards, and resumed my former name of Dunsick.[9]

The specific ethnicity of Africans enslaved in North America and the Caribbean poses some difficulty. Period sources reveal numerous possibilities, by no means all-encompassing. First, a single shipment of kidnapped Africans was not necessarily monolithic. One Englishman wrote in 1689, "the means used by those who trade to Guinea [west coast of Africa], to keep the Negroes quiet, is to choose them from several parts of ye Country, of different Languages; so they cannot act jointly." Daniel Horsmanden wrote of the Africans involved in the 1741 New York insurrection, "they are brought from different parts of Africa."[10] Of the participants, Linebaugh and Rediker note:

The leading cell was made up of Africans from the Gold Coast of West Africa, the Akan-speaking people who were known by the name of the slave-trading fort from which they were shipped: Coromantee (or, in Fante, Kromantse). Many a "Coromantee" had been okofokum, a common soldier trained in firearms and hand-to-hand combat in one of the mass armies of West Africa's militarized, expansionist states (Akwamu, Denkyira, Asante, Fante), before being captured and shipped to America.[11]

Other participants in the New York uprising originally belonged to the Papa (near Whydah on the Slave Coast—present-day Togo, Benin, and western Nigeria), Igbo (Niger River vicinity), and Malagasay (from Madagascar) ethnic groups.[12]

Some slaveowners had their preferences, affecting regional enslaved populations. Charleston port records show that 39 percent of enslaved Africans originated in Angola, 20 percent from Senegambia, 17 percent from the Windward Coast, 13 percent from the Gold Coast, 6 percent from Sierra Leone, and 5 percent (combined) from Madagascar, Mozambique, and the Bights of Benin and Biafra. Africans of the Congo and Angola ethnicities formed the core of the insurgents in the 1739 Stono Rebellion near Charleston, South Carolina. Those groups were present in eighteenth-century Virginia as well, but records indicate that 38 percent originated in the Bight of Biafra, and included Igbo, Tiv, Asante, Ibibio, Fon, and other ethnicities. Jeffery Brace, a Connecticut Revolutionary veteran and former slave, wrote of his African home, located in the modern country of Mali, but his specific ethnic group is unknown.[13]

More easily known than specific ethnicities is that Africans transported by British and American carriers to North America and the Caribbean came from these regions:

West-Central Africa, 27 percent of North American/
    Caribbean slave trade (modern Congo, Angola)
Senegambia, 22 percent (Senegal, Gambia, Guinea-Bissau)
Bight of Biafra, 17 percent (Southeast Nigeria,
    Cameroon, Gabon)
Gold Coast, 12 percent (Ghana)
Sierra Leone, 11 percent (Sierra Leone, Guinea)
Windward Coast, 6 percent (Liberia, Ivory Coast)
Bight of Benin, 3 percent (Togo, Benin, Southwest Nigeria)
Southeast Africa, 2 percent (Madagascar, Mozambique)[14]

These were the points of embarkation where the grandparents or great-grandparents of the Black soldiers we are studying, or perhaps the soldiers themselves, had their last sight of the land of their birth.

Charleston, South Carolina, entry port for hundreds of thousands of slaves, was the only city with a strict regulatory system for hiring out enslaved people that required them to wear standardized identification tags. Each "slave tag," suspended from the neck, was inscribed with the city's name, serial number, year issued, and wearer's occupation. Known examples bear the occupations servant, house servant, porter, fruiterer, fisher, and mechanic. To participate in the program, slaveholders paid a one-year licensing fee, which varied according to the bearer's occupation. When leased to an individual, business, or local government, the slave was required to wear the tag constantly and could perform only the listed vocation. (Benjamin Weiss, "Medallic History of Slavery: Racial Oppression as Chronicled by Historical and Commemorative Medals," 54–57.)

2. *"The thundering of the great guns"* [1]

French and Indian War (1754–1763)

The Seven Years' War, instigated by events in North America, was fought across the world; in Europe, on the coast of Africa, the Indian subcontinent, and into the Pacific, with corresponding and crucial naval actions. The conflict was largely a white man's war, though it would certainly affect colonial possessions and the people of color, free and enslaved, in their populations. The Native inhabitants of North America allied themselves according to which side they considered as best serving their interests. As one theater of the larger conflict, from 1754 to 1762 the American mainland and Caribbean saw numerous military operations, the bulk of which were centered in northern New York and French Canada. French and British regular regiments contained only white soldiers, but for the latter, free and enslaved Blacks served as officers' waiters, wagon and packhorse drivers, and general laborers. During the 1762 siege of Havana, Cuba, the British purchased or hired slaves from Jamaica, Antigua, St. Christopher, and Martinique islands to assist in building siege-works and relieve soldiers from some arduous duties. But men of African descent, free and enslaved, served as armed soldiers in most American Provincial units. Free Blacks, liable for militia service, generally saw themselves as both British and African, and an integral element of the empire; enslaved men served with little or no choice of their own. [2]

The American French and Indian War witnessed enslaved Africans enlisted as soldiers and sailors, with or without their owners' permission. Because of the large disparity between French Canada (approximately 4,000 slaves—some 2,800 Indians and 1,200 Africans) and British North America (in 1750, some 242,000 enslaved Africans), King George's regular and Provincial forces resorted to enslaved labor on a much larger scale than French forces. Fortification and roadbuilding, carrying water, cutting and hauling wood, caring for and herding livestock: These are only a few of the much-needed tasks Black slaves and freedmen performed. [3]

Enslaved men were impressed into the Royal Navy, or joined of their own volition to escape bondage. In October 1762 Vice-Admiral Alexander Colville took aboard HMS *Northumberland*, without permission, several slaves to replace "thirty of her best Seamen [dead] by a Malignant Fever" and "a much greater number at the Hospital." He informed the admiralty secretary, "these Negroe Slaves shared the same Fate with such freeborn White Men, as we could pick up at a very critical time, for his Majesty's Service." Slaveowners who demanded their property be returned were often refused. Slaves belonging to ship's officers often augmented the crew; African and late-eighteenth-century abolitionist Olaudah Equiano, who purchased his freedom in 1766, at one time belonged to British lieutenant Michael Pascal. He was in several naval actions, and at the sieges of Louisbourg and Havana. While aboard the ship *Roebuck*, Equiano helped work the vessel, at sail and in combat. Jeffrey Brace (named after British commander in chief Jeffrey Amherst), who was manumitted after service as a Continental soldier in the War of the Revolution, belonged to a ship's captain, also served as a seaman, seeing action off the American coast and Cuba. [4]

The first British campaign in the Americas was Major General Edward Braddock's 1755 expedition to capture Fort Duquesne, an important French outpost at the confluence of the Ohio, Monongahela, and Allegheny Rivers (present-day Pittsburgh, Pennsylvania). Leaving Fort Cumberland, Maryland, on May 29, the army needed to march northwest, while at the same time building a road through a wilderness of trees and mountains, 115 miles in all. Two British regular regiments formed the core of Braddock's army; they were seconded by Provincial units from Virginia, Maryland, and North and South Carolina. Little is known of the composition of the last three states' military organizations in the 1755 campaign, but Virginia's companies did contain some Blacks. [5]

An advertisement in the February 28 *Virginia Gazette* called for the return of two men, possibly belonging to the Virginia Regiment:

> Deserted the following Recruits, from King-William County . . . Joseph Coupland, about 20 Years of Age . . . a Shoemaker by Trade, stoops pretty much in his Walk . . . [and] William Holmes a Mullatoe, about 45 Years of Age, is about six feet high, Whoever secures the said Deserters . . . shall have a Guinea [21 shilling] Reward for Copeland, and a Pistole [sixteen shillings] for Holmes. [6]

William Holmes left his unit prior to the summer 1755 expedition, but we know that the Virginians did enlist or hire free Blacks as packhorse drivers and officers' personal servants. Despite their menial role, and the state stricture against arming African Americans, as the column marched farther into enemy territory, General Braddock ordered that all menials be issued and carry arms. When disaster befell British and Provincial forces on July 9, some eight miles from Fort Duquesne, the packhorse drivers, Black and white, were involved in the action and a number were killed and wounded. [7] In 1788 an enslaved African turned up in Carlisle, Pennsylvania, claiming to have taken part in Braddock's expedition:

> taken up . . . a [Negro] male, named William, supposed to be above forty years old, from the following assertions:— That he came from Guinea to America, and served as a

waiting boy at Braddock's defeat, the taking of Canada, the seiges of the Havana [*sic*], and was part of that time in the retinue of General, then Colonel Washington; is about five feet six inches high, has many scars in his back, from severity of whipping, and remarkable for the abridgement of his fingers by frost; more particularly those of his right hand; wears a broken coarse woolen coattee and a much worn royal rib buff breeches . . . [he belongs] to a Mr. Thomas Violet, nine miles from Winchester, Virgina [*sic*], and departed thence about three weeks ago . . . [currently lodged at] Carlisle Gaol.[8]

From 1754 to 1757, and 1759 to 1762, Virginia had only a single Provincial regiment; two regiments were authorized for Brigadier General John Forbes's 1758 Expedition against Fort Duquesne. Following the July 1755 disaster, Colonel Washington, Virginia Regiment commander, complained of a shortfall in white enlistment; with authorization from the Virginia assembly, on December 27 he wrote one of his captains, "I think it will be advisable to detain both Mulatto's and Negroes in your Company; and employ them as Pioneers or Hatchet-men." Those roles signified military laborers; if occupied by Black men, they would enable more whites to serve as arms-bearing soldiers. Unlike packhorse drivers and servants, the men who served in these positions wore the uniform of their company or regiment. The practice continued till the war's conclusion, but due to the fear of slave insurrection, Southern men of African descent were sometimes denied the opportunity to serve in any soldierly role. Research has revealed seven Black men in the Virginia Regiment in 1756 and 1757. The listings provide some descriptive information; the men's ages ranged from seventeen to forty years old, and all but one were planters. In August 1757 Captain Thomas Waggener's company contained William Combs, a mulatto, age thirty-nine, height five feet, six inches, and James Pompey, "Negro," five foot four, and twenty-two years old. That same year Samuel Howel, a mulatto, twenty-five years of age, five feet ten inches high, and a sawyer by trade, was in Captain Robert Spotswood's Company.[9] Another man, "free negro" Matthew Roberts, had been a Virginia soldier, and was "entitled to 50 acres of land by His Majesty's Proc. of 1763. Dec. 16, 1773. [signed] Dunmore."

North American slaveowners were justifiably concerned about slave uprisings. Marcus Rediker notes, "Between 1730 and 1742 unfree workers [in North America and the Caribbean] organized more than eighty conspiracies, insurrections, and mass runaways—six or seven times as many as in the dozen years before or after." The 1739 Stono Rebellion, near Charleston, South Carolina, was the mainland's largest, involving some seventy-five slaves and ending with the deaths of twenty whites and forty-four Blacks. And in 1741 a conspiracy between Irish soldiers and free and unfree Africans resulted in an aborted uprising in New York City. In the aftermath, thirty Blacks and four whites were tried and executed.[10]

North Carolina had several foot and garrison companies, and, at times, a single regiment or battalion. North Carolina troops were largely deployed to protect the colony's frontier, but one company supported Braddock's expedition, four

companies served in New York in 1756, and a battalion took part in Forbes's 1758 campaign. Fourteen Black soldiers have been found in three North Carolina companies. In 1755 Captain Abner Neale's Craven County, North Carolina, company contained five "Free Negroes" listed separately from the white soldiers: James Black, Abel Carter, John Carter, Jacob Copes, and Peter George.[11]

Maryland's militia law exempted "all Negroes and slaves" from training, effectively barring them from military service, and Pennsylvania seems to have had little to no Black presence in their military units. The Pennsylvania Regiment (authorized in summer 1756) resorted to enlisting European indentured servants, paying their masters a small sum, plus allowing them half their former bondsmen's military pay in recompense. South Carolina, Georgia, and Virginia were backward in contributing troops for Crown campaigns, blaming recruitment shortages and fear of insurrection; in 1756 South Carolina governor William Lyttelton told Commander in Chief John Campbell, Earl of Loudoun, of "the number of Negro's [*sic*] in this province which greatly overbalances that of the whites & who in case of an Attack might prove an Intestine Enemy."[12] Despite that, South Carolina armed free Blacks and slaves for militia service to make up for a shortfall in white recruits. Maria Bollettino relates several examples, including,

"A General Return of the Officers and Men in the Charles Town Regiment of Foot" [that] reveals that Colonel Othniel Beale commanded five militia companies in 1756, which together consisted of 744 effective private men, 137 alarm men, and 608 slaves. Each militia company enrolled between 100 and 150 enslaved black men alongside an only slightly higher number of white militiamen. Moreover, it is likely that black slaves in reality often outnumbered white privates, as fewer white men joined their companies at musters than were enumerated on the rolls.[13]

While Southern colonies' militaries were sidetracked by manpower difficulties, fear of slave rebellion, and, in 1760 and 1761, warfare with the Cherokee nation, provinces from New Jersey northward were heavily involved in the war for empire. One result was that, as Maria Bollettino writes, "Northern black men participated in battles from Nova Scotia to Cuba, affording them the opportunity to scope out new lands for purchase or new prospects for employment."[14]

While the Delaware Provincial troops are at present too-little known, Charles Fithian has been attempting to rectify that shortfall. The colony was a singular political entity, in that it was headed by the governor of Pennsylvania, but had its own separate legislative assembly. The colony's three counties (termed the Lower Counties, as regards Pennsylvania) provided only logistical support for Braddock's 1755 expedition, and the expired militia law was not reinstituted until March 1756. When the militia was organized, New Castle County had two regiments, while Kent and Sussex Counties each had one. In 1758 they raised troops, sending 300 men, including Black and Indian soldiers, to take part in Brigadier General John Forbes's expedition to take Fort Duquesne. An October 1758 inspection roll dated Rays Town (on the Juniata River, halfway between Lancaster and Fort Duquesne) shows 215 men in three Delaware companies "on advanced posts" or "on the frontier." In 1759 "3 Companies of the Lower Counties" were serving as part of the Pennsylvania Regiment's 3rd Battalion. Fourteen Delaware soldiers fought at or near Fort Duquesne on September 14, 1758; two were listed "killed or missing." Only a few Black Delaware soldiers are known, though more likely served: Suthy Jackson of Worcester, Maryland, black complexion, twenty years old, shoemaker, and Suthy Pride of Indian River, Sussex County, brown complexion, age eighteen, farmer, both of Captain John McClughan's company, May 22, 1758. Suthy Pride may have been all or part Native American; four other men were listed as Indian.[15]

New Jersey fielded a single Provincial regiment that saw hard service in the Northern campaigns, plus several ranger, frontier guard, and garrison companies. The colony's General Assembly was proactive in recruiting free Blacks, passing legislation in April 1755 titled, "An act to encourage the Enlisting of Five Hundred Freeman or Well-affected Indians . . . for his Majesty's Service in the Present Expedition" against Crown Point, New York. There is no evidence those men were ever recruited in any substantial number, and information on individual New Jersey soldiers of color remains yet to be discovered.[16]

Men of color (Black, mulatto, mustee, and Native) were scattered throughout New York's Provincial contingent. Edward H. Knoblauch studied preparations for the 1760 campaign, when New York asked for volunteers, then, still needing troops, drafted men from the militia to serve in the colony's three Provincial regiments. Their goal was to reinforce Crown forces in Canada. Regarding that, the 1760 Army Act stated "that all free Negroes, and mustee and mulattoe Freemen, within this Colony, shall be and hereby are made liable to be detached on the aforesaid Service . . . notwithstanding any Indenture or Indentures of Servitude they, or any of them may be under." Knoblauch notes, "that the [New York] muster rolls of 1760 indicate that 2,277 men were of European ancestry, 59 were native North American, 24 African, 16 of mixed European and African ancestry, and 12 of mixed [Native] American and African ancestry."[17] He then goes into more detail:

> Men of non-European ancestry who joined the provincial forces were not evenly distributed from county to county. Suffolk County [Long Island] raised 280 men, not counting officers. Those of European descent account for 226 (80.7 percent); those of native North American descent for 43 (15.4 percent); men described as "Mustees" [mixed African-Indian] for 9 (3.2 percent); and those called "Mulattoe" for 2 (0.7 percent). Jonathan Baker's company, raised from the Eastern battalion of the Suffolk County Militia, was 25 percent of non-European descent.[18]

Suffolk County muster rolls from 1758 and 1759 show a similar mix of "Negro," "Molato" (aka "Yellow"), "Mustee," and Indian soldiers. All the men were listed with a modicum of personal data—here are some of African descent in the 1760 companies: John Johnson ("Negro"), age twenty-one, born on the island of Nevis, by trade a cooper; Peter Calumpoe ("Negro"), age thirty, born in Spain, and worked as a "mariner"; the same for his two companions Theodo Twawoolshead ("Negro"), and Peter Jamey ("Dark Mulatto"); and lastly, Josiah ("Mustee"), thirty years old, born in Southold, Long Island, a laborer. Three other men of color were born in Pennsylvania; Schenectady, New York; and Stockbridge, Massachusetts Connecticut.[19]

Enslaved men in this period, and through the War of the Revolution, occasionally tried to find freedom in the army by enlisting. The May 19, 1760, *New-York Gazette* advertised, "Run Away from his Master Theodorius Van Wyck, of Dutchess County . . . a Negro man names James, age about 22 Years, a short, well made Fellow . . . supposed [to be going] to Albany to inlist into the Army." He was captured near Livingston Manor, but managed to escape. In November that same year Toby Hazard left his owner; possibly of mixed Afro-Indian heritage, he had "hair not like a Negro's, but a little longer," somewhere "between an Indian and a Negro." Passing as a free man, Hazard joined a New York provincial company and after receiving his pay or bounty, "absconded, in order as 'tis supposed to escape by Sea."[20]

Without exception, the New England colonies allowed Black men to serve under arms. Total numbers are unknown, but after the first large battle in the North, at least one man gave them kudos. Six New England Provincial regiments (three Massachusetts, two Connecticut, and one Rhode Island), plus three New York companies and a New Hampshire detachment, fought under Major General William Johnson at the Battle of Lake George on September 8, 1755. After a daylong, hard-fought series of actions, Crown forces were victorious. In a September 10 letter, an anonymous gunner serving under William Eyres (director of Johnson's artillery and captain, 44th Regiment) claimed that during the action, "our Blacks behaved better than the Whites."[21]

For most of the war Rhode Island's military contingent consisted of a single regiment, increased to two only in 1756 and 1757. In 1762 a three-company "Cuba Detachment" participated in the June to August siege of Havana (Provincial troops from New Jersey, New York, and Connecticut also took part). A compilation of Rhode Islanders who served in the Seven Years' War includes twenty-two men of African descent, including eight who sailed on privateers in 1757 and 1758, nine who served in 1757, one enlisted in 1758 and 1759, one in 1760, and three in 1762. Among them were George Mew of Warwick, taken prisoner at the capture of Fort William Henry, and Pomp Greenman, who on September 6, 1762, died in Havana.[22]

New Hampshire contributed two regiments for the war's first full year, one regiment (captured at Fort William Henry) and a battalion in 1757, and a single regiment for all other years, plus ranger and garrison companies. Several veterans of color are known. Free Black Samuel Perham constructed batteaux in 1755, before joining William Johnson's forces at Lake George, where he fought in the September battle. Caesar Nero, who served in Captain Richard Emery's company, was captured at Fort William Henry in August 1757. Owned by Exeter resident John Gilman, Nero was held for three years and was returned to slavery upon his 1760 release. And Cuffe Noakes took part in the 1756 operations against Crown Point, New York.[23]

For most of the war Connecticut fielded four Provincial regiments, plus a number of other company-size and larger units. As for Connecticut's soldiers of color, Harold Selesky writes:

> Black men, both slave and free, also enlisted, but their numbers are difficult to determine. In 1756, the year the census counted 3,019 black people in the colony, there were 25 soldiers with names like Prince Negro, Jupiter Negro, and Solomon Scipio in the regiments, roughly 1 percent of the total [black population]. More black men undoubtedly served, but they are impossible to distinguish by name alone. An advertisement for deserters . . . described twenty-three-year-old Hezekiah Wright of Norwich as a "molatto," but the fact that he was a black man is evident nowhere else in the record.[24]

Connecticut free Black Prince Goodin served as a sailor on Lake George in 1757; captured and sold into slavery by the French or their Native allies, he remained so for three years until Montreal was taken, when he was released to return home. Gershom (Garshom) Prince, enslaved by Connecticut lieutenant Robert Durkee, accompanied Durkee on campaign and participated in the 1755 Lake George battle, as well as the 1762 Havana siege. During the War of the Revolution Prince may have served with Captain Robert Durkee's Connecticut Independent company until that officer's resignation from Continental service in May/June 1778. Incorporated with the local militia, Prince Gershom and Robert Durkee were both killed at the July 3, 1778, Battle of Wyoming.[25]

Regarding numbers, we know that Connecticut called for 2,500 men in 1756, but were only able to raise 2,339; taking the minimum of twenty-five Black soldiers found for that year shows that they made up *at least* 1 percent of the total. This can be compared with the August 1778 "Return of the Negroes in the Army," which covered fifteen brigades of General George Washington's army, totaling 20,771 troops. The percentage of men of African descent (possibly only the enslaved soldiers) for the whole was 3.63 percent; in Samuel Parsons's and Jedediah Huntington's Connecticut brigades, Black soldiers counted comprised 9.31 and 4.90 percent respectively.[26]

As the largest province above the Mason-Dixon Line, and with a bigger white population than Virginia, Massachusetts likely fielded more Black soldiers in the war than any other province. In 1756 the colony called for 3,000 men in six regiments, the next year only 1,800 soldiers, but for the campaigns of 1758 and 1759 authorized 7,000 men for each year.[27]

One man, John Bush, and his family, will serve to represent Black Massachusetts provincials. Bush first served in the latter stages of King George's War (1744–1748), at times being stationed at Fort No. 4 and Fort Dummer on the Connecticut River in New Hampshire. John had two brothers who took part in the 1750s war; Joseph served with Brown's Regiment in the 1755 Crown Point Expedition and died in April 1756, likely of an illness contracted in camp, while George enlisted in April 1759 and "died in service . . . [in] October 1759." John, a mulatto, enlisted in Dwight's Massachusetts Regiment in November 1755, likely serving at Fort William Henry until November 1756. On March 14, 1756, he transferred as

a "centinel" (private soldier) to Captain Joseph Ingersoll's company, and that October was appointed captain's clerk. John Bush signed on again in 1757, serving in Colonel Jonathan Bagley's Massachusetts Regiment at Fort William Henry, on the southern end of Lake George in New York. While serving in the military, John augmented his pay by engraving powder horns for fellow soldiers (his first known carved horn dates from 1747). Among others, he decorated horns for Captain Robert Rogers (of Rogers' Rangers) and Ranger Captain Israel Putnam, later a major general in the Continental Army. John Bush was with the Fort William Henry garrison during the six-day August siege, surrendering with the garrison on the 9th. Rumors spread afterward of wholesale massacre by French-allied Natives as the defeated British marched from the fort, and that Black members of the army were the first to be taken and killed. In fact, the Indians and some French, knowing Black slaves were valuable, pulled men of African descent from the ranks in order to sell them later. There *were* horrible depredations, but they were exaggerated, and of the 1,500-man garrison, some 385 soldiers and civilian followers were killed, and another 300 to 500 taken captive. Somehow, perhaps because he was a very light-skinned mulatto, John Bush was not enslaved, but remained with the other prisoners redeemed from the Indians.[28]

Having lost one son already and worried about John, George Bush Sr. wrote the Massachusetts governor:

Shrewsbury Sept ye 14th 1758

Honrl. Sr. I have a Son In Captivity at Cannady if he be Living that was Taken Last year at Lake George when yt was redused / I never have heard from him since he was Taken, only when our men etonedt hay say he was not killed but Carried of[f] by the Indens: his Naime is John Bush a melattor [i.e., mulatto] Fellow about 30 years of Eage: pray sr. if their be any opportunity to Exchang[e] Captives let my Son be Remembred

In So Doing your Honbl. Sarvent will Be much obliged George Bush[29]

Unfortunately, John Bush's luck did not hold. The October 12, 1758, *Boston News-Letter* published a list of men who had been shipped overseas, including Bush and five others who had "died on board in their Passage to France." As his father pleaded, "let my Son be Remembred."[30]

1757, Massachusetts Provincial Soldier

The New England regiments formed the backbone of British North American Provincial forces during the 1754–1763 French and Indian War. Massachusetts Bay edged out Connecticut in numbers of troops contributed, but both colonies had proportionately substantial numbers of Black men serving in the ranks throughout the conflict.

In 1754 Massachusetts governor William Shirley set in train a campaign against French Fort Saint Frédéric, on Crown Point, at the Lake Champlain narrows. In August 1755 Major General William Johnson led a force of 3,500 Massachusetts, Connecticut, Rhode Island, and New York Provincials, plus a few hundred allied Natives, as far as the foot of Lake George. There they set up camp. On September 8 a large Provincial scouting detachment was ambushed and forced to retreat to Johnson's main body. Eight hundred French and Canadians, with some 700 Indians advanced to attack the camp, which was crudely fortified with upturned batteaux and wagons. After a desultory five-hour action, during which the French commander was wounded and captured, and their allied Caughnawagas lost their leader, the attack was repulsed.

Artillery was a crucial factor in winning the day. William Eyre, Johnson's engineer and a captain of the British 44th Regiment, moved four guns to cover the road over which French forces initially advanced toward the Provincial encampment. Halting at the wood's edge, French commander Major General Jean-Armand, Baron de Dieskau decided to charge the cannon with two companies of grenadiers from the Regiments Languedoc and La Reine. Historian Fred Anderson relates the result: "From the clearing to the mouth of Captain Eyre's battery was perhaps 150 yards. Dieskau's grenadiers . . . charged along the road . . . with bayonets fixed, six abreast, in a column 100 yards long. . . . They were not half-way to their goal when the grapeshot . . . of the English guns cut 'Lanes, Streets, and Alleys' though them, annihilating their order and forcing them back." This incident likely brought about a laudatory comment about African soldiers or slaves, likely assigned to help work the artillery; two days after the battle an anonymous gunner with Eyre's artillery claimed that during the action, "our Blacks behaved better than the Whites." The Battle of Lake George induced Johnson, also wounded, to call a halt to the campaign and begin constructing a new fortification nearby, eventually named Fort William Henry.

Two years later French major general Louis-Joseph, Marquis de Montcalm, led an expedition against Fort William Henry. After coalescing at Carillon (later known as Fort Ticonderoga) in July, Montcalm's force of 6,000 French and Canadians, and almost 2,000 Natives reached Fort William Henry in the first days of August. The fort's garrison, commanded by Lieutenant Colonel George Monro, numbered about 1,500, including five companies of Monro's own British 35th Regiment, plus 900 New York, New Hampshire, and New Jersey Provincial troops. Fearing for the fort, Major General Daniel Webb, commanding at Fort Edward, sent reinforcements in the form of 200 soldiers of the 60th Royal American Regiment and Lieutenant Colonel Joseph Frye's 800 Massachusetts Provincials, who reached William Henry on August 2. Frye's men moved into the fortified Provincial camp, built on a height some 250 yards southeast of the fort.

The siege began on August 3, 1757, and, after a gallant defense, ended six days later. Accorded the honors of war, the British and Provincial troops were to remain under parole for eighteen months, and be allowed to march to Fort Edward with colors flying and one brass fieldpiece, retaining small arms and personal effects. On the 9th the fort's garrison made its way to the Provincial entrenched camp, and the next day the combined garrison set off for Fort Edward. That was when the "massacre" took place, later described succinctly by Colonel Frye, "they [the Natives] killd & Scalpt all the Sick & wounded before our faces, then took out from Our troops, all the Indians and negroes and carried them off."

By the end of 1757 at least 300 of the fort's garrison, plus untold numbers of sutlers, women, and other army followers remained missing. Black soldiers and servants were especially prized for their value as slaves, a point made by Louis Antoine de Bougainville, Montcalm's aide-de-camp, on August 15:

> Will they in Europe believe that the Indians alone have been guilty of this horrible violation of the capitulation, that desire for the Negroes and other spoils of the English has not caused the people who are at the head of these nations to loosen the curb, perhaps to go even further? The more so since one today may see one of these leaders, unworthy of the name of officer and Frenchman [a Canadian officer], leading in his train a Negro kidnapped from the English commander under pretext of appeasing the shades of a dead Indian, giving his family flesh for flesh. That is enough of the horror, the memory of which I would hope be effaced from the minds of men.

Among those who suffered that fate were Massachusetts slave-soldiers Caesar, Canada Cuggo, Jacob Lindse, and Jock Linn; Caesar and Jock were returned to their masters in 1760, but the others were never heard of again. Free Blacks James Bristol, John Bush, and Thomas Hinds were also taken. Hinds was also exchanged in 1760, while Bush was transported to France, dying at sea en route; James Bristol was still missing in 1758.

Sources: Fred Anderson, *A People's Army: Massachusetts Soldiers & Society in the Seven Years' War* (Chapel Hill: University of North Carolina Press, 1984), 8–13; Fred Anderson, *The Crucible of War: The Seven Years' War and the Fate of Empire in British North America, 1754–1766* (New York: Alfred A. Knopf, 2000), 110–57, 179–201; Ian K. Steele, *Betrayals: Fort William Henry & the "Massacre"* (New York and Oxford: Oxford University Press, 1990), 96–98, 140, 187–96; Edward P. Hamilton, *Adventure in the Wilderness: The American Journals of Louis Antoine de Bougainville, 1756–1760* (Norman: University of Oklahoma Press, 1964), 175; Scott Padeni, "The Role of Blacks in New York's Northern Campaigns of the Seven Years' War," *Bulletin of the Fort Ticonderoga Museum*, vol. 16 (1999), 158–59.

1760, Capture of Detroit, Rogers' Rangers

The year 1760 witnessed the culmination of six hard-fought years in the contest for North America, between Great Britain, France, and their associated Native American allies. The conflict was marked by irregular warfare and savagery on both sides, European linear combat, and formal siege operations, as well as the successful exercise of George II's much-vaunted Royal Navy in support of American land campaigns.

The previous year Major General James Wolfe followed up on the 1758 siege and capture of Fortress Louisbourg, at the mouth of the Gulf of Saint Lawrence, by moving up the Saint Lawrence River. That September, Wolfe's army effected a landing near Quebec City, battling and defeating Major General Louis-Joseph, Marquis de Montcalm's French and Canadian forces on the adjacent Plains of Abraham (both commanding generals were mortally wounded during the action). Five days later the city capitulated. Earlier in 1759, Fort Niagara, crucial for communication and supply between French Canada and the western posts and Native tribes, was taken by Brigadier General John Prideaux's British and Provincial forces, aided by a thousand Iroquois warriors led by Sir William Johnson.

Almost one year after Wolfe's bittersweet victory, three armies converged on French-held Montreal; North American commander in chief Jeffrey Amherst's forces advanced eastward from Oswego down the Saint Lawrence, while Brigadier General William Haviland's troops moved from Crown Point up the Lake Champlain corridor. Closing the trap, Brigadier General James Murray moved west, up the Saint Lawrence from Quebec: in all 18,000 British and Provincial troops. The largest portion of the army in New France, commanded by Brigadier General François-Gaston, Chevalier de Lévis, garrisoned Montreal, under the overall leadership of Governor General Pierre de Rigaud, Marquis de Vaudreuil. Those forces, numbering some 2,100 troops, surrendered on September 9, 1760, but not before the Chevalier had their regimental flags burned to save them from capture. The terms of capitulation called for the surrender of all posts from Michilimackinac in the west to the Restigouche River in the east. Most important for the indigenous tribes, the treaty stipulated, "The . . . Indian allies of his most Christian Majesty, shall be maintained in the Lands they inhabit, if they chose to remain there; they shall not be molested on any pretence whatsoever, for having carried arms, and served his most Christian Majesty; they shall have, as well as the French, liberty of religion."

The 60th Royal American Regiment and Major Robert Rogers' Ranger corps advanced on Montreal with General Haviland's column. Following the surrender, Rogers, with two Ranger companies and a single 60th company, was sent west to take possession of the French forts there. One of the most important was the trading site at Michilimackinac, in the Mackinac straits, linking Lakes Huron and Michigan. Two hundred and sixty miles south was Detroit, on the river of the same name, with access into Lake Erie. Detroit was, as historian René Chartrand notes, "truly a frontier metropolis . . . a bustling place whose population had doubled to over eight hundred souls in the last decade, besides hundreds of traders and Indians that constantly visited the town. It was the most important business and administrative center after Quebec and Montreal."

Detroit's small garrison was commanded by Captain François-Marie Picoté de Belestre, senior French commander on the frontier. Despite his Native allies' surprise that he would not fight, Captain de Belestre knew the terms of the Montreal Articles of Capitulation, and formally surrendered the town on November 29, 1760. Major Rogers noted of the occasion, "The French garrison laid down their arms, English colours were hoisted, and the French taken down, at which about 700 Indians gave a shout, merrily exulting."

There were several Black rangers in Rogers' corps, though how many were at Detroit is not known. One was Boston Burn, who joined by agreement of his master James Burn of Massachusetts. Boston was captured in 1758, while on a scouting mission near Fort Carillon; James Burn tried to recover him, but his success in doing so is unknown. Another was Castor (or Caesar) Dickinson; also enslaved, he gained his freedom after the war. A notice in the July 30, 1759, *New-York Mercury* told of one more African ranger:

> Taken up . . . in Orange County, a Negro Man named (as he says) Jacob; has a Scar from his Chin under his under Lip; has the Negro Mark with a Cut on each Cheek in his own Country [Africa]; has had the Small-pox, and a little pitted with it; has a Scar on his right Wrist, he says it was shot with a Ball; is five Feet seven Inches and a Half high, is about 25 or 30 Years old, has a green Jacket lined with red, Buckskin Breeches, blue Indian Stockings, fine white Shirts, with Chitterlings; has a Gun iron mounted, spotted Silk Handkerchief; he says he was in Rogers's Rangers three Years, and was at the Battle of Ticonderoga; that he belonged formerly to one Daniel McCoy, in New York, who lived near the Old-Sly, and that his Master had given him freedom for serving three Years in the Rangers.

A fourth man, Prince, "property of Major Rogers," possibly served with the Rangers when they destroyed the Abenaki town of Saint Francis in 1759.

Sources: Fred Anderson, *The Crucible of War: The Seven Years' War and the Fate of Empire in British North America, 1754–1766* (New York: Alfred A. Knopf, 2000); *John Borrows, "Wampum at Niagara: The Royal Proclamation, Canadian Legal History, and Self Government," in* Michael Asch, ed., *Aboriginal and Treaty Rights in Canada: Essays on Law, Equity, and Respect for Difference* (Vancouver: University of British Columbia Press, 1997), *170–71; Robert Rogers, Journals of Major Robert Rogers* (New York: Corinth Books, 1961), 159–60, 165; Maria Alessandra Bollettino, "Slavery, War, and Britain's Atlantic Empire: Black Soldiers, Sailors, and Rebels in the Seven Years' War, Dissertation, University of Texas at Austin, December 2009, 74–76, 92 (note 206); John L. Bell, "'A Negro servant Man, belonging to Major Robert Rogers'" (January 4, 2013), https://boston1775.blogspot.com/2013/01/a-negro-servant-man-belonging-to-major.html.

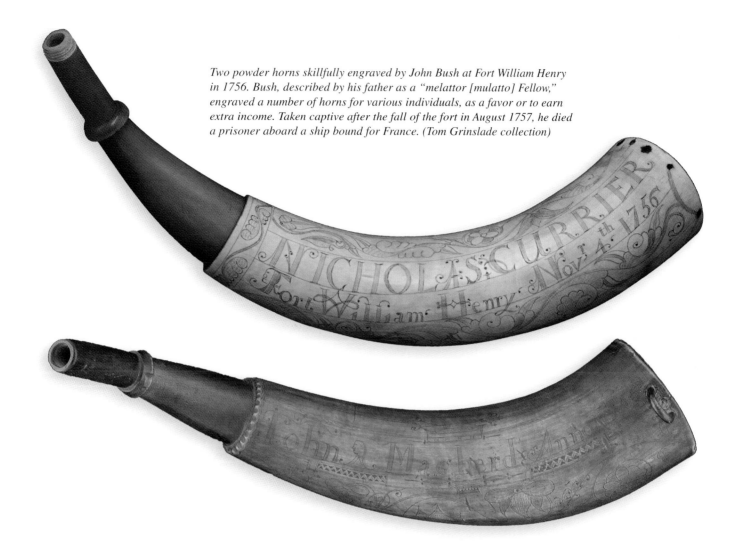

Two powder horns skillfully engraved by John Bush at Fort William Henry in 1756. Bush, described by his father as a "melattor [mulatto] Fellow," engraved a number of horns for various individuals, as a favor or to earn extra income. Taken captive after the fall of the fort in August 1757, he died a prisoner aboard a ship bound for France. (Tom Grinslade collection)

RAN away from Capt. Samuel Cottnam, laſt Sunday Night, the Ninth Inſtant, a Negro Man Slave called Nicola; when he went away he had on a blue lappelled Coat, a ſcarlet Waiſtcoat and grey Breeches, all with yellow Metal Buttons, a white Shirt ruffled at the Boſom, black Ribbon about his Neck, talks a little ſmattering of French. If any Perſon takes up ſaid Negro, and brings him to his Maſter in Winter Street, near the Common in Boſton, he ſhall have THREE DOLLARS Reward, and all neceſſary Charges paid: And publick Notice is hereby given to forewarn all Maſters of Veſſels, and others, not to take on board or harbour ſaid Negro, otherwiſe they may depend on being proſecuted as the Law directs.   Boſton, May 11. 1756.

1756 Boston newspaper notice calling for the return of an enslaved Black man in what may be a regimental uniform

1760, Capture of Detroit, Rogers' Rangers

3. *"Life, Liberty, and the Pursuit of Happiness"*[1]

The War of the American Revolution (1775–1783)

The story of Black men fighting in the forces for American Independence is wide-ranging and often mistold, as has been the tale of the enslaved people who heeded Crown commanders' promises of "full Security" and left bondage behind to claim it. Men of African descent in Continental regiments and American (Whig) militias served under arms in much greater numbers than those with British or Loyalist units, where they more often handled a fife, drum, or horn, pick and shovel, or worked as wagoners, packhorse drivers, or servants. Still, while enslaved men serving the American cause were usually emancipated as a result, those numbers were far fewer than those who gained their freedom merely by joining campaigning Crown forces or entering British-held territory.[2]

Continental Army and State Militias

Black soldiers fighting for American Independence, Continentals and militia, took part in every major battle of the war, and in most, if not all of the lesser actions. And of those who began their Continental service as enslaved men, the greatest part were manumitted at the end of their enlistment, while the remainder received their freedom postwar.

On June 14, 1775, the Second Continental Congress formally authorized the inception of the Continental Army, formed around the New England regiments already serving around Boston, augmented by six rifle companies from Pennsylvania, Maryland, and Virginia.[3] In autumn 1775 the fledgling Continental Army's commanders were debating whether to bar men of African descent from military service. Massachusetts brigadier general John Thomas responded to the proposed prohibition:

> I am Sorrey to hear that any Prejudice Should take Place in any of the Southern Colony's with Respect to the Troops Raised in this [the Army of Observation investing Boston]; I am Certain the Insinuations you Mention are Injurious; if [unless] we Consider with what Precipitation we were Obliged to Collect an Army [following the events of April 19, 1775]. [In] The Regiments at Roxbury [Massachusetts], the Privates are Equal to any that I Served with Last war, very few Old men, and in the Ranks very few boys, Our Fifers are many of them boys, we have Some Negros, but I Look on them in General

Equally Servicable with other men, for Fatigue and in Action; many of them have Proved themselves brave.[4]

The prejudice Thomas mentions was aimed at the New England army as a whole and, as he notes, the derogatory comments emanated from the "Southern" colonies, an umbrella which included Pennsylvania, where the Continental Congress met and deliberated.

In May 1775 Massachusetts authorities debated whether enslaved men should be enlisted, the colony's Committee of Safety recommending, "the admission . . . as soldiers, into the army now raising . . . only such as are freemen," but the Provincial Congress never brought it to a vote. Despite that, Adjutant General Horatio Gates's July 10, 1775, instructions for Massachusetts recruiting officers were distinctly emphatic: "You are not to Enlist any Deserter from the Ministerial Army, nor any Stroller, Negro [i.e., slave] or Vagabond, or Person suspected of being an Enemy to the Liberty of America, nor any under Eighteen Years of Age." And when at an October 1775 Council of War General George Washington posed the question, "whether it will be advisable to reenlist any Negroes in the new Army or whether there be a Distinction between such as are Slaves and those who are free?," the officers "agreed unanimously to reject all slaves & by a great Majority to reject Negroes [sic] altogether." As a result, November 12 army orders directed, "Neither Negroes, Boys unable to bare Arms, nor old men unfit to endure the fatigues of the campaign, are to be enlisted. It must also be noted that in late eighteenth-century America the term "Negro" legally denoted an enslaved person; some foregoing and ensuing quoted statements go against that convention."[5]

The previous September, New Jerseyan Richard Smith told of regional differences during congressional deliberations on the matter:

> Tuesday 26 Septr. Com[mitt]ee. Brought in a Letter to Gen Washington, in the Course of it E[dward] Rutledge [of South Carolina] moved that the Gen. shall discharge all the Negroes as well Slaves as Freemen in his Army, he (Rutledge) was strongly supported by many of the Southern Delegates but so powerfully opposed that he lost the Point.[6]

A pragmatic change of policy was possibly in part instigated by news of Lord Dunmore's Loyalist regiment of freed slaves in Virginia; at the end of December 1775 General

George Washington, noting he had been "informed, that Numbers of Free Negroes are desirous of inlisting . . . [gave] leave to recruiting Officers to entertain them, and promises to lay the matter before the Congress, who he doubts not will approve it." With limitations, that approval was forthcoming on January 16, when the Continental Congress decided "that the free negroes who have served faithfully in the army at Cambridge, may be re-inlisted therein, but no others." In any event, free African Americans remained in the army during the eight-month paper exercise of deciding if they should be soldiers. And, given the desperate need to fill Continental regiments, General Washington's decree was expanded to include newly enlisted African Americans, and the Continental Army continued as it began, a racially integrated organization to the war's end.[7]

Black Americans were in the fight from the first. Massachusetts militia men of color, free and enslaved, fought alongside their white comrades from Lexington to Concord, and back to Boston, on April 19, 1775. To date we have the names of thirty-five Black men present that day, at least eighteen seeing combat: one, Prince Estabrook, was wounded while with Captain John Parker's company on Lexington Green. John Hannigan notes that, given incomplete records, it is likely that as many as forty to fifty African Americans were with the militia on the war's first day.[8] Another was twenty-six-year-old Cuff Whittemore, slave to William Whittemore. A 1907 history of Arlington, Massachusetts, recounted an eyewitness account from April 19:

> Cuff was on the hill with the Menotomy militia [under Capt. Benjamin Locke]. . . . Solomon Bownan was lieutenant, and on the opening of the fight at that point . . . [Whittemore] acted cowardly, and in his alarm turned to run down the hill. But the lieutenant threatened to shoot him with a horse pistol, and pricked him in the leg with the point of his sword. This brought Cuff to his senses and the negro "about facing" fought through the contest, as the colonel [Ebenezer Thompson] said, like a wounded elephant, making two "cuss'd Britishers" bite the dust.[9]

At the end of the day's action Lieutenant Frederick Mackenzie, British 23rd Regiment of Fusiliers, noticed another Black participant. "As soon as the troops had passed Charlestown Neck the Rebels ceased firing. A Negro (the only one who was observed to fire at the Kings troops) was wounded near the houses close to the Neck, out of which the Rebels fired to the last."[10]

Two months later, at least eighty-eight Black and fifteen Indian soldiers are known to have served at the Bunker Hill battle; one historian estimates the total may have been as high as 150, roughly 5 percent of American troops involved.[11] Cuff Whittemore had enlisted in the newly formed New England army on June 4, 1775, and fought at Bunker Hill two weeks afterward. An 1826 book included this passage:

> [Whittemore] fought bravely in the redoubt. He had a ball through his hat . . . fought to the last, and when compelled to retreat, though wounded, the splendid arms of the British officers were prizes too tempting for him to come off empty handed, he seized the sword of one of them slain in the redoubt, and came off with the trophy, which in a few days he unromantically sold.[12]

Another soldier, Salem Poor, stands out among the many involved in the Bunker Hill battle. He was lauded for his actions that day, and honored in a testimonial signed by Colonel William Prescott, commander of the Bunker Hill redoubt, and thirteen officers from five different regiments. The document was addressed to "The Honorable General Court of the Massachusetts Bay" and reads:

> The Subscribers beg leave, to report to your Honble House, (which wee do in justice to the Caracter of So Brave a Man) that under Our Own observation, Wee declare that A Negro Man Called Salem Poor of Col Fryes Regiment Capt Ames Company in the late Battle at Charlestown, behaved like an Experienced officer, as Well as an Excellent Soldier, to Set forth Particulars of his Conduct Would be Tedious, Wee Would Only beg leave to Say in the Person of this . . . Negro Centers a Brave & gallant Soldier. The Reward due to So great and Distinguisht A Caracter, Wee Submit to the Congress ___ Cambridge Decr 5th 1775[13]

We do not know what Poor did to earn that encomium, but George Quintal notes, "it is a strong [but unsubstantiated] local tradition in Andover that he shot Lt. Col. James Abercrombie of the grenadiers, the highest-ranking British officer to have been killed . . . that day. To have performed this act, Salem Poor would have had to remain in the front ranks in the redoubt probably much longer than was prudent." Poor reenlisted for a second year in 1776, and in April 1777 signed on for three years in Colonel Edward Wigglesworth's (13th) Massachusetts Regiment. With that unit he participated in the Saratoga campaign, wintered over at Valley Forge, and took part in the 1778 Monmouth campaign as well.[14]

In autumn 1775, during the debate over the worthiness of Black men as soldiers, Massachusetts brigadier general William Heath described the trend for New England regiments, colony by colony. All but New Hampshire would see an increase in soldiers of color as the war went on.

> There are in the Massachusetts Regiments Some few Lads and Old men, and in Several Regiments, Some Negroes. Such is also the Case with the Regiments from the Other Colonies, Rhode Island has a Number of Negroes and Indians, Connecticut has fewer Negroes but a number of Indians. The New Hampshire Regiments have less of Both. The men from Connecticut I think in General are rather stouter than those of either of the other Colonies. But the Troops of our Colony are Robust, Agile, and as fine Fellows in General as I ever would wish to see in the Field.[15]

Southern Black men also began to serve early on. William Flora, a free Black Virginia militiaman, fought at the December 1775 Battle of Great Bridge, a Whig victory near Norfolk and the first action where African soldiers fought against each other on opposite sides. Flora went on to enlist for three years in November 1776, serving in the 15th, 11th, and 5th Virginia Regiments. Nathan Fry, "a man of Color, and native of Virginia . . . was born free in the County of Westmorland—enlisted in the minute Service under Dennis Duval of Henrico County in the year 1775—went to Savannah in Georgia and served under Col. [Samuel] Elbert [2nd Georgia Regiment] against the Creek Indians in the capacity of a Drummer."[16] That was only the beginning for Fry. After serving as a drummer,

He was taken out of that to wait on Major Duval [probably Major Peter De Veaux] who was aid-de-camp or Brigade Major to [Brigadier] General [Lachlan] McIntosh. He attended the Major Duval in the capacity of a waiter until he accompanied General McIntosh to the Army under General Washington [McIntosh joined the army at Valley Forge in December 1777, and took command of the North Carolina brigade] and remained with him until he was taken into the service of the Baron Steuben with whom he remained as a waiter or Batman [a servant in charge of a "bat" or packhorse] until after the siege of York in Virginia. He was then transferred to [Pennsylvania] General [Arthur] St. Clair by whom he was discharged in the course of the winter [1781–1782]. His discharge is lost. He says that during the whole of this service he remained a soldier under his first enlistment in 1775 and that he continued a soldier and was uninterruptedly in service from the time of his enlistment to the time of his discharge.[17]

Of all the Black Southern Continentals found for this study, Virginian Andrew Pebbles had perhaps the most varied career. Self-described as "a poor unlearned Mulatto," Pebbles enlisted in the 15th Virginia Regiment in September 1777, and later served with Lieutenant Colonel Henry "Light Horse Harry" Lee's Legion. In his own words,

he enlisted . . . under Captain George Lee Turberville [15th Virginia] of Westmoreland County who was a recruiting Captain. . . . He joined the Camp at Valley Forge and was placed under the Command of Captain Lewis Booker [likely Samuel Booker, with the 15th Virginia from November 1776 to September 1778, when that unit was incorporated with the 11th Regiment]. . . . He belonged to the 15th Virginia Regiment . . . for two years. . . . At Trenton he was detailed to serve in the artillery. . . . He was commanded by a Capt [John] Dandridge [1st Continental Artillery: Dandridge was a captain from February 1777, captured at Charleston in 1780] and served one year in the Artilory. . . . Captain [William] Miller commanded the gun with 12 men to which he belonged. . . . He served for two years under Capt Michael Rudolph [of Maryland, captain as of November 1779] in the light infantry commanded

by Colo Harry Lee whose command was composed of infantry & Cavalry [Lee's Legion, authorized by Congress in April 1778, near full strength by November the same year]. . . . He was in three general actions, at Monmouth [June 28, 1778], Gilford Courthouse [March 15, 1781] & at Eutau Springs [September 8, 1781]. . . . At Eutau Springs he received three wounds he was wounded in the shoulder slightly lost the thumb of the left hand and was bayonetted in the belly. . . . He was discharged on Combahee River honorably. . . . The day before he was discharged he was in a battle in which Colo Lawrence [John Laurens] who commanded in the absence of Colo Lee was killed [August 27, 1782]. . . . Colo Lee had gone home to be marryed [in April 1782, to Matilda Ludwell]. . . . At Petersburg in Virginia he had his knee much injured by the wheel of a field piece.[18]

Stacey Williams was one of some fifty free Black soldiers who served in the Pennsylvania line during the war. He briefly stated in a 1820 Federal pension deposition that, "he served in the Revolutionary War . . . In the 6th. Regiment commanded by Col. [Henry] Bicker and afterwards by Col. [Josiah] Harmar Pennsylvania Line and in the Company commanded by Capt. [Jacob] Humphries." Two years earlier Williams noted, "he was in many engagements during the war one of which was the battle of Monmouth." At that battle he would have participated in the hard-fought late-afternoon attack on the 1st Battalion British Grenadiers, which ended in the Pennsylvanians' bloody defensive action at the Parsonage Farm.[19]

Two 6th Regiment officers, former lieutenants James Glentworth and John Markland, submitted testimonials supporting Williams. Markland wrote, "I do certify that Stacy Williams, the bearer hereof, was a soldier in capt. Jacob Humphreys company 6th Pennsylvania Regiment, in April 1777, enlisted for the war; and that he served faithfully, until he was discharged at the barracks in Philadelphia, November, 1783, soon after our return from South Carolina, under col. [Josiah] Harmar."[20]

One detail the old soldier did not tell was recorded in a compendium on the Pennsylvania regiments: he was, "wounded in the right thigh, at Brandywine." Despite his brevity, Private Williams is an excellent representative for the entirety of Pennsylvania common soldiers. He enlisted in April 1777 and served until autumn 1783. During that time, he was very likely present at all the actions or operations his regiment took part in: Short Hills, June 26, 1777; Brandywine, September 11, 1777; Germantown, October 4, 1777; Monmouth, June 28, 1778; Bull's Ferry Block House, July 20–21, 1780; Green Spring, July 6, 1781; Yorktown, September 28 to October 17, 1781. His military travels took him from West Point, New York, to Charleston, South Carolina, on foot the entire way.[21]

John Francis, "a negro man," signed up for a long-term enlistment, but his military career was cut short, and his later life circumstances show the potential enduring effects of wartime service. Several depositions were submitted to support his application for a state pension. This first, from William Neely in October 1786, states: "These are to Certify that John Francis was an Inhabitant of Solesbury Township Bucks County When

Inlisted by Lieut. [Jacob] Drake." We do not know when Francis first joined, but the moment that changed his life came in late summer 1777, as evidenced by a wartime document: "This is to Certify whome it may Concern that John Francis of the 3 Regt of Pennsylvania in Capt [Henry Epple's] Company was wounded and Taken Prisoner at Brandiwine on the Eleventh of [September 1777] & is Now on his Parole [several illegible words] the 3d Day of February 1778." Private Francis was discharged from the Lancaster military hospital in late March 1778, unable to serve out his enlistment. Two of his neighbors testified to his incapacity in the mid-1780s: "We . . . do hereby Certify that John Frances from the Wounds in his Legs is frequently laid by from his Ordinary Labour, and that he is thereby rendered incapable of procuring the necessary support for himself and Family." And Mary Stockdale related, "it is my opinion the wound in John Franceses leg will never Be . . . sound . . . for when he Caim to me frequently dressing his leg I tuck out agreat many Bones."[22] Mr. Francis also spoke for himself.

To the Honourable the Judges of the Supreme Court of the Commonwealth of Pennsylvania holding Court of Oyer and Terminer and [?] prices at Newtown for the County of Bucks May 21st Anno Domini 1787

The Petition of John Francis —

Humbly Sheweth That Your Petitioner was a Soldier in the Army of the United States, That in the Battle of Brandywine on the 11th day of Septembr AD 1777 He was unfortunately wounded and taken Prisoner, that He was paroled by the Enemy & was a Considerable Time in the Hospital at Lancaster / One of his Legs (both of which were wounded) being much shattered & little hopes of recovering so as to be fit for Military Duty, that He was suffered to return Home, since which time, He has been subjected to great Expences & still remain unable to procure a Livelihood for Himself & Family Consisting of a Wife & three small Children, He therefor prays Your Honors would take his Case into Your Consideration & grant Him such Relief as You in Your Wisdom shall see Meet And Your Petitioner as in Duty Bound will pray
his
John UW Francis
Mark [23]

Despite early and ongoing strictures barring enslaved men enlisting, many found their way into the ranks. As in the French and Indian War, some seized on the opportunity to pass themselves off as free, with varied success; others served in place of their masters. Unlike many New England soldiers of color, it seems most Southern Black Continentals were free rather than enslaved. There were exceptions. In one instance an intoxicated Virginia farmer, Rolling Jones, was induced to enlist; regretting his action when sober, he sent his slave Tim in his place. Tim Jones (taking his master's last name) served with the 3rd Virginia Regiment, seeing action at the battle of Camden and the Yorktown siege, where he "lost his leg by a musket ball." He "was given his freedom by the Country for the faithful discharge of his duty as a soldier." Writing of men who enlisted while still in bondage, John Hannigan notes that "military service offered enslaved men limited opportunities to negotiate their freedom, either with white owners, local officials, or army officers."[24] On one occasion,

in March 1781, a nineteen-year-old enslaved man named Richard Hobby enlisted to serve three years in the Continental Army. Hobby marched to West Point where he remained until the winter of 1783 when his owner, Jonathan Hobby, appeared in camp to retrieve his wayward servant. Claiming that Richard had enlisted without permission, Jonathan demanded the slave be released from the army into his custody. A military court composed of white officers determined that Richard had legally enlisted and any prior claims on his servitude were secondary to the army's claim on his soldiering. Frustrated, Jonathan Hobby left West Point empty handed and Richard Hobby remained in the army.[25]

As with the 1750s war, non-enlisted enslaved men were used to support military operations. With a much larger population of people in bondage, Southern military authorities more often resorted to slave labor, particularly in South Carolina. Fort Sullivan, some 500 feet long and sixteen feet wide, protecting Charleston, was entirely built by slaves; constructed of spongy palmetto logs, the fort served to repulse a British fleet in June 1776. Four years later, in the face of a threatened British siege, enslaved laborers, working alongside Continental and militia soldiers, refurbished the Charleston defenses, razed houses to clear fields of fire, and hauled 200-plus cannon into position. Having landed on Simmons Island in February 1780, Crown forces opened the siege on the evening of April 1. Soon after that, garrison commander Major General Benjamin Lincoln ordered gun emplacements built at the mouth of the Wando River, at Cainhoy and Lampriers Point; once again, slaves were allotted to do the labor. During the siege the American defenders "inlisted" slaves for artillery crews, to perform navvy work and repair crumbled embrasures and other defenses, mostly by night. Brigadier General Lachlan McIntosh noted these laborers had, "to be pressed daily, & kept under guard, as the masters as well as the Slaves, were unwilling they should work."[26]

After the controversy of the war's first year, derogatory comments about American soldiers of African descent were few and far between; in fact, Continental Army integration was largely a success, in that white, Black, and Indian soldiers melded together to make a whole, and post-1776 comments lauding or denigrating the troops referred to that whole, without singling out subsets by skin color. In December 1777 a German officer wrote of the American Revolutionary forces, "The negro can take the field in his master's place [meaning they were enlisted as substitutes]; hence you never see a regiment in which there are not a lot of negroes, and there are well-built, strong, husky fellows among them."[27] And Baron Ludwig von Closen, aide-de-camp to French General Rochambeau, wrote in July 1781:

I had a chance to see the American Army, man for man. It is really painful to see those brave men, almost naked with only some trousers and little linen jackets, most of them without stockings, but, would you believe it, very cheerful and healthy in appearance. . . . It is incredible that soldiers composed of men of every age, even children of fifteen, of whites and blacks, unpaid and rather poorly fed, can march so fast and withstand fire so steadfastly.[28]

From von Closen, a captain with twelve years' experience in the Royal Deux-Ponts Regiment and from a military family, this was high praise indeed.[29]

Black soldiers' motivations for joining the Continental Army and their treatment while serving are important to any discussion of their military experience. Their reasons largely mirrored those of their fellow white and Indian soldiers. Many fought for national independence and hoped-for opportunities in a new republic. Some joined for the adventure of military service, sometimes connected to the prospect of serving alongside family or friends; others were at least partly enticed by the lure of an enlistment bounty or regular pay. And, with the ideals espoused in the Declaration of Independence, some men fought for their own freedom, or for that of their loved ones. Enslaved men joined as unpaid substitutes, taking their owners' place in the ranks. Forced service was another factor. If they were on the militia rolls, both white and Black men periodically faced the chance of being drafted for a short-term stint in a Continental regiment. Whites were occasionally compelled to enlist, but enslaved African Americans were more often coerced or forced by their masters to serve. Many, especially in New England, were promised freedom in return for military service; most of those promises were honored, but some veterans were kept in bondage after leaving the army. Of course, the major dividing line between white and Black common soldiers was the American system that enslaved 95 percent of the country's African Americans, and relegated free Blacks to underclass status.[30]

In light of their treatment in civilian society, one remarkable result of researching Black Continental soldiers is finding that they largely received the same considerations as their white comrades. At the most basic level, soldiers of color (both African and Native Americans) received the same pay, provisions, clothing, and equipment as white soldiers. Both whites and soldiers of color suffered together in times of scarcity and jointly enjoyed the rare times of bounty. The most glaring case of unequal treatment was that Black soldiers were, with some few exceptions, barred from serving in any rank other than drummer, fifer, or private soldier. There were other inequities. Early in the war, Africans were occasionally singled out for labor details, but that ended by the conflict's middle years. There are also indications that Black enlisted men served as officers' waiters (servants) more often than white soldiers, but that remains unsubstantiated. Finally, while there were likely difficulties due to officers' or fellow soldiers' personal or race animus, to date no such instances have come to light.[31]

1778: "Return of the Negroes in the Army"

At the onset of the War for Independence approximately 480,000 African Americans lived in the colonies, of whom roughly 24,000 were free, meaning some 456,000 (95 percent) were enslaved. Total American population at the time was approximately 2.5 million; using these numbers, free Blacks comprised 0.96 percent of the overall population, and slaves formed 18.24 percent. By comparison, roughly 5,000 to 7,000 African American soldiers and sailors, free and slave, served the Revolutionary cause.[32]

Service of African American soldiers alongside their white counterparts is strikingly illustrated in the August 24, 1778, "Return of the Negroes in the Army," listing 755 Black soldiers in fifteen brigades of General George Washington's main army at White Plains, New York. That force totaled 20,771 rank and file (sergeants, corporals, music, and private soldiers), making men of African descent 3.6 percent of the whole. While that proportion may seem small, by themselves Black soldiers would form two understrength regiments, each equal to, or larger in size than, most other serving Continental regiments.[33]

All the listed brigades were integrated organizations; the only segregated unit having only African and Native American privates (with white officers and noncommissioned personnel) was the newly re-formed 1st Rhode Island Regiment, then serving in its home state. Reciprocally, the only purposely segregated whites-only unit was the 2nd Rhode Island Regiment, following the transfer of Captain Thomas Arnold's veteran Black and Indian company to the 1st Rhode Island in July 1778.[34]

A caveat regarding this discussion: A recent analysis by Matthew C. White asks why the August 1778 return was made, and convincingly argues that in that and many other references "Negroes" was a synonym for slave. Among other points, Mr. White's contention is supported by his finding at least forty Blawck soldiers serving with the Pennsylvania brigades in August 1778, far more than the two listed. If true, it would mean there were 755 enslaved soldiers in Washington's main army, plus unknown numbers of free Black men serving.

British and Loyalist Corps

Our final section on Revolutionary War soldiers of African descent will look at those serving with British and Loyalist units, including the slaves and former slaves who left America with Crown forces at the conflict's end.

In March 1776 Sir William Howe, North American commander in chief, stated that,

being desirous that the Provincial Forces should be put on the most respectable Footing, and according to his first Intention be composed of His Majesty's Loyal American Subjects, has directed that all Negroes, Molattoes, and other Improper Persons who have been admitted into these Corps be immediately discharged;

"Return of the Negroes in the Army," August 24, 1778

Brigades	Present	Sick Present	On Command	Total	Percentage of Brigade Strength (Rank & File)
North Carolina	42	10	6	58	4.81%
Woodford (Virginia)	36	3	1	40	3.18%
Muhlenberg (Virginia)	64	26	8	98	6.88%
Scott (five Virginia regiments and one from Delaware)	20	3	1	24	1.65%
Smallwood (Maryland)	43	15	2	60	4.06%
2nd Maryland (three Maryland regiments and the German Regiment)	33	1	1	35	2.04%
Wayne (Pennsylvania)	2	0	0	2	0.16%
2nd Pennsylvania	0	0	0	0	0%
Clinton (New York)	33	2	4	39	2.85%
Parsons (Connecticut)	117	12	19	148	9.31%
Huntington (Connecticut)	56	2	4	62	4.90%
Nixon (Massachusetts; including one militia levy regiment)	26	0	1	27	1.62%
Patterson (Massachusetts)	64	13	12	89	5.80%
Late Learned (Massachusetts)	34	4	8	46	3.91%
Poor (three New Hampshire regiments and the 2nd Canadian Regiment)	16	7	4	27	1.85%
Total	586	98	71	755	3.63% of the whole

20,771 rank and file in fifteen brigades (above)
755 Black soldiers = 3.63% of rank and file in the listed brigades
(1 of every 28 soldiers was Black)

Brigade strength numbers do not include officers and staff, as Black soldiers could not serve in those ranks. Men listed as on furlough, or dead, deserted, or discharged are also not included. (Note: New Jersey and Rhode Island are the only states not represented that had units serving with General George Washington's army. In 1778 only ten Black soldiers are known to have served in New Jersey's four Continental regiments. Rhode Island had just that spring reconstituted its 1st Regiment, filling it with some 190 soldiers of color (182 Black, six Indian, and two African/Indian mix), serving with the rank of drummer, fifer, or private soldier. Of that total, some fifty-five were veterans, and the remainder were former slaves, freed upon enlistment. The 2nd Rhode Island contained only white soldiers.)*
*Daniel M. Popek, *They ". . . fought bravely, but were unfortunate": The True Story of Rhode Island's "Black Regiment" and the Failure of Segregation in Rhode Island's Continental Line, 1777–1783* (Bloomington, IN: AuthorHouse, 2015), 1778 1st Regiment company listings, 169–205.

the Inspector Genl. of Provincial Corps [former British captain Alexander Innes] will receive particular Orders on this Subject to Prevent such Abuses in future.[35]

In short, this order meant that Black men serving in Loyalist units on the Establishment were to be ejected; this was eventually amended informally, so that blacks could serve in those same corps as musicians, pioneers, wagon or packhorse drivers, and other unarmed positions. But still they fought. Butler's Rangers, a largely white unit formed along the New York–Canadian frontier in December 1777, had some armed Black soldiers in its ranks, but only a few are known by name: Thomas Tin Brook (Ten Broeck?) was a private soldier, residing in Canada postwar; Richard Pierpont, native of Bundu (present-day Senegal) and former slave, also served with the Canadian "Coloured Corps" and fought at the October 13, 1813, Queenston Heights battle; and Peter Becket, formerly

of Philadelphia, served from December 1777 to May 1778, being then discharged "unfit for service." He and his widowed mother were awarded 300 acres of land postwar. Two men are known to have served with another Canada–New York Loyalist regiment. John Powell (aka Jacques or Jean Paul), possibly from Guadeloupe, and his African-born wife Elizabeth served with the "regiment du brigadier Janson" (Sir John Johnson's King's Royal Regiment), and were allotted land after the war. Rubin Middleton, a "negroe" or "mulattoe man," was sentenced to a fine and nine months' imprisonment after being convicted of rape. Pleading for a pardon, in return for which Middleton offered to enlist in the King's Royal Regiment, he was freed, enlisted as promised, survived the war, and also received a land grant for his service.[36]

British and Loyalist regiments sometimes had Black musicians, often by special permission. The 29th Regiment of Foot famously enlisted Black drummers in numbers sufficient to provide one for each company. The position of other men is uncertain: George Crane is merely noted as an 84th Regiment (aka Royal Highland Emigrants) veteran, described postwar as "a man of Colour, by trade a Saddler." Hilaire Lamour was an officer's enslaved servant; as such he had been in military service with Daniel Robertson, formerly of the 42nd Regiment, since 1762. After spending five years as commander at Michilimackinac, Captain Robertson, 84th Regiment, returned to Montreal; having purchased Lamour on Martinique during the Seven Years' War, Robertson manumitted him after twenty-five years "true and faithful service." Lamour's wife Catherine still being enslaved by the captain, Hilaire was able to borrow or amass £100—the highest recorded price in that city for a female slave—to purchase his spouse. If the purchase cost was indeed borrowed and not repaid, Catherine would likely be forcibly sold in response.[37]

The Queen's Rangers began with a Black company commanded by Robert Cook, but even before General Howe's orders precluding men of color from serving, a deserter advertisement mentioned, "Captn. Cook's Company of Negroes are (all but three or four) dead." In 1778 John Graves Simcoe became commander of the regiment and led it on an enviable career. Just after the 1780 capture of Charleston, the Queen's Rangers had, one way or another, acquired several enslaved men. Lieutenant Colonel Simcoe, having been informed that a "Mrs. Elliot is to apply to the Comr. in Chief for four Negro boys now with the Queens Rangers," wrote deputy adjutant general Major John André, "to explain to this matter. The Boys are Taylors & Musicians, & are at this time clothed in the Rebel Artillery Uniform, which her Husband commanded." Mrs. Elliot was the wife of Lieutenant Colonel Barnard Elliott, commander of the 4th South Carolina (Artillery) Regiment, captured at Charleston. Another man, Bernard Griffiths, served as an armed cavalry trumpeter.[38] Known as "Trumpeter Barney" in Simcoe's memoirs, the colonel wrote this recommendation letter in March 1789:

Sir,
B E Griffiths has applied to me for his Discharge from the Queens Rangers. The Particulars of his Situation I take the Liberty of Submitting to you, & entreating the Protection of the War Office on his behalf.

He joined the Queens Rangers at The Siege of Charles Town, & was very useful as a Guide; He served as a Dragoon & was frequently distinguished for his Bravery & Activity—in particular at the action near Spencer's Ordinary, by his presence of mind when sentinel, He was principally concerned in betraying the Enemy into an unfavourable [situation], & in the consequent Charge of Cavalry was distinguished by Fighting hand to hand with a French Officer who commanded a Squadron of the Enemy & taking him Prisoner. When the Cavalry afterwards charged the Rebel Infantry, He by his gallantry preserved the Life of his Captain & was severely wounded. His Activity had made him so remarkable That I personally interfered with The Baron Steuben at the Surrender of York Town to obtain that He might not risk the Hazard of being sent Prisoner into the Country [where he would likely have been enslaved]—& had I been with The Regiment when it was disbanded, I should have felt it my Duty to have recommended him as a proper Object for his Majesty's Bounty of Chelsea, not having that Power, I humbly hope that you will direct him to be examined; in particular, as being a Loyal Negro, He has no other means of reaping the Protection his Services in The Opinion of Every Officer of the Corps as well as mine most amply merit . . . J G Simcoe

Lt. Coll. Comdt. (late) Q Rangers[39]

The King's American Dragoons were raised in 1781 and counted several Black trumpeters in its ranks. Six are named in the first volume of the Book of Negroes, a record of Black evacuees from New York in 1783. All embarked on the ship *Lady's Adventure*, destined for St. Johns, Nova Scotia, as follows: Nathaniel Lindsay, twenty years old, a "stout man . . . Free born in the Grenades"; Edward Lloyd, nineteen years of age, "formerly the property of Ebenezer Cowley of Fairfield [Connecticut] who gave him his freedom"; Dick Jackson, twenty-one years, "formerly the property of Col. Lloyd of Maryland"; Charles Terrill, twenty-one, "formerly the property of Mr. John Murphy, Richmond, Virginia"; John Frederick, twenty-one-and-one-half years, "formerly the property of Lord Baltimore who gave him his freedom"; Hector Micuro, twenty-three years old, a "stout mulatto . . . Formerly servant to Mr. Pyate at Charlestown; left it with Col. [Benjamin] Thompson [commander, K.A.D.]" Also listed are seven Black regimental pioneers. One of the named trumpeters was twenty-year-old Daniel Green, made "free by Captain Williams, Master of a Transport in England." After service with the King's American Dragoons, he reenlisted as a drummer in the 38th Regiment of Foot, remaining until discharged April 14, 1801; his certificate notes he was forty-five and born in Charleston, South Carolina, and states he "Hath served honestly and faithfully in said Regiment 18 Years . . . And in the Kings American Dragoons three years & a half, but being rendered unfit . . . by a Broken Leg and being worn out in the service, he is hereby Discharged, and humbly recommended as a proper Object of His Majesty's Royal Bounty of Chelsea Hospital."[40]

One roster indicates the jobs allotted to 773 black refugees at Charleston in mid-July 1780; 266 were with the Royal artillery, 192 with the Pioneers, and the rest spread among the "Royal Fusiliers" (7th Regiment of Foot), German regiments, the commissary general, and hospital. A 1791 "List of the Blacks of Birch Town who gave in their Names for [emigration to] Sierra Leone" provides some indication of the proportion of male refugees who had experienced military service; of 151 adult men, sixty-eight had served as soldiers, sailors, or pioneers, 45 percent of the whole.[41]

Many Black men served in Loyalist irregular units and militias, too. Todd Braisted mentions several, including the Armed Boat Company, operating off Long Island, and the Associated Loyalists. He notes the most integrated was the Loyal Refugee Volunteers; originally formed early in 1780 to provide wood for New York's garrison, they occasionally executed small raids; in May, 150 Loyal refugees occupied

PUBLIC SALE.

BY virtue of an order of the Orphan's Court of Frederick County, the undersigned, as Administrator of Sarah Garrott, late of said County, deceased, will offer at Public Sale, at the late residence of the deceased, on the Merryland Tract, Frederick County, within 1 mile of Knoxville, all the NEGROES belonging to the estate of the said deceased, viz:

32 NEGROES,

EIGHT NEGRO MEN, good Farm hands, one a good Blacksmith, one a good Shoemaker, and three are good Wagoners; several

Negro Women,

some of whom are good Cooks and Washer Women, and several are good House Servants; several BOYS & GIRLS, aged from infancy to 18 years.

By order of the Court and by the assent and concurrence of the heirs, none of the above mentioned Negroes will be sold to traders or to their agents.

☞—Sale to commence ON WEDNESDAY THE 31st DAY OF JANUARY, 1849, at 10 o'clock, A. M., and to continue from day to day, till all are sold.
TERMS OF SALE PRESCRIBED BY ORDER OF THE COURT.---The purchaser or purchasers to give his, her or their note, with security to be approved by the Administrator, payable six months after date, bearing interest from date.   EDWARD GARROTT,
                    Administrator of Sarah Garrott, deceased.

January 23, 1849.

[Printed at the Office of the " Republican Citizen," Frederick City, Md.]

Poster from Maryland slave auction of female slaves.
(Don Troiani Photo, Connecticut Museum of History Collection)

the Hudson River post at Bull's Ferry, New Jersey, building a blockhouse as a base for their incursions. On July 21 Brigadier General Anthony Wayne's Pennsylvania regiments cannonaded and then attacked Bull's Ferry. Inside were ninety-two white refugees plus "20 Negroes," who repulsed Wayne's men and forced them to retreat, with sixty casualties. Perhaps the best known Loyalist band were the "refugees" commanded by Colonel Tye, earlier known as Titus when enslaved by a resident of Shrewsbury, New Jersey. Tye freed himself in November 1775 and went on to lead a group of Black and white Loyalists operating from the fortified Sandy Hook lighthouse. He and his men (known colloquially as the "Black Brigade") harassed local Whigs from early 1779 until Tye's death from wounds in autumn 1780. Tye's "Brigade" disintegrated after his death, but Loyalist African American partisans, with their white counterparts, continued to operate along the New Jersey coast.[42]

The Loyalist Ethiopian Regiment was the first Black-centered corps to serve in the war, but it had a troubled existence, and, because of the British high command's distaste for arming slaves, was disbanded having served only one year. (Note: The Revolutionary War artwork sections contain detailed information on the four Black regiments that served from 1775 to 1783—Loyalist, Whig, Spanish, and French.) The question of using still-enslaved men as soldiers led to North American commander in chief Sir Henry Clinton issuing his July 1779 Philipsburg proclamation, to wit, "Whereas the Enemy have adopted a practice of enrolling Negroes [i.e., slaves] among their Troops; I do hereby give Notice, That all Negroes taken in Arms, or upon any military Duty, shall be purchased for a stated Price; the money to be paid to the Captors." That was a rejoinder to the news that the preceding March the Continental Congress had authorized the formation of armed slave battalions in South Carolina and Georgia. Never mind that many states' regiments already had enslaved in their ranks, or that the Southern Black battalions never came to fruition, the mere thought of escalating the war by wholesale slave enlistments was, to their minds, beyond the pale. In the words of a consortium of British "Gentlemen, Merchants and Traders" who petitioned George III in October 1775, they had no wish to unleash the horrors of a slave rebellion on "our American brethren."[43]

News of Lord Dunmore's November 1775 decree of freedom for "all indented Servants, Negroes, or others, (appertaining to Rebels,) free that are able and willing to bear Arms" quickly spread, and enslaved people soon saw all British forces as their saviors. That was almost four years before Clinton's 1779 proclamation promising "every Negroe who shall desert the Rebel Standard, full Security to follow within these Lines, any Occupation which he shall think proper." The British seem to have been judicious in honoring their perceived offer of freedom, and thousands of slaves confiscated from rebels in the American South were not included and left to the mercy of their former masters or ended in bondage in the British Caribbean and elsewhere.[44]

Of course, those on the side of American independence were no better. Perhaps a thousand or more enslaved men served as Continental soldiers and eventually received their freedom in return, but that reward did not extend to their families. And, north and south, thousands upon thousands of Black men, women, and children were still enslaved by those extolling freedom; as Samuel Johnson wrote in 1775, "how is it that we hear the loudest yelps for liberty among the drivers of negroes?"[45]

At war's end the men of two Loyalist organizations were evacuated to the British West Indies. The largest was the Southern contingent of the Black Pioneers; created by engineer Colonel John Moncrief in late 1778, they served in the 1779 Savannah and 1780 Charleston sieges. The Pioneers continued in service until the December 1782 evacuation of South Carolina. The Black Dragoons was an all–African American cavalry unit of some fifty men, formed in late 1781. It was one of only two armed Black corps that served on the mainland, the other being the 1775–1776 Ethiopian Regiment. When the British left Charleston in autumn and early winter 1782, they took with them about 300 men of both units; landing in Grenada, they were formed into a single armed organization called the Carolina Corps.[46]

The British copy of the two-volume "Book of Negroes" lists 3,000 Black emigrants (1,336 men, 914 women, and 750 children) who evacuated New York with British forces in 1783; the United States's copy, housed in the National Archives, contains 2,679 names, 321 less than the British version.[47] Michael White provides a breakdown:

> Of the total [less 3] 2,997 people of African descent evacuated from New York City, the largest two groups recorded by the British were 1,135 freed by military proclamation and 812 who were categorized as escaped slaves. . . . Additional smaller groups among the evacuees included 371 who were born free; 205 who had been emancipated by their masters; 44 acquired their freedom from their master's death; [and] 28 [who] had free or unknown status. Among those with unfree status among the evacuees were 366 slaves, 29 who were indentured, and 7 who had been abandoned by their masters. Thus, some 2,595 people found in the Book of Negroes had free status (87 percent of the total), while some 402 were unfree.[48]

The Black emigrants embarking from New York City from May to November 1783 were among about 27,000 British subjects, Black and white, plus 30,000 British and German troops, all who left the city by ship. These were not the only Black emigrants who left the United States in 1782 and 1783. Numbers for the Southern exodus are open to dispute and difficult to reconcile; Cassandra Pybus provides an estimate of freedmen refugees, placing the total at 20,000 British-emancipated Blacks, with some 12,000 originating in the South; that total includes those recruited into the navies, serving with army and navy officers, and those enlisted in British and German regiments (plus families), estimated at 5,000, plus some 300 South Carolina Black soldiers and military laborers. Dr. Pybus also includes in her estimate some 8,000 Black refugees who died of disease. Pybus's numbers must be viewed with skepticism, but do provide some idea of the magnitude of the refugee situation and the difficulties it caused for British authorities.[49]

Various scholars agree that the British left behind most of the slaves confiscated from Southern Whig plantations, to be taken up again by their former masters and re-enslaved, and there is an alternate view of the numbers of formerly enslaved Blacks who evacuated with British forces and gained their freedom, one based on some documentation. If, as Cassandra Pybus claims, "the British did not renege on their promises of freedom," in the Southern ports they seem to have had a narrow view of who they were obliged to permanently emancipate.[50] Garry Sellick writes:

> Unlike in New York, where Carleton personally oversaw the evacuation of over 3000 black Loyalists to Nova Scotia and Britain at the end of the conflict, very few blacks from Charlestown [sic] achieved freedom. While several hundred black Loyalists . . . reached New York and then Nova Scotia, thousands were simply abandoned to re-enslavement. Outside of the Carolina Corps, the number of slaves who found freedom through Charlestown certainly numbered no more than 500.[51]

This author would add that the small number of Blacks who emigrated into freedom via Charleston exceeded those who did so from Savannah.

The number of still-enslaved Africans taken out of New York at war's end was relatively modest compared to the Southern ports. Exact figures are unknown, but John Pulis states British ships transported "some 5,000 slaves (along with an estimated 2,000 white Loyalists), and perhaps as many as 65,000 blacks seized as contraband" from North America to Jamaica, from 1782 to 1785. Most of those slaves sailed out of Savannah and Charleston in 1782, and later, Spanish East Florida, an authorized haven for Southern Loyalists and their chattel.[52] Two months before the December Charleston departure date, military governor Major General Alexander Leslie ordered that all Whig-owned slaves who had not served the British military would be left behind; Gary Sellick notes,

> this meant that nearly all of the slaves who had earned their freedom within the British lines by this late stage in the conflict would be returned to bondage, with only loyalist slaves [, those belonging to officers of the army and navy,] and the small number of actively serving blacks in the military, including the Carolina Corps, being evacuated.[53]

Two days prior to departure, 9,127 civilians were placed aboard ship, including 5,333 Black people, all or most enslaved. Of the latter number, 2,613 were destined for Jamaica, 2,211 for East Florida, 350 to St. Lucia, 56 to England, 53 to Halifax, and 50 to New York.[54]

Twenty-three-year-old Boston King will have the last word, giving the British more credit than they deserve. King was "formerly the property of Richard Waring of Charlestown, South Carolina; left him 4 years ago," and seems to have joined the Loyalist New York Volunteers (3rd American Regiment).[55] He took a ship from New York in 1783, and recalled:

> The English had compassion upon us in the day of distress, and issued out a Proclamation, importing, That all slaves should be free, who had taken refuge in the British lines, and claimed the sanction and privileges of the Proclamations respecting the security and protection of Negroes. In consequence of this, each of us received a certificate from the commanding officer at New-York, which dispelled all our fears, and filled us with joy and gratitude. Soon after, ships were fitted out, and furnished with every necessary for conveying us to Nova Scotia. We arrived at Burch Town [Nova Scotia] in the month of August, where we all safely landed. Every family had a lot of land, and we exerted all our strength in order to build comfortable huts before the cold weather set in.[56]

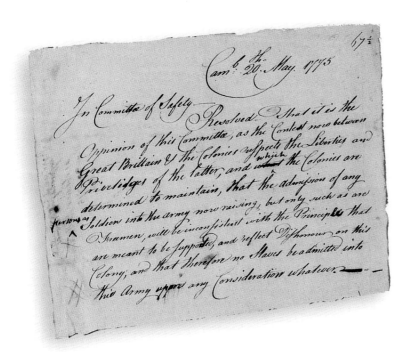

Massachusetts Committee of Safety document forbidding enlistment of slaves into the American army surrounding Boston. In late autumn 1775 free Black men were also barred from serving; that ban was soon reversed, and eventually many states allowed slaves to enlist.

1775, Drummer, 29th Regiment of Foot

By the time of the War of the American Revolution the British 29th Regiment was a venerable organization. First formed in 1694, the regiment was disbanded four years later, then re-formed in the second year of the War of the Spanish Succession (1701–1713).

The regiment first arrived in America late in 1745, landing in Virginia before being sent the next year to garrison Louisbourg in Nova Scotia. Four years later, the 29th sailed for Ireland, where it remained until June 1765. During that time Lieutenant Colonel George Boscawen was appointed commander (1752), and in 1759 the regiment received several men of African descent to serve as drummers. According to Hugh Everard, the regiment's chronicler,

> Admiral [Edward] Boscawen being at the surrender of Guadeloupe, and thinking that blacks would prove very ornamental as drummers, procured eight or ten boys, whom he brought home and gave to his brother, who then commanded the 29th Regiment. Col. [John] Enys [ensign in 1775] . . . states: "His Majesty's permission was obtained to retain them in that capacity, and when I joined the regiment in 1775, there were three, if not more, of the original blacks in the corps, who were remarkable good drummers."

The Island of Guadeloupe capitulated on May 2, 1759, a time when Admiral Boscawen was with a fleet en route to Europe, which calls into question that origin story. We do know that three Black drummers joined the regiment prior to 1759: John Charloe, from St. Kitts, served from 1751 to 1780; John Bacchus, born on Jamaica, served 1752 to 1780; and Joseph Provence of Santo Domingo from 1755 to 1790. It may be that the colonel himself decided to add enough Black drummers to ensure one for each company; however they joined, by April 1774 there were ten Black drummers with the regiment, including the three already mentioned.

Black musicians or servants were a status symbol in European courts, households, and military units, so it is no surprise that the 29th's commander took the opportunity to add these men to his corps. And being soldiers with a special and important talent, drummers and fifers (even slaves) were paid 50 percent more than private soldiers. In July 1765 the regiment returned to Nova Scotia and, with the 1767 Townsend Acts stirring trouble in Boston, sailed there, landing on October 5, 1768. The 29th Regiment and other troops marched in "with drums beating, fifes playing, and colours flying."

The day after they arrived, several soldiers having incurred punishment, it was administered by the 29th Regiment drummers, that duty being associated with their rank. Flogging was always a barbarous sight, but in this instance it was Black men, normally servants or slaves, inflicting it on white men, and the citizens of Boston were shocked. The whippings were called "indignities [that] are a Disgrace to the human Nature"; another witness stated, "to behold Britons scourg'd by Negro Drummers, was a new and very disagreeable Spectacle." Worse, the following week,

> in the forenoon one Rogers, a New-England man, sentenced to receive 1000 stripes, and a number of other soldiers, were scourged in the Common by the black drummers, in a manner, which however necessary, was shocking to humanity; some gentlemen who had held commissions in the army, observing, that only 40 of the 170 lashes received by Rogers, at this time, was equal in punishment to 500, they had seen given in other regiments.

A year and a half later, on the evening of March 5, 1770, heightened tensions led to a confrontation between soldiers of the 29th and a large Boston crowd; rocks and other missiles were thrown and the troops fired, killing three and wounding eight others. Two of the wounded later died. At the soldiers' civil trial 29th drummer Thomas Walker, "a tall negro," testified to the hatred aimed at the British military in the months leading up to the "massacre."

The use of Black drummers in British regiments was not widespread during the period, but we do know at least one other regiment, the 38th, had three drummers of African descent in 1765. Those numbers can be compared to twenty-nine known drummers, fifers, and trumpeters of color in Loyalist units, and at least eighty-three Black drummers and three fifers in German corps.

In 1771 the 29th Regiment sailed to Florida, where it was stationed at Pensacola and Mobile. Over a year later it returned to England, only to be sent to Canada in spring 1776. The regiment's main body played a support role in 1777, with only the grenadier and light infantry companies taking part in the ill-fated Saratoga campaign. The regiment remained in Canada until October 1787, when it took a ship back to England.

With the onset of the nineteenth century, individual Black men began to enlist in British regiments as arms-bearing private soldiers, several being present at the Battle of Waterloo and other famous actions. But the 29th continued its custom of Black drummers for almost eighty-four years; the last known veteran 29th Regiment drummer of African descent died on July 15, 1843.

Sources: Hugh Everard, *History of Thomas Farrington's Regiment: Subsequently Designated the 29th (Worcestershire) Foot, 1694–1881* (Worcester, UK: Littlebury & Company, Worcester Press, 1891), 46–50, 53, 55, 56, 58, 71, 77–104; John D. Ellis, "Drummers for the Devil? The Black Soldiers of the 29th (Worcestershire) Regiment of Foot, 1759–1843," *Journal of the Society of Army Historical Research*, vol. 80, no. 323 (Autumn 2002), 188, 200; Don N. Hagist, "Black Drummers in a Redcoat Regiment," *Journal of the American Revolution* (online), February 22, 2022, https://allthingsliberty.com/2022/02/black-drummers-in-a-redcoat-regiment/; Steven M. Baule, "Drummers in the British Army during the American Revolution," *Journal of the Society for Army Historical Research*, vol. 86, no. 345 (2008), 29–30; David Niescior, "'to behold Britons scourg'd by Negro Drummers, was a new and very disagreeable Spectacle': The Army, Race, and Slavery in Boston During the Townshend Acts Crisis" (Rutgers University, 2014), 11–19, https://www.academia.edu/14097529/_to_behold_Britons_scourg_d_by _Negro_Drummers_was_a_new_and_very_disagreeable_Spectacle_The_Army_Race_and_Slavery_in_Boston_During_the_Townshend_Acts_Crisis; John L. Bell, "Black Drummers of the 29th Regiment," May 2, 2007, https://boston1775.blogspot.com/2007/05/black-drummers-of-29th-regiment.html; John D. Ellis, "They Were There Too—Black Soldiers in the British Army at the Battle of Waterloo," https://www.academia.edu/43352940/They_were_there_too_Black_Soldiers_in_the_British_Army_at_the_Battle_of_Waterloo); Ellis, "From Nova-Scotia to Liverpool, via the Battlefields of the Napoleonic War: The Travels and Travails of Drummer George Wise of the 29th (Worcestershire) Regiment of Foot," https://www.historicalroots.com/ george-wise-from-nova-scotia-to-liverpool-via-the-battlefields-of-the-napoleonic-wars/.

Above: British soldier's brass waist belt plate, 29th Regiment of Foot (Private Collection)

June 17, 1775, The Battle of Bunker Hill

Following the April 19, 1775, British raid on Concord, American militia companies and regiments surrounded the Crown-occupied city of Boston. Beginning that day thousands of militia troops from all the New England colonies converged on the area. Some reached the scene of action on the 19th; all as they arrived were eventually formed into what became the New England Army of Observation, which morphed into the Continental Army when General George Washington took command on July 3, 1775.

The Charlestown peninsula lies across the Charles River, north of Boston; Charlestown proper sits at the southern base of Breed's Hill. Prior to the June 17 battle the peninsula was unoccupied ground, though well in range of British warships. Still, American forces occasionally made their appearance there. In the afternoon of June 13 Major General Israel Putnam led a force of "between 2 and 3,000 of the Rebels" across the neck joining the peninsula to the mainland, over Bunker's Hill to Breed's Hill "where they kept parading a long time." Putnam then marched his troops down into Charlestown, upon which the sixty-four-gun HMS *Somerset* prepared for action. On this occasion cooler heads prevailed, with American soldiers shouting a "War-hoop" before withdrawing across Charlestown Neck.

To forestall a leaked British plan of attack slated for execution on June 18, on the 15th the Massachusetts Committee of Safety directed that "the hill called Bunker's Hill, in Charlestown, be securely kept and defended, and also some one hill or hills on Dorchester Neck [south of Boston] be likewise secured . . . [the militia to be prepared] to march on the shortest notice, completely equipped, having thirty rounds of cartridges per man." Colonel William Prescott later wrote, "on the 16th June, in the evening, I received orders to march to Breed's Hill." Taking position on Breed's rather than Bunker's hill meant occupying forces with artillery could command the north end of Boston and its adjacent harbor, thus ensuring a British reaction.

In that manner, twenty-eight days after Lexington and Concord, the second major action of the war was about to take place. Lieutenant Paul Lunt described it succinctly:

> Friday, 16th. — Our men went to Charlestown and intrenched on a hill beyond Bunker's Hill. They fired from the ships and Copp's Hill all the time.
>
> Saturday, 17th. — The Regulars landed a number of troops, and we engaged them. They drove us off the hill, and burnt Charlestown. Dr. [Joseph] Warren was lost in the battle: the siege lasted about three hours. They killed about 50 of our men, wounded about 80: we killed of the king's troops 896,— 92 officers, 104 sergeants.
>
> Sunday, 18th. — We intrenched on Prospect Hill [just west of Charlestown Neck].

On the night of June 16 Colonel Prescott led "about one thousand" Massachusetts and Connecticut soldiers onto the peninsula, making their way to the top of Breed's Hill, where they commenced digging. They would fight from behind fortifications; Israel Putnam said of the amateur soldiers, "Americans are not at all afraid of their heads, though very much afraid of their legs; if you cover these, they will fight forever." In the end a rough redoubt was built atop the hill, 132 feet square with a narrow opening on the north side for access. Made of "dry and loose" heaped soil, it was "raised to the height of 6 or 7 feet, with a small ditch at its base, but it was yet in a rude or imperfect state." Protecting the south side were American marksmen in vacated Charlestown. Before the British assault, New Hampshire and other troops took post to the north behind "a fence half of stone and two rayles of wood" and "a breastwork made with strong railing taken from the fences and stuffed with Hay." To fill gaps in the northern defense line, three small V-shaped fleches were built, likely from rails. Additional troops took post behind a stone wall on the Mystic River beach.

Of the three to four thousand American troops on the peninsula during the battle, the names of eighty-eight Black and fifteen Indian soldiers are known; historian George Quintal Jr. estimates the total may have been as high as 150, roughly 4 to 5 percent of American forces involved. One anonymous Black combatant steeled the heart of a white militia soldier about to join the fray. John Greenwood noted,

everywhere the greatest terror and confusion seemed to prevail. . . . As I ran along the road leading to Bunker Hill it was filled with chairs and wagons, bearing the wounded and dead. . . . Never having beheld such a sight before, I felt very much frightened. . . . I could positively feel my hair stand on end. Just as I came near the place, a negro man, wounded in the back of his neck, passed me and, his collar being open and he not having anything on except his shirt and trousers, I saw the wound quite plainly and the blood running down his back. I asked him if it hurt him much. . . . He said no, that he was only going to get a [bandage] put on it, and meant to return. You cannot conceive what encouragement this immediately gave me; I began to feel brave and like a soldier from that moment, and fear never troubled me afterward during the whole war.

Sources: Robert K. Wright Jr., *The Continental Army* (Washington, DC: Government Printing Office, 1983), 3, 12–20, 22–24; John R. Elting, *The Battle of Bunker's Hill* (Monmouth Beach, NJ: Philip Freneau Press, 1975), 3, 6, 10–13, 17, 19–21, 24, 26–27, 30–35, 37–38; Samuel A. Green, ed., *Paul Lunt's Diary, May–December 1775* (Boston: Privately printed, 1872), 6; George Quintal Jr., *"A Peculiar Beauty and Merit": African Americans and American Indians at the Battle of Bunker Hill* (Privately printed: 2006), 39–41.

June 17, 1775, The Redoubt (Battle of Bunker Hill)

About 3:30 p.m. Major General Sir William Howe ordered his troops forward against the fortifications on and adjoining Breed's Hill. In this first attack a column of British light infantry was sent along the beach in the supposition it was not fortified. Meeting heavy fire coming from behind a stone wall in that narrow space, the lights fell back, leaving ninety-six dead upon the beach, "as thick as sheep in a fold." Going against the fence line and fleches, Howe wrote that his battalions were disordered "in getting over some very high fences of strong railing under a heavy fire, well kept up by the Rebels, they [the British, then] began firing, and by crowding fell into disorder, and in this state the 2d Line mixt with them." Brigadier General Robert Pigot's British battalions going against the redoubt also stalled in disorder, and fired back at the Americans. After withdrawing to a safe distance Howe sent his forces forward in a second failed attack.

Changing tactics for his third advance at 4:30, the light infantry were deployed in open order, holding the Americans in place at the fence line, while Sir William's main body enveloped the redoubt. With the New Englanders exhausted and running low on ammunition, they stood as long as possible, but as Howe's soldiers poured over the ramparts a harried withdrawal began.

Of the 2,500 British troops engaged, nineteen officers and 207 enlisted men were killed, seventy officers and 738 enlisted wounded, for a total loss of 1,034; that does not include some lightly wounded who remained on duty, or those who died of their wounds. The New England forces engaged are difficult to enumerate, perhaps 2,000 in the redoubt, adjacent fence lines and rail fleches, possibly a total of 4,000 if those who took post on Bunker's Hill are included. Colonel Artemas Ward recorded American losses at 115 killed, 305 wounded, and thirty captured; total casualties were likely between 400 and 600.

For many of the ninety or so men of African descent who fought at Bunker's Hill we have only brief accounts; a neighbor described Asahel Wood as a "Coloured Man," and noted "[he] stated to me [he] . . . was in the Battle of Bunker Hill." Others gained some repute. Cuff Whittemore "fought bravely in the redoubt. He had a ball through his hat . . . fought to the last, and when compelled to retreat, though wounded, the splendid arms of the British officers were prizes too tempting. . . . He seized the sword of one of them slain in the redoubt, and came off with the trophy, which in a few days he unromantically sold." Aaron Smith was positioned at a rail fence "strengthened" with bundles of new-cut hay. He told of, "a man at his side, a negro, so crippled by a shot in the leg that he could not rise up to discharge his gun, but he could load and re-load, which he continued to do, both Smith's and his own, and then hand them to Smith to fire, until their ammunition was expended, when he undertook to carry the negro off the field on his back, but was obliged to leave him to his fate."

Without proof, Salem Poor is often credited with killing Marine major William Pitcairn. Poor did perform some extraordinary action at Bunker Hill. A testimonial was signed by Colonel William Prescott and thirteen officers from five different regiments:

The Subscribers beg leave, to report to your Honble House, (which wee do in justice to the Caracter of So Brave a Man) that under Our Own observation, Wee declare that A Negro Man Called Salem Poor of Col Fryes Regiment Capt Ames Company in the late Battle at Charlestown, behaved like an Experienced officer, as Well as an Excellent Soldier, to Set forth Particulars of his Conduct Would be Tedious, Wee Would Only beg leave to Say in the Person of this Sd Negro Centers a Brave & gallant Soldier. The Reward due to So great and Distinguisht A Caracter, Wee Submit to the Congress—Cambridge Decr 5th 1775

Historian George Quintal posits, "It is a strong [unsubstantiated] local tradition . . . that he shot Lieutenant Colonel James Abercrombie of the grenadiers, the highest-ranking British officer to have been killed . . . that day. To have performed this act, Salem Poor would have had to remain in the front ranks in the redoubt probably much longer than was prudent."

Of the Black soldiers known to have been at the Bunker Hill battle, three were wounded and three killed that fateful day. In the nineteenth century one veteran's family suffered the iniquity of American slavery, and the descendants of two others fought to end that institution. Jude Hall's three sons

were kidnapped and sold into enslavement in the nineteenth century; a testimonial by a Boston gentleman recorded that Jude, who was deceased, "was a pensioner of the United States. . . . He was alive when [his son] James was first heard of in slavery; but he did not live to hear from William [who had escaped and was in England]. Nobody has ever heard from Aaron." Jeffrey Hemenway and Barzillai Lew had descendants who served in the American Civil War all-Black 54th and 55th Massachusetts Regiments; Zimri Lew Jr. was in the 55th Regiment, while Alexander Freeman Hemenway and Cornelius Henson, both in the 54th, were in the attack on Fort Wagner, July 18, 1863, where Cornelius was captured.

Sources: John R. Elting, *The Battle of Bunker's Hill* (Monmouth Beach, NJ: Philip Freneau Press, 1975), 26–27, 30–38; George Quintal Jr., *"A Peculiar Beauty and Merit": African Americans and American Indians at the Battle of Bunker Hill* (Privately printed: 2006), 45, 100–101, 129–30, 135, 153, 159–61, 201; Andrew H. Ward, *History of the Town of Shrewsbury, Massachusetts from Its Settlement in 1717 to 1829 . . .* (Boston: S.G. Drake, 1847), 55–56; J. L. Bell, "Peter Salem—Salem Poor, Who Killed Major John Pitcairn," *Journal of the American Revolution* (June 18, 2018), https://allthingsliberty.com/2018/06/peter-salem-salem-poor-who-killed-major-john-pitcairn/; "Zimri Lew II," https://www.wikitree.com/wiki/Lew-50); "The 54th Massachusetts Regiment: C to H," https://www.nga.gov/collection/sculpture/fifty-fourth-regiment/fifty-fourth-c-h.html).

1775–1776, Ethiopian Regiment

The short-lived Ethiopian Regiment was the American Revolutionary War's first Black-centered combat unit; as with the segregated 1st Rhode Island Regiment (an integrated unit prior to March 1778, and integrated again as of January 1781), it was born of necessity and centered around freed slaves.

John Murray, fourth Earl of Dunmore, became Virginia's Royal governor in 1771. In 1774 the rebellious First Virginia Convention pledged support for Boston, banned British trade, and elected delegates to the First Continental Congress. In April of the next year, with Virginians actively raising militia companies, Lord Dunmore removed a large quantity of gunpowder from Williamsburg; the stores were taken aboard the HMS *Magdalen*, but the confiscation only increased antipathy toward the governor. By early June Dunmore and his family had fled to the safety of the armed ship *Fowey* in the York River. With that action he permanently relinquished his governance of the colony.

Dunmore's armed forces consisted of seamen and Marines from the few British warships in the area, plus a small number of loyal Virginians. In autumn he was reinforced by the understrength British 14th Regiment (comprising about five companies, numbering thirteen officers and 156 enlisted men). To remedy his predicament more troops were needed and the governor decided on a plan that would add to his little corps, simultaneously hitting the rebellious Virginians materially and financially. During the April 1775 Gunpowder Crisis Dunmore threatened to "declare Freedom to the Slaves, and reduce the City of Williamsburg to Ashes." In autumn 1775 he went one step further and created a corps of freed slaves, the Ethiopian Regiment. On November 30, 1775 Lord Dunmore wrote Major General Sir William Howe, commander in chief in America, "you may observe by my proclamation that I offer freedom to the blacks of all Rebels that join me, in consequence of which there are between two and three hundred already come in, and those I form into Corps . . . giving them white officers and non commissioned officers in proportion." On December 2 the *Virginia Gazette* published the following notice: "Since Lord Dunmore's proclamation made its appearance here, it is said he recruited his army, in the counties of Princess Anne and Norfolk, to the amount of about 2000 men, including his black regiment, which is thought to be a considerable part, with this inscription on their breasts: 'Liberty to Slaves.'" Along with the exaggerated estimate of Dunmore's army, there is some question whether the use of that motto was true or a bit of Whig rabble-rousing; whatever the case, the phrase was extremely provocative. Eventually, at least a portion of the freedmen-soldiers were issued surplus 14th Regiment coats.

On November 15, 1775, Dunmore had gained a minor victory over local Whig forces at Kemp's Landing, near Norfolk (during this action two Black soldiers purportedly captured a Virginia officer). While some Black troops participated in that affair, their first real combat was at Great Bridge where Crown and Whig forces had erected fortifications on opposite sides of a causeway. On December 9 Dunmore, wishing to forestall a Rebel attack, sent his own forces against the opposing breastworks. The assault, led by the 14th Regiment, supported by contingents from the Queen's Own Loyal Virginians and the Ethiopian Regiment, was a disastrous failure. While the Ethiopians saw little action at Great Bridge, among the casualties were two of Dunmore's newly freed slaves, now soldiers: wounded and taken prisoner were James Anderson, hit "in the Forearm—Bones shattered and flesh much torn," and Casar, wounded "in the Thigh, by a Ball, and 5 shot—one lodged." With that defeat, Lord Dunmore's troops were forced to abandon the mainland and return to their small fleet, occasionally occupying remote islands or isolated, defensible land. (As a side note, William Flora, a free Black Virginia militiaman, opposed the attack on the bridge, making it the first-known instance in that conflict of African Americans facing each other in battle.)

The following months were spent harassing and plundering waterside Whig properties, and foraging for food and other necessities. By late winter 1776 there was a new foe for Dunmore's men to reckon with, variola major, otherwise known as smallpox. The men of the Ethiopian Regiment were hit hard; as the disease spread, Dunmore's forces established an inoculation camp on Tucker's Island, near Portsmouth. During that lengthy process, they needed a more defensible position, so moved to Gwynn's Island, in the Chesapeake Bay at the end of May 1776. One British captain claimed most of the Black soldiers had been inoculated while still at Norfolk and were felled by an unrelated fever, perhaps typhus, during that spring and summer. Several others noted that inoculations occurred on Gwynn's Island. Whatever the case, the soldiers died in great numbers. In June, Lord Dunmore wrote, "Had it not been for this horrid disorder I should have had two thousand blacks." By the time the Royal governor abandoned Virginia, roughly 150 Black soldiers, plus 150 women and children, sailed north with him.

Reaching New York in late August 1776, the Ethiopian Regiment disembarked on Staten Island. The corps soon disbanded and its members dispersed. Some likely attached joined the Black Pioneers, the only Black corps to be placed on the official Provincial Establishment.

Sources: Todd W. Braisted, "The Black Pioneers and Others: The Military Role of Black Loyalists in the American War for Independence," in John W. Polis, ed., *Moving On: Black Loyalists in the Afro-Atlantic World* (New York and London: Garland Publishing, Inc., 1999), 3–37, https://tinyurl.com/Braisted-Black-Pioneers; James Corbett David, *Dunmore's New World: The Extraordinary Life of a Royal Governor in Revolutionary America—with Jacobites, Counterfeiters, Land Schemes, Shipwrecks, Scalping, Indian Politics, Runaway Slaves, and Two Illegal Royal Weddings* (Charlottesville: University of Virginia Press, 2013); Benjamin Quarles, *The Negro in the American Revolution* (New York, London: W.W. Norton & Company, 1973), 19–32; John U. Rees, *"They Were Good Soldiers": African-Americans Serving in the Continental Army, 1775–1783* (Warwick, UK: Helion and Company, 2019; U.S. distributor, Casemate Publishing), 13–16; Elizabeth A. Fenn, *Pox Americana: The Great Smallpox Epidemic of 1775–82* (New York: Hill and Wang, 2002); "Ethiopian Regiment Morning Reports," *Virginia Gazette*, (Williamsburg), August 31, 1776, http://www.royalprovincial.com/military/rhist/ethiopian/ethreports.htm);
Virginia Gazette, February 3, 1776, No. 1278, "Williamsburg, Feb. 3. Six white men and four negroes, last week, landed near to Mr. Narsworthy's, in Isle of Wight County, in order to carry off some sheep which they knew were on the plantation, and likewise seize Mr. Narsworthy, for whose ransome they expected a large quantity of stock. A negro man, who happened to be in the yard, discovering a negro dressed in the uniform of the 14th regiment, immediately went and informed his master that some of the Governor's men had landed; he dispatched the negro to a guard who were stationed at a small distance; they pursued them, took the negro in uniform, and drove the others into their boat without any stock."; John U. Rees, "'I offer freedom to the blacks of all Rebels that join me': Lord Dunmore's Loyalist Ethiopian Regiment, 1775–1776," https://www.academia.edu/44364250/_I_offer_freedom_to_the_blacks_of_all_Rebels_that_join_me_Lord_Dunmores_Loyalist_Ethiopian_Regiment_1775_1776).

1777, American Militia Soldier, Northern or Middle States

American militias were often the only military organizations available to protect state frontiers, land and sea, as well as other locales. Militias provided a much-needed auxiliary force for the Continental Army, serving to guard supply lines, provide extra labor, or augment forces on campaign and in action. They could also screen an army's movements or even stand in a line of battle. Continental regiments were the backbone of the new nation's military forces, more reliable in a European-style battle or special operations, but their numbers were small compared to state militias. One drawback of the militia was their limited term of service, counted in days, weeks, occasionally months, as opposed to the years-long enlistments Continental soldiers signed on for. Another was their oft-exhibited lack of discipline.

Militia forces assisted the Continental Army in another way. Beginning as early as 1777 and continuing into 1782, states could conscript men from the militia to serve in Continental regiments for a term of from six to eighteen months. Early on this was done by Connecticut and Virginia to garner men for their long-term regiments. In 1778 the first congressionally authorized draft was implemented, allowing eleven states (South Carolina and Georgia excepted), to draft men into their Continental regiments for a term of nine months, but only if the state wished to do so. The conscription legislation first relied on volunteers, then substitutes purchased by men who did not wish to serve, and finally drafted men. Many thus enlisted had already seen extensive service in the militia or in an early-war regular regiment, and proved good soldiers.

Most state militias had seen some campaign service: In 1777 large numbers of New England militia were with Major General Horatio Gates's army contending against the British at Saratoga, and by 1781 the militias of South Carolina had already fought for several years against Indian, Loyalist, and British forces. The New Jersey militia had wide-ranging experience gained during the spring 1777 Forage War, and again in the New Jersey and Philadelphia campaigns that same year. The 1778 Monmouth campaign and battle provided further hardening. They were so effective in the June 1780 New Jersey battles of Connecticut Farms and Springfield, that Jäger captain Johann Ewald was later moved to write:

What can you do to those small bands who have learned to fight separate, who know how to use any molehill for their protection, and who, when attacked, run back as fast as they will approach you again, who continuously find space to hide? Never have I seen these maneuvers carried out better than by the American militia, especially that of the province of Jersey. If you were forced to retreat through these people you could be certain of having them constantly around you.

One early 1777 action illustrates the mode of warfare at which militia were most proficient. On January 20, 500 Crown troops, British and German, left New Brunswick, New Jersey, to gather food and forage at the Van Nest mill on the Raritan River, nine miles away. Two Connecticut Independent companies and some militia were stationed nearby and tried to push the British back, but did not have sufficient men. Meanwhile, the alarm had been raised and militia forces began to arrive, eventually numbering about 400. Lieutenant Cornelius Van Horn was among them, recounting that as they reached the river, "our Colonel [Mark] Thompson on horse at our head road a cross the water brakeing the ice at the shore with his Sword wee his men waided through after him, the water to our waistbands and after crossing a field about 40 rods wide to a road where wee took 36 Inglish Wagons loaded with hay & grain & large inglish horses."

Militia soldier Samuel Sutphen noted,

I piloted Davis' Co[mpany] and as many others as we could assemble to a fording place over the S[outh] branch, and hurried on to the mills. They had plundered the mill of grain and flour, and were on their way back to Brunswick, but had not got out of the lane leading from the mill to the great road. We headed them in the lane. The team laden with the flour was the first we fell in with; the lane, 100 yards, was filled with 4-horse teams. Davis ordered us to fire, and then we shot part of the 1st team, which stopped the whole drove. The drivers left their teams and run. A guard escorting the teams made their escape. We took, as was said, about 40 horses, and all the waggons, about 10, which were all sent off under an escort to Morristown.

Sutphen, who belonged to the 1st Regiment, Somerset County militia, was enslaved by Casper Berger of Readington, who enlisted him to serve in his place. Mr. Sutphen claimed to have been at the Battle of Long Island in August 1776, and then temporarily transferred to a New York militia company to take part in Major General John Sullivan's 1779 punitive expedition against the Iroquois. Free mulatto James Ray, another New Jersey militia soldier with lengthy experience, was also with Sullivan.

At the end of the war Samuel Sutphen "demanded" his freedom from Berger. Instead, Berger sold him to another man. Samuel stated, "[I] bought my freedom after the additional servitude of 20 years under different masters."

Sources: Larry R. Gerlach, *New Jersey in the American Revolution, 1763–1783: A Documentary History* (Trenton: New Jersey Historical Commission, 1975), 354–57; John U. Rees, "'The pleasure of their number': 1778, Crisis, Conscription, and Revolutionary Soldiers' Recollections," Part I: "'Filling the Regiments by drafts from the Militia.': The 1778 Recruiting Acts," https://www.academia.edu/13926796/_Filling_the_Regiments_by_drafts_from_the_Militia_The_1778_Recruiting_Acts. Part II: "'Fine, likely, tractable men.': Levy Statistics and New Jersey Service Narratives," https://www.academia.edu/13926835/_Fine_likely_tractable_men_Levy_Statistics_and_New_Jersey_Service_Narratives. Part III: "'He asked me if we had been discharged . . .': New Jersey, Massachusetts, New York, Maryland, and North Carolina Levy Narratives," https://www.academia.edu/13926847/_He_asked_me_if_we_had_been_discharged_New_Jersey_Massachusetts_New_York_Maryland_and_North_Carolina_Levy_Narratives); John U. Rees, "'The road appeared to be full of red Coats . . .': The Battle of Millstone, 20 January 1777: An Episode in the Forage War," *Military Collector & Historian*, vol. 62, no. 1 (Spring 2010), 24–35, https://www.academia.edu/4595164/_The_road_appeared_to_be_full_of_red_Coats_The_Battle_of_Millstone_20_January_1777_An_Episode_in_the_Forage_War_).

September 11, 1777, Battle of Brandywine

After a brief campaign in New Jersey, on July 20, 1777, General Sir William Howe's British, German, and Loyalist forces put to sea from the waters off Staten Island, New York, destination unknown. For the remainder of July and the beginning of August, portions of General George Washington's Continental Army marched and countermarched, led by news and rumors as to whether the fleet had gone north or south. Vice Admiral Richard Howe's ships, having sailed to the northern end of the Chesapeake Bay, found a landing place at Turkey Point, Maryland, and on August 25 began disembarking troops. There followed a series of maneuvers and failed defensive stands, Washington finally settling on a position along the Brandywine Creek, in Pennsylvania, where his troops arrived on September 9.

On September 11 General Howe's forces moved to attack. As the action opened, General Washington and Major General the Marquis de Lafayette rode the defensive lines arrayed along the northeast side of the Brandywine. Brigadier General Anthony Wayne's 2,000-man Pennsylvania division took post at Chadd's Ford, supported by the guns of Colonel Thomas Procter's 4th Continental Artillery Regiment. (In the image, the 7th Pennsylvania Regiment is seen cheering, with officers and support personnel of the 4th Artillery on the right.) Most

of Procter's cannon and crews were spread along the high ground north of Chadd's Ford. Procter also located four guns overlooking that crossing point, on a height behind the John Chad house in an earth-and-log fortification.

In mid-morning fifteen-year-old Jacob Nagle, a volunteer with the 4th Artillery, stood by as, "General Washington came riding up to Col. Procter with his Life Guards . . . and enquired how we came on." Procter told him of two bothersome masked British fieldpieces, and the general ordered intense counterbattery fire which seemed to silence the enemy guns.

The 4th Artillery cannon were still in place above the Chad house when German and British troops attacked across the ford, a little after 5:00 p.m. This assault was delayed to allow General Howe's flanking column to hit the American right, which had occurred about one hour previously at and near Birmingham Hill, approximately six miles north of the ford. Caught between two pincers, American forces along the Brandywine began a fighting withdrawal. Procter's men fought to the last. Jacob Nagle observed British troops advancing on the artillery redan, saying that, "though our artillery made a clear lane through them as they mounted the works . . . they filled up the ranks again." In that action at least three American artillerymen were wounded, the regimental quartermaster killed,

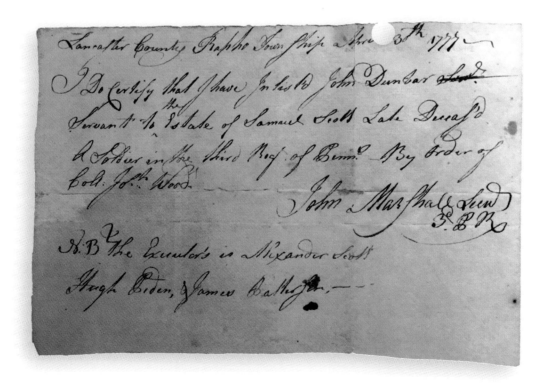

Enlistment authorization of John Dunbar, a soldier of the 3rd Pennsylvania Regiment. Dunbar was formerly enslaved by Samuel Scott, a Pennsylvania soldier who died in April 1777. Pennsylvania did not allow the enlistment of slaves by masters, so the document is proof that Dunbar was freed by the provisions of Samuel Scott's will. (Information courtesy of Matthew C. White)

and Colonel Procter's horse shot under him. The unit lost three brass field pieces and a howitzer in this action. Soon after, the 1st Pennsylvania Regiment's Colonel James Chambers saw that the enemy had "advanced on the hill, where our [artillery] park was," ordering a musket volley to clear them out. Chambers then had "two field pieces [taken] up the road protected by about sixty . . . men, who had very warm work, but brought them [off] safe." Jacob Nagle saw a group of soldiers having "swampy ground to cross with the artillery to get into the road, and the horses being shot, the men could not drag the pieces out."

Edward (Ned) Hector, a wagon driver, was among the retreating melee of soldiers and vehicles. Hector had previously been a bombardier with Procter's Regiment, but either reenlisted in his new role or had been demoted because, as a Black man, it would have been unacceptable for him to outrank white matrosses (artillery laborers). Late in life, Mr. Hector was recognized for his actions that evening. While he never applied for a federal pension, he was denied a state annuity. The year before his death he was awarded a one-time forty-dollar gratuity for his service. His death notice, published in the January 1834 Norristown *Free Press*, noted:

> His conduct on one memorable occasion, exhibited an example of patriotism and bravery which deserves to be recorded. At the battle of Brandywine he had charge of an ammunition wagon attached to Colonel Proctor's regiment, and when the American army was obliged to retreat, an order was given by the proper officers to those having charge of the wagons, to abandon them to the enemy, and save themselves by flight. The heroic reply of the deceased was uttered in the true spirit of the Revolution: "The enemy shall not have my team; I will save my horses and myself!" He instantly started on his way, and as he proceeded, amid the confusion of the surrounding scene, he calmly gathered up a few stands of arms which had been left on the field by the retreating soldiers, and safely retired with his wagon, team and all, in face of the victorious foe.

Two other Pennsylvania Black Continentals are known to have fought at Brandywine. Sixth Pennsylvania soldier Stacey Williams was "wounded in the right thigh" fighting at or near Birmingham Hill, on the American left. John Francis, in the 3rd Regiment, same brigade as Williams, "was wounded and Taken Prisoner at Brandiwine" with "one of his Legs (both of which were wounded) being much shattered & little hopes of recovering so as to be fit for Military Duty."

Sources: Michael C. Harris, *Brandywine: A Military History of the Battle That Lost Philadelphia but Saved America, September 11, 1777* (El Dorado Hills, CA: Sava Beatie, 2014), 57, 67, 152, 169–70, 210, 243, 324–25, 327–30 (note 16); John B. B. Trussell Jr., *The Pennsylvania Line: Regimental Organization and Operations, 1776–1783* (Harrisburg: Pennsylvania Museum and Historical Commission, 1977), 9–20, 85–91, 189–210; National Archives, Pension files (microfilm), reel 2265, William Stacey (40688); John B. Linn and William H. Egle, eds., *Pennsylvania Archives*, Series 2, vol. 10 (Harrisburg: Lane S. Hart, State Printer, 1880), 606; NA , Pension, reel 2265, William Stacey (40688), deposition of John Markland; (Pennsylvania) Record Group 33 Records of the Supreme Court Eastern District Revolutionary War Soldiers Claims, 1781–1789, images 216–222, John Francis, https://digitalarchives .powerlibrary.org/psa/islandora/object/psa%3A1795845?overlay_query=RELS_EXT _isMemberOfCollection_uri_ms%3A%22info%3Afedora%2Fpsa%3Arwscrp1786%22& fbclid=IwAR0FZ9L09mk12kuV90XqbEIdzuWHJ5_8S_XY4tsjthCHqbwi4U0-nuF6v68.

September 11, 1777, Battle of Brandywine

1777 Saratoga Campaign, 4th New York Regiment

In spring 1777 American Continental and militia forces in northern New York were preparing for an all-too-certain British invasion. The previous October, Brigadier General Benedict Arnold's improvised flotilla confronted a British fleet near Valcour Island on Lake Champlain. Though Arnold lost the battle, along with most of his ships, that action delayed the Crown incursion for another seven months. In mid-June 1777 Lieutenant General John Burgoyne's army of British, German, and Loyalist troops, augmented by a mixed force of some 500 Native Americans, moved south. By early July American soldiers had evacuated Fort Ticonderoga and its subsidiary post Mount Independence, with Burgoyne's forces following.

Major General Arthur St. Clair's retreating Continental regiments took the road to Castleton, Vermont, via Hubbardton, On the morning of July 7, British brigadier general Simon Fraser's 850-man advance force caught up with Massachusetts colonel Ebenezer Francis's rear guard. Francis's men were preparing to set off and quickly formed battle lines. The ensuing hour-and-a-half battle resulted in 137 Americans killed and wounded, and 240 captured, while Fraser's forces were severely mauled. Among the prisoners was Aaron Oliver, a mulatto. He had served with Colonel James Reed's New Hampshire Regiment in 1775, taking part in the Bunker Hill battle, was at Fort Ticonderoga with Colonel Enoch Hale's regiment the next year, and enlisted for three years in March 1777 with Colonel Alexander Scammell's 3rd New Hampshire Regiment. Conditions during captivity were harsh. Silas Pratt and John Welch were also taken that day. Welch recalled being "first kept in the guard house at Ticonderoga," while his messmate stated he "was kept in captivity for about 15 months; that during . . . his captivity, he suffered almost everything but death, aboard . . . the prison ships, at St. Johns, Quebec, & Halifax, & in the gaols of Quebec & Halifax, but was eventually exchanged at Boston." Oliver returned from captivity on April 3, 1778, in ill-health, and died on April 30 at Bennington, Vermont. (The August 1778 "Return of . . . Negroes in the Army" shows twenty-seven black soldiers in the brigade containing three New Hampshire regiments, plus the 2nd Canadian Regiment.)

In mid-August a 500-man foraging force under German lieutenant general Friedrich Baume was defeated at the Battle of Bennington, near Walloomsac, New York; six days later the siege of Fort Stanwix ended with a British retreat. As Burgoyne's troops moved south they suffered irreplaceable losses, while American forces, resisting when possible, gained increasing reinforcements.

With these American victories behind them and after Major General Horatio Gates's accession to command, between August 19 and September 8 Continental and militia forces began coalescing at Stillwater, New York. A few days later their defensive positions were resituated three miles north, at Bemus Heights on the Hudson, the army's main camp for the upcoming stand against Burgoyne's invasion force.

Previously stationed in the Hudson Highlands, in late August 1777 the 2nd and 4th New York Regiments moved north to Loudon Ferry, on the Hudson River between Albany and Stillwater. That September they were assigned to Brigadier General Ebenezer Learned's brigade of Major General Arnold's division, major portions of which fought in the battles of Freeman's Farm (September 19) and Bemus Heights (October 7). Major General John Burgoyne's army surrendered on October 17.

Exact numbers of Black soldiers in the New York regiments during the Saratoga campaign are uncertain, but in August 1778 the four-regiment New York brigade had thirty-nine men of African descent, making 2.85 percent of total rank and file present. While there were likely ten or more Black men serving with the 2nd and 4th Regiments in the battles against Burgoyne, only two are certainly known by name: 2nd New York soldier John Patterson (aka Peterson), "a Man of Colour," and Cato Moulton, drummer with Captain Benjamin Walker's 4th New York company.

During the autumn 1777 campaign, 4th New York Regiment soldiers wore linen hunting or "rifle" shirts instead of woolen regimental coats; many were issued blue knit-wool "Mill'd Caps" for headwear in lieu of military cocked hats.

Sources: Philip K. Lundeberg, *The Gunboat Philadelphia, and the Defense of Lake Champlain in 1776* (Basin Harbor, VT: Lake Champlain Maritime Museum, 1995), 21–35; Eric Schnitzer and Don Troiani, *Don Troiani's Campaign to Saratoga: The Turning Point of the Revolutionary War in Paintings, Artifacts, and Historical Narrative* (Guilford, CT: Stackpole Books, 2019), 28–32, 48, 52–60, 112–37, 143–46, 149–53; Michael Barbieri, "Fort Ti's Evacuation and the Battle of Hubbardton," *Journal of the American Revolution* (online), July 24, 2014, https://allthingsliberty.com/2014/07/tis-evacuation-and-the-battle-of-hubbardton/; Michael Barbieri, "Aaron Oliver," 2017, Compiled for Hubbardton Battlefield State Historic Site, Hubbardton, VT; Elsa Gilbertson, "Aaron Oliver" (Research compilation), Regional Historic Site Administrator, Vermont Division for Historic Preservation, for Hubbardton Battlefield State Historic Site, Hubbardton, VT, 2016–17; "Aaron Oliver (b. 1750, d. 30 Apr 1778)," https://www.genealogy.com/ftm/s/u/r/Gary-A-Surrell-NH/WEBSITE-0001/UHP-0043.html; John U. Rees, "*They Were Good Soldiers": African-Americans Serving in the Continental Army, 1775–1783* (Warwick, UK: Helion & Company Limited, 2019), 83–84; "African Descended Soldiers at Fort Schuyler & in the Mohawk Valley," https://www.nps.gov/articles/000/patriots-of-color-at-fort-schuyler-in-the-mohawk-valley.htm; New-York Historical Society, The Horatio Gates Papers, 1726–1828 (microfilm edition), George Measam to Gates, September 5, 1777, roll 5, frame 459; New-York Historical Society, Early American Orderly Books: 1748–1817 (microfilm), Maj. Ebenezer Stevens' Independent Battalion of Continental Artillery (September 11 to December 23, 1777), General Orders, October 7, 1777, reel 5, no. 50 (clothing information courtesy of Eric Schnitzer); Compiled Service Records of Soldiers who Served in the American Army During the Revolutionary War (National Archives Microfilm Publication M881), Record Group 93 (Massachusetts), Second New York Regiment, John Peterson, Fourth New York Regiment, Cato Moulton; National Archives, Revolutionary War Pension and Bounty-Land Warrant Application Files (National Archives Microfilm Publication M804), Records of the Department of Veterans Affairs, Record Group 15, Washington, DC, reel 1887, John Patterson/Peterson (S43783); William C. Nell, *Property Qualification or No Property Qualification: A Few Facts from the Record of Patriotic Services of the Colored Men of New York, During the Wars of 1776 and 1812* . . . (New York: Thomas Hamilton, 1860), 7–9.

1777, 2nd Rhode Island Regiment

Rhode Island's Continental cohort was small, beating only Delaware in size. Still, during the *rage militaire* of 1775 the colony contributed three one-year regiments (commanded by colonels James Varnum, Daniel Hitchcock, and Thomas Church) to the New England army. Varnum's and Hitchcock's units were retained in 1776, respectively renamed the 9th and 11th Continental Regiments. Two existing state regiments, William Richmond's and Christopher Lippett's, were added to the national army in September 1776. Lippett joined Washington's forces at New York that October, while Richmond's men remained in Rhode Island. With the Continental Army's 1777 rebirth only the 1st and 2nd Rhode Island Regiments remained, recruited with men enlisted (or reenlisted) for three years or the duration of the war. All these regiments, from 1775 through 1777, contained Black and Indian soldiers serving alongside their white comrades.

In 1777 Rhode Island brigadier general James Varnum commanded a brigade with four regiments, his home state's own two, plus the 4th and 8th Connecticut regiments. All would take part in the autumn fight to keep the Delaware River closed to the British, in order to deny shipborne supplies to Crown forces occupying Philadelphia. Leaving their posts in and around Peekskill, New York, on September 28 Colonel Christopher Greene's 1st Rhode Island was eventually directed to march and occupy Fort Mercer on the Delaware River, while Israel Angell's 2nd Regiment continued to General George Washington's Pennsylvania headquarters. A few days later Angell's troops were also sent to Fort Mercer, arriving on October 18, seven days after Greene's Regiment.

The siege of Fort Mifflin, south of Philadelphia, had begun on September 26, 1777, the same day British forces captured Philadelphia. Fort Mercer in New Jersey, opposite Mifflin, was built by Pennsylvania militia the preceding summer. The fortification was far too large for the forces slated to occupy it, so, under direction of French volunteer artillery Captain Thomas-Antoine de Mauduit du Plessis, a wall was erected across the fort, making a new defensive redoubt ("the Citidel") of the original work's southern third. Meanwhile, detachments of Rhode Island soldiers were ferried to Mud Island to reinforce Fort Mifflin, and on October 12 a 1st Rhode Island captain led a portion of the garrison in an attack on a British gun emplacement on the Pennsylvania shore. Ten days later, Fort Mercer was attacked.

[October 21] Next Day untill Night—we were Inform'd that a Party of Regulars had Landed at [Coopers] ferey to attacke our fort—we Remov'd all our tents & baggage into the Citidale & Every man was Employd at worke on the fort to fortify the same. . . . We Cut Down an orchard by the fort & hald trees Round the fort to Keep off the Enemy—

At that point both Rhode Island regiments contained 379 musicians and privates (the only ranks soldiers of color could hold), including forty-eight African and Native American soldiers. Soldiers of color formed 12.6 percent of the total, Black soldiers alone comprising 10.3 percent.

On October 22, 1777, 2,300 Hessian grenadiers attacked Fort Mercer. First Rhode Island sergeant John Smith gave this account:

Every Person [was] in the fort by 2 O clock & about 3 or 4 O Clock the Enemy advanc'd to the woods adjoining the fort when the Hesian . . . Commander Sent a flag & Demanded the fort['s surrender] or they were ordred to . . . Put all to Death if they overcame us—Colo. Olney Gave them Answer that we ask'd no mercy nor Did we Expect any . . . the flag Returnd & the Enemy began the Attack immediately—they began a brisk fire with their field Peces & then advancd up to the fort. . . . We began a smart fire with our Artillery & our small armes & Continued firing 47 [minutes] as smart as Ever was Known [the unoccupied portion of the fort was turned into a killing ground, with naval artillery firing chain-shot contributing to the slaughter]—the firing began [when] the sun [was] half an hour high & Continued till Dark—we Lost [one officer, four sergeants, and a fifer dead] . . . & Several Privats Killd Belonging to both Regemts.—We Killd Dead of the Hesians . . . one Lt Colo. & several Officers 70 or 80 Non Commissiond Officers & Privats . . . & about 70 or 80 wounded Privats teaken Prisoners —the Rest of the [enemy] army made the best of their way off teaking with them 3 or 4 wagons Loaded with the wounded Hesians. . . . The whole Garrison were up all Night Dressing the wounded & teaking Care of them.

Following this small but seminal action, the Rhode Islanders continued sending men to reinforce Fort Mifflin, until it was evacuated on the night of November 15/16. Lieutenant Loftus Cliffe, British 46th Regiment, viewed the fort on November 16, 1777: "such ruin would amaze you, that a Man should be left alive in it, indeed they must have suffered greatly . . . for I am told that when our People came on it, it was one clot of Blood; every Corner containes Limbs Skin & Gutts. Is supposed they lost 70 men in it; the few that were in it must have been brave fellows." Following the siege, Varnum's brigade rejoined the main army above Philadelphia, taking part in the Whitemarsh operations and Valley Forge winter camp.

Sources: John U. Rees, *"They Were Good Soldiers": African-Americans Serving in the Continental Army, 1775–1783* (Warwick, UK: Helion & Company Limited, 2019), 72; Rees, "'None of you know the hardships of A soldiers life …': Service of the Connecticut Regiments in Maj. Gen. Alexander McDougall's Division, 1777–1778," https://www.academia.edu/14059235/_None_of_you_know_the_hardships_of_A_soldiers_life_Service_of_the_Connecticut_Regiments_of_Maj_Gen_Alexander_McDougall_s_Division_1777_1778, Bibliography, tinyurl.com/CT-troops-77to79; Robert C. Bray and Paul E. Bushnell, eds., *Diary of a Common Soldier in the American Revolution: An Annotated Edition of the Military Journal of Jeremiah Greenman* (DeKalb: Northern Illinois University Press, 1978), 75–88; Map and diagram of the Hessian assault on the fort at Red Bank, NJ, October 22, 1777, Johann Ewald, Hessian jäger captain, Joseph P. Tustin Papers, Special Collections, Harvey A. Andruss Library, Bloomsburg University, Bloomsburg, PA); John W. Jackson, *The Pennsylvania Navy, 1775–1781: The Defense of the Delaware* (New Brunswick, NJ: Rutgers University Press, 1974), 146, 232–33, 241; Norman Desmarais and Edward Field, eds., "The Diary of Colonel Israel Angell Commanding Officer, 2nd Rhode Island Regiment, Continental Army" (1777–1781), https://www.academia.edu/29739571/The_Diary_of_Colonel_Israel_Angell_Commanding_Officer_2nd_Rhode_Island_Regiment_Continental_Army; Bob McDonald, ed., "'Thro Mud & Mire Into The Woods': The Diary of Sergeant John Smith, 1st Rhode Island Regiment, July 18, 1777–January 9, 1778," https://revwar75.com/library/bob/smith2.htm; Robert A. Selig, PhD, "African-Americans, the Rhode Island Regiments, and the Battle of Fort Red Bank, 22 October 1777," Sponsoring Organization County of Gloucester, New Jersey, 2019 (plus, reconciliation of soldier of color numbers at the Fort Mercer assault, and computed proportion of the whole, by John U. Rees); Lt. Loftus Cliffe, (British 46th Regiment) to Bat, "Camp Philadelphia 12 Novr. 1777," (letter discusses events up to November 23, 1777), Loftus Cliffe Papers, William L. Clements Library, University of Michigan, Ann Arbor; John U. Rees, "'We began a smart fire with our Artillery & our small armes': African and Native Americans in the Rhode Island Regiments, 1775–1783," https://www.academia.edu/112997530/_We_began_a_smart_fire_with_our_Artillery_and_our_small_armes_African_and_Native_Americans_in_the_Rhode_Island_Regiments_1775_1783).

1778, 1st Rhode Island Regiment (segregated)

The two Rhode Island regiments were hard-hit during the 1777 Philadelphia campaign, and new men were sorely needed. The Rhode Island legislature met in early February, resolving that any "negro, mulatto, or Indian man slave in this State may inlist into either of the . . . two battalions to serve during the continuance of the war." In actuality, the recruits joined only the 1st Regiment, which would comprise only African or Native American private soldiers, with white commissioned officers, sergeants, and corporals. In early May the assembly set a June 10, 1778, cutoff date for slave recruiting, though free Blacks could continue to enlist. In all, approximately 117 bondsmen were purchased by the Rhode Island legislature in 1778. Including veteran soldiers, only 190 men of color joined the segregated 1st Regiment, and it was never able to form a full battalion for service with General Washington's main army.

While the 1st Regiment was recruiting, white enlisted personnel remaining at Valley Forge were incorporated into the 2nd Regiment. At the same time, the veteran Black soldiers from both regiments were formed into a single segregated company under Captain Thomas Arnold. Arnold's company belonged to the absent 1st Regiment, but while with the main army fielded with Colonel Israel Angell's 2nd Rhode Island. In May 1778 the Rhode Islanders were issued "froks [hunting shirts] hats & overhalls" (their well-known leather caps were not issued until June 1781). At the June 28 Monmouth battle, the Rhode Islanders (including Arnold's company) fought a rearguard action against the advancing British Grenadiers and light horse. Lieutenant Colonel Jeremiah Olney recounted:

> After retiring something more than a Mile [under Major General Charles Lee] . . . Gen. [James] Varnum's brigade was ordered to halt, and form by a cross Fence, to cover two pieces of artillery, which were in Danger of being lost. We there exchanged about ten Rounds, and were then obliged to retire with considerable Loss, but not until the Enemy had out-flanked us, and advanced with charged Bayonets to the Fence by which we had formed. Our Brigade suffered more than any that was engaged: The Loss in our Regiment was Lieutenant [Nathan] Wicks, a Sergeant and 8 Privates killed; Captain Thomas Arnold and 7 privates wounded, and 4 privates missing. . . . The Enemy did not pursue us far in our Retreat; observing our Army formed on the Heights in our Rear, [they halted on a Height, and began a brisk Cannonade, which lasted upwards of an Hour.

During this action, Captain Arnold was wounded in the leg, which was later amputated, and at least one of his men, African-born former slave Richard Rhodes, was wounded.

At the end of July Colonel Christopher Greene's entire segregated 1st Regiment numbered 182 Black, six Indian, and two Afro-Indian privates. They participated, alongside the 2nd Regiment, in the August 29, 1778, battle of Rhode Island. The action was at times hard-fought, and the 1st Rhode Island was in the thick of it; the regiment did not, however, repel three Hessian assaults, as claimed by nineteenth-century and some modern accounts. Drummer Winthrop Robinson of Peabody's New Hampshire State Regiment noted, "Col. Green had a regiment of negroes who were in the same engagement, fought bravely, but were unfortunate." Acting 1st Rhode Island commander Major Samuel Ward wrote,

> early yesterday morning the Enemy . . . and took possession of the Heights in our Front they sent out parties . . . and we made detachments to drive them back. After a skirmish of three or four hours with various successes, in which each party gave way three or four times and were reinforced we drove them quite back to the ground they first took in the morning, and they have continued there ever since. . . . I am so happy as to have had only one Capt. slightly wounded in the hand. I believe a couple of the blacks were killed and four or five wounded but none badly.

Any shortfall in performance is understandable, given that the unit had only forty-four veteran soldiers (23.2 percent), and 146 newly enlisted men. Still, one 1st Rhode Island company, most likely Captain Jonathan Wallen's veterans, did receive some notice that day. During an advance by General Solomon Lovell's Massachusetts militia brigade, Major Samuel Lawrence was caught between the battle lines and saved by a 1st Rhode Island company, which moved forward and stood firm long enough for the major to escape.

The 1st Rhode Island Regiment existed as a segregated unit from February 1778 to July 1780, two years and five months. Formed into five companies in 1778, in 1779 it was reduced to four. In June 1780, with only 124 private soldiers, the corps was formed into two large companies. That July a 400-man eight-company battalion of Rhode Island Six Month Levies was formed; they were joined with the two 1st Rhode Island companies to form a single temporary battalion commanded by Colonel Greene. One white levy soldier, Abner Simmons, recalled, "Capt. [Elijah] Lewis commanded the Black Company [actually two companies] which took post on the right of the regiment," the place of honor. In the meantime, Col. Henry Sherburne's Additional Regiment was disbanded and thirty-two Rhode Islanders from the unit, including several Black soldiers, were transferred to the 2nd Rhode Island, thus ending its existence as a segregated organization.

Above: *Pewter soldier's button of the integrated one-year Rhode Island 9th Continental Regiment. In January 1777 the regiment was reorganized and redesignated the 1st Rhode Island Regiment. (Troiani Collection)*

Near left: *British Long Land Pattern flintlock musket. This was the main infantry arm of the British Army during the Revolution. Thousands fell into the hands of Continental Army and militia soldiers via capture of British supply ships, and after American victories such as Princeton, Saratoga, and Yorktown. (Troiani Collection)*

Sources: Daniel M. Popek, *They ". . . fought bravely, but were unfortunate": The True Story of Rhode Island's "Black Regiment" and the Failure of Segregation in Rhode Island's Continental Line, 1777–1783* (Bloomington, IN: AuthorHouse, 2015), 81–83, 86–87, 102–3, 169–95, 206–11, 220, 224–37, 270–84, 317, 318, 347; "At the General Assembly . . . of the State of RhodeIsland . . . begun on the Second Monday in February," 1778 (Attleborough, MA: S. Southwick, Printer, 1778), 14–17; "State of Rhode-Island . . . in General Assembly, May second session, A.D. 1778," begun May 28, 1778 (Attleborough, MA: S. Southwick, Printer, 1778), 3–5; "State of Rhode-Island . . . in General Assembly, May first session, A.D. 1778," begun May 6, 1778 (Attleborough, MA: S. Southwick, Printer, 1778), 15; Robert C. Bray and Paul E. Bushnell, eds., *Diary of a Common Soldier in the American Revolution: An Annotated Edition of the Military Journal of Jeremiah Greenman* (DeKalb: Northern Illinois University Press, 1978), 119; John U. Rees, "'We began a smart fire with our Artillery & our small armes': African and Native Americans in the Rhode Island Regiments, 1775–1783," https://www.academia.edu/112997530/_We_began_a_smart_fire_with_our_Artillery_and_our_small_armes_African_and_Native_Americans_in_the_Rhode_Island_Regiments_1775_1783.

1778, 3rd South Carolina Regiment

South Carolina authorized the formation of three units in June 1775, the 1st and 2nd South Carolina as foot regiments, and the 3rd as mounted infantry assigned to the western region to counter Indian incursions. The following February the 4th (artillery) Regiment was formed, as well as two small rifle regiments, the 5th and 6th South Carolina. All but the rifle regiments were taken into the Continental establishment in June 1776.

In the war's first two years South Carolina may have been considered a backwater, but its soldiers were busy, from their first strike in the fight for independence at the capture of Fort Charlotte, to operations against Loyalist forces and the Cherokee Nation, actions in Georgia and Florida, and the successful defense of Charleston against a British fleet and land forces. The next two years were relatively quiet in the South, though the capture of Savannah, Georgia, in December 1778 was a precursor of increased British focus. With that new base of operations, in 1779 Crown forces' activity increased and the year ended with the unsuccessful Allied attempt to retake Savannah.

Colonel William Thomson's 3rd Regiment, popularly known as Thomson's Rangers, was enlisted from the state's western districts, and initially recruited some 450 men. In February 1776 the assembly increased the size of Thomson's Regiment, and decreed that it "be composed of *expert* Rifle-men, who shall act on horseback, or on foot, as the service may require; each man, at his own expence, to be constantly provided with a good horse, rifle, shot-pouch and powder-horn, together with a tomahawk or hatchet." A further stipulation was that the new recruits "be approved by the commanding officer . . . as *expert Rifle-men.*"

Colonel Thomson's men were active from the first, seeing action in their home state and Georgia, at least six times in 1775, three more times in 1776 (including the June British attack on Sullivan's Island, outside Charleston), but only once in 1777. In December 1778 the regiment took part in the failed defense of Savannah. The following year the 3rd South Carolina fought again in Georgia, and then participated in the September/October Savannah siege. That affair culminated with an unsuccessful joint Franco-American assault on the city's right-flank fortifications. Thomson's regiment attacked that day, and one of his soldiers, Drury Harris, a light-complexioned mulatto, was noted for his bravery. His 3rd Regiment comrade John Davis stated, "in the fight at Savannah [October 9, 1779], I saw no man, officer nor private, more Activer nor braver, than Drury Harris was, also Seeing and knowing him, to receive two wounds, a shot wound in the thigh, and a bayonet in the arm, in trying to scale the walls of his Inamy,"

By January 1780 Thomson's Regiment had joined the Charleston garrison, in expectation of a British attack. At that time South Carolina's original Continental contingent had been reduced to three foot battalions, plus the artillery battalion. From April 1 to May 12 Crown forces besieged the town, with the South and North Carolina light companies detached to form a mobile light infantry battalion, and the three South Carolina regiments manning the left flank of the Charleston fortifications. When the city fell in mid-May all were captured and imprisoned. No serious attempt was made by the state afterward to form new Continental regiments, though state troops continued to fight.

Drury Harris either missed being captured, or was paroled or exchanged; in April 1781 he enlisted for ten months as a light dragoon in Lieutenant Colonel Wade Hampton's State Regiment, Brigadier General Thomas Sumter's Brigade, and fought at Eutaw Springs that September. Six other African Americans are known to have served as 3rd South Carolina soldiers: Gideon and Morgan Griffin, Edward Harris, and Allen, Berry, and Osborne Jeffers. Drury Harris was eligible for "Sumter's bounty," an ad hoc policy that awarded late-war state troops "one grown negro" for their service. Brigadier General Thomas Sumter in early 1781 took it upon himself to make this offer in an effort to gain troops for state service. Harris seems not to have received (or accepted) this reward, but his neighbors and fellow-soldiers Gideon Griffin, the Jeffers brothers, and cousin Edward, all mulattoes, did.

The 3rd South Carolina soldier is pictured as equipped in 1778. His knapsack, gaiters, and firearm are all French-made, imported by the United States's new ally. The regiment's rifles were exchanged for muskets and bayonets beginning in August 1777, finally accomplished a year later. During that time they were transformed from mounted cavalry to a foot regiment. The initial three South Carolina regiments wore "a silver crescent on the front of their caps," and one veteran recalled, "a plate on the cap of the 3rd S.C. Regiment inscribed 'LIBERTY OR DEATH.'" The latter is corroborated by another postwar recollection; prior to the June 1780 skirmish at Alexander's Old Field in the Camden District, "'three of [John] Gaston's sons . . . arose upon their feet and [vowed] . . . that liberty or death, from that time forth, should be their motto!' . . . these young men had served three years in the company of Eli Kershaw . . . Third Regiment of South Carolina . . . with the above motto inscribed on the front of their military caps."

Sources: John U. Rees, *"They Were Good Soldiers": African-Americans Serving in the Continental Army, 1775–1783* (Warwick, UK: Helion & Company Limited, 2019), 112–16; Michael C. Scoggins, *The Day It Rained Militia: Huck's Defeat and the Revolution in the South Carolina Backcountry, May–July 1780* (Charleston, SC: History Press, 2005), 26, 31–32, 38; "SC Third Regiment (Rangers)," https://www.carolana.com/SC/Revolution/revolution_sc_third_regiment.html; Patrick O'Kelly, *Nothing but Blood and Slaughter: The Revolutionary War in the Carolinas*, vol. 1, 1771–1779 (Trenton, GA: Booklocker.com, 2004), pp. (1775) 35 (Fort Charlotte), 36 (Ninety-Six), 39 (Seneca Town), 51 (Congaree River), 59 (Ninety-Six), 71 (Great Cane Brake), (1776) 74 (Sullivan's Island), 110, 133 (June, Sullivan's Island), 157 (Seneca), (1777) 172 (Fort McIntosh, Ga.), (1778) 214 (Girardeau's Plantation, GA), 216 (Savannah), (1779) 224 (Fort Morris, GA), 292 (Stono Ferry), 313 (Savannah, GA). O'Kelly, *Nothing but Blood and Slaughter: The Revolutionary War in the Carolinas*, vol. 2, 1780 (Trenton, GA: Booklocker.com, 2004), pp. (1780) 37 (Charleston, March to May), 130 (Gibbes Plantation, March), 167 (Alexander's Old Field, June 1780), 392 (two or three British prisoners taken who had been taken at Charleston and joined the Queen's Rangers; Carl P. Borick, *A Gallant Defense: The Siege of Charleston, 1780* (Columbia: University of South Carolina Press, 2012), 38–39, 104, 126; Philip Katcher, *Uniforms of the Continental Army* (York, PA: George Shumway Publisher, 1981), 165–66.

Above: Pewter soldier's coat button, 3rd South Carolina Regiment (Troiani Collection)

1777–1778, 3rd Connecticut Regiment

In response to questions regarding the ability of African Americans as soldiers, Brigadier General John Thomas wrote in October 1775 that in "the Regiments at Roxbury [Massachusetts], the Privates are Equal to any that I Served with Last war, very few Old men, and in the Ranks very few boys. . . . We have Some Negros, but I Look on them in General Equally Servicable with other men, for Fatigue and in Action; many of them have Proved themselves brave."

Black men had indeed already proved themselves, in the war's opening day on April 19, 1775, and at Bunker Hill that June, Connecticut soldiers of color among those at the latter action. Connecticut quickly answered the Bay colony's April 1775 call for more troops, and that year eventually fielded eight provincial regiments manned by eight-months men. Two years later the state's contingent was still as large, comprising the 1st through 8th Connecticut regiments.

A few 1777 3rd Connecticut African soldiers had served in the 1775 and 1776 campaigns, with their hard-fought actions and forced marches, but the unit's ensuing experiences echoed this time-honored military truism by Surgeon Jabez Campfield: "How hard is the soldier's lott who's least danger is in the field of action? Fighting happens seldom, but fatigue, hunger, cold & heat are constantly varying his distress." Soldiers' duties outside of combat are often the most crucial, revolving around daily chores needed to keep an army in being, routemarches, and garrison duty, including building defensive works. From 1777 onward, the men of Colonel Samuel Wyllys's 3rd Regiment had their full share of all those. That year, as part of the Continental Army new establishment enlisting soldiers for terms of three years, or during the war, the 3rd

Connecticut was organized anew. In April the regiment was sent to the Hudson River Highlands (an area roughly from Verplanck's Point to Newburgh, New York), where it would remain until late summer of 1778, barring a June/July 1777 New Jersey hiatus.

Third Regiment captain Samuel Richards's diary provides insights into the corps' activities. In 1777 the regiment, as a whole or in part, frequently occupied Peekskill, New York, just above the major Hudson River crossing at King's Ferry. Their month in New Jersey was spent watching the British as they threatened to advance across the state, and when Sir William Howe's Crown forces took ship from the coast, Richards noted,

a part of our army was left in the vicinity to oppose their predatory excursions. Our regiment was part of the force thus left; and most of the summer passed in our moving from one post to another as the movements of the enemy dictated. This kind of service was very harassing. . . . We marched three times across Jersey from the North river towards the Delaware, and back.

Back in the Hudson Highlands that August, regimental detachments operated on the river's east side, and just as they readied to cross to reinforce the garrison, observed the fall of Fort Montgomery, just below West Point. A month later, marching to join Major General Horatio Gates's army, they heard of the British surrender at Saratoga, Captain Richards writing, "in the afternoon the troops were formed into a hollow square and the official news having been received—was read to us by the Adjutant General while on horse back." He continued:

Below: "Garshom Prince his horn made at Crownpoint Septm ye 3rd day 1761/Prince+Negro his horn M." Gershom (Garshom) Prince's powder horn, worn when he was killed at the Battle of Wyoming in Pennsylvania, July 3, 1778. He was identified solely by the horn attached to his body. Prince was a veteran of the French and Indian War, and reputed to have enlisted with Colonel Zebulon Butler's 4th Connecticut Regiment during the Revolution. He does not appear on any of the 4th Regiment muster rolls, nor those of the three Wyoming Valley independent companies serving with that regiment and detached in June to return and defend their homes. It is likely Gershom Prince was a member of a militia company present at the July 1778 action. Black Revolutionary soldiers left few personal objects that survive, but powder horns seem to be the most numerous. (Image courtesy of Mary Walsh, Luzerne County Historical Society)

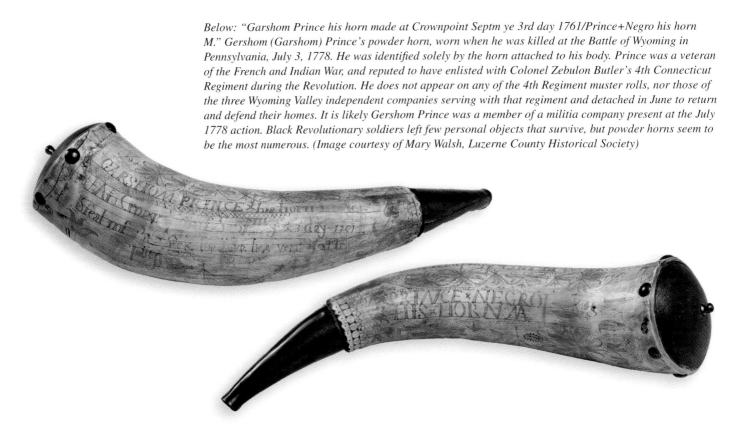

Our warm and joyfull feelings were dampened the next day by a severe North East rain storm which continued two or three days, and being without tents, and in an open country where cover could not be obtained we suffered severely, being previously worn down by severe duty and exposure. After the ending of the storm . . . we commenced our march back toward the highlands.

Taking post across the river from West Point, at the Beverly Robinson Farm, the men of Wyllys's Regiment began building winter huts. Having gotten settled, in February the regiment was ordered across the river to work on the newly planned West Point fortifications. After building new huts, "as spring approached we set ourselves to collect the rough stone which we found on the surface of the ground—to use in erecting the fortification" and, amid rattlesnake dens, "we soon began to erect fort Putnam far up the mountain." That May, Major General Friedrich Wilhelm de Steuben arrived "to introduce into our army the prussian discipline," during and after which work on fortifications, including the main bastion, Fort Clinton, continued. In July, having moved to Fishkill, the 3rd Connecticut Regiment, marched to join General George Washington's army at White Plains.

During this time, there was mention of one of the regiment's Black soldiers, Sergeant Simon Giffen writing, "Thirsday Febury 5 [1778] . . . a bout fore o clock [there] was a Negor Man was whipped 23 Lashes he be longed to Coll Wyillis Regt." In August 1778 at General Washington's order a "Return of the Negroes in the Army" was compiled; Major General Samuel Parson's four-regiment Connecticut brigade, including the 3rd Connecticut, tallied 148 Black soldiers, making on-average thirty-seven for each eight-company regiment.

Sources: John U. Rees, *"They Were Good Soldiers": African-Americans Serving in the Continental Army, 1775–1783* (Warwick, UK: Helion & Company Limited, 2019), 29, 37–38, 57; Journal of Surgeon Jabez Campfield, Spencer's Additional Regiment, August 4, 1779, *Journals of the Military Expedition of Major General John Sullivan Against the Six Nations of Indians in 1779* (Glendale, NY: Benchmark Publishing Co., 1970), 53; Samuel Richards, *Diary of Samuel Richards, Captain of Connecticut Line, War of the Revolution, 1775–1781* (Philadelphia: Press of the Leeds & Biddle Co., 1909), 43–44, 47–59; James M. Johnson, "West Point Becomes a Fortress," The Hudson River Valley Institute, https://www.hudsonrivervalley.org/documents/401021/1055071/jmj_west_pt_january+1778.pdf/116d4b2b-4964-4df8-9a93-69b0e7d0dd01; Merle Sheffield, ed., "Giffin's Diary: The First Fortification of West Point," https://www.hudsonrivervalley.org/documents/401021/1055071/GiffinDiary.pdf/7d746083-f521-455c-a4a1-51ad5e43ed15; Rees, "'None of you know the hardships of A soldiers life . . .': Service of the Connecticut Regiments in Maj. Gen. Alexander McDougall's Division, 1777–1778," https://www.academia.edu/14059235/_None_of_you_know_the_hardships_of_A_soldiers_life_Service_of_the_Connecticut_Regiments_of_Maj_Gen_Alexande"_McD'ugall_s_Division_1777_1778, Bibliography, tinyurl.com/CT-troops-77to79.

1779, Chasseur Volontaires de Saint-Domingue

French recognition of the United States in February 1778 was a declaration of war on Great Britain. Seen by many as retribution for the loss of Canada and Louisiana in the Seven Years' War, that act was not without risk, particularly for His Majesty Louis XVI's West Indian possessions. In the second year of the 1778–1783 coalition, Louis's forces embarked on a Franco-American military operation against British-held Savannah, Georgia. One element in that 3,000-man expedition was the Chasseurs Volontaires (Volunteer Light Infantry) de Saint-Domingue, first authorized in March 1779.

French Saint-Domingue (later Haiti) was, like many Caribbean islands, a slave-supported society, but one with a sizable number of middle-class and well-to-do free men of color. Saint-Domingue Black citizens were class and color-conscious, and extremely protective of their rights as free men. All these concerns were played upon in procuring volunteers for the new regiment. The Chasseurs' white commander, Colonel Laurent de Rouvray, proud of his men, who joined without enlistment bonuses, asked for the abolishment of "humiliating and degrading distinctions" differentiating them from white troops. He wished his men's creed would be, "I must make the whites blush for the scorn they have heaped on me in my civil status and for the injustices and tyrannies they have continually exercised over me with impunity. I must prove to them that as a soldier I am capable of at least as much honor and courage and of even more loyalty." The uniform of French regiments formed in the home country and manned by native-born men were white coats, with facings (cuffs, sometimes lapels) and trim of varying regimental colors. French West Indian troops wore blue uniforms; the Chasseurs Volontaires' coats had yellow collars, with green cuffs and trim, that color signifying light infantry troops.

By July 1779, via voluntary and coerced enlistment, the Chasseurs were fully formed, with Blacks and mulattoes accorded their own companies. Beginning with almost 1,000 men, when the fleet of Admiral Charles, comte d'Estaing, set sail on August 16 the Chasseurs were reduced to 545. Alluding to possible problems within his army, the admiral gave orders that the "people of color be treated at all times like the whites. They aspire to the same honor, they will exhibit the same bravery." Before leaving Saint-Domingue, an aide to d'Estaing noted the Chasseurs "maneuvered perfectly, were well disciplined and well appointed and served wonderfully." Despite their proficiency on the parade ground, the Saint-Domingue Chasseurs and (white) Grenadiers were described as "raised recently . . . and not to be employed for more than trench work."

Disembarking near Savannah in mid-September, by the 24th junction was made with American forces and the siege-works begun. The right of the French line was commanded by Brigadier General Arthur, vicomte de Dillon; on the far right, were "M. de Rouvray with his Volunteer Chasseurs," and to their right, a bit further forward was "M. Des Framais, commanding the Grenadier Volunteers and two hundred men of different regiments." That day British forces made a sortie against the French trenches; some portion of the two Saint-Domingue regiments took part in this action, with the Chasseurs suffering twenty-five casualties. First, they and other French troops repelled the British assault, then the Chasseurs' second in command led a rash counterattack. That officer was said to be intoxicated, that "his natural courage and the excitement caused by the wine carried him beyond the proper limits which had been prescribed. His indiscreet impetuosity [in leading six companies in a counterattack] cost us one hundred and fifty men placed hors de combat, of whom forty were killed, struck down in their retreat by the enemy's artillery."

After that, Chasseur detachments helped man artillery and mortar batteries. At midnight on October 4 the bombardment began, but after four days of ineffective cannonading, Admiral d'Estaing decided to assault Savannah. The bloody attack on the British right, centered on the Spring Hill redoubt, took place on October 9, but there is no indication the Chasseurs participated. They more likely took part in the concurrent feint assault on the British left.

The two weeks following the October 9 bloody reverse were spent tending the wounded and preparing to abandon the siege. The last French troops boarded their transports on October 21, 1779. A large part of the Chasseurs Volontaires were delayed in their journey home. Two hundred were put aboard the ship *Languedoc*, destined for France. They arrived at Brest that December, and set sail for Saint-Domingue in May 1780. About forty were noted to be serving on two seventy-four-gun ships in spring 1780, possibly acting as marines. On December 1, 1779, 148 Chasseurs arrived at Grenada, where they were stationed at Fort Royal. Reduced to 108 soldiers by August 1782, these men likely remained on the island until it was ceded to the British in January 1784. A few more wayward Chasseurs, perhaps sixty-two in all, may have accompanied soldiers wounded at Savannah to Charleston, South Carolina. Historian René Chartrand writes the escort at Charleston is known to have been from Saint-Domingue, but could have been Chasseurs, Grenadiers, or a mixed detachment of both. Whoever the Saint-Domingue soldiers were, they reportedly fought well during the May 1780 siege, and were exchanged not long after British forces captured the city. The Chasseurs were not reconstituted after the Savannah campaign, being discharged upon reaching home.

Source: John U. Rees, "'The most promising young men present themselves for service': A Black Regiment from French Saint Domingue in the War of the American Revolution," https://www.academia.edu/103394461/_The_most_promising_young_men_present_themselves_for_service_A_Black_Regiment_from_French_Saint_Domingue_in_the_War_of_the _American_Revolution.

1780, Black Pioneers

In August 1776 the Virginia-raised Ethiopian Regiment disembarked on Staten Island, was disbanded, and its members dispersed. Some likely joined the Black Pioneers, the only African American corps to be placed on the official Provincial Establishment.

The Black Pioneers were first formed near Wilmington, North Carolina, in spring 1776, when General Sir Henry Clinton's British forces were stationed on the Cape Fear River. Clinton noted that April: "Forty or fifty Negros . . . found a way to get on board the shipping previous to my arrival. . . . I have determined to form a Company of them with an intention of employing them as Pioneers and on working Parties and have given the Command to Lieut. [George] Martin of the Marines."

Small numbers of Pioneer troops were included in British regiments, but they were armed and could take an active part in siege or other warfare. The Black Pioneer company was unarmed, and conformed more to this 1778 military dictionary entry, in which pioneers were defined as, "such as are commanded in from the country, to march along with an army for mending the ways, for working on intrenchments and fortifications, and for making approaches [in a siege] ."

Yet, the Black Pioneers were on the Provincial Establishment, paid the same as other Loyalist soldiers (sixpence a day), and issued uniform clothing. At Philadelphia in 1778 they received, "1 Great Coat, 1 Small sailor Jacket, 1 pair of woolen Trousers, 1 White Shirt, [and] 1 Hatt," in addition to what they already had or wore.

Their commander from July 1777 to June 1780 was Captain Allan Stewart, Loyalist and half-pay French and Indian War Scottish officer. When he took command, the company numbered one lieutenant, one ensign, two sergeants, three corporals, and seventy-two privates, plus fifteen women and eight children. The Pioneers had been in New York City from September to December 1776, after which they took part in the occupation of Newport, Rhode Island. During their residence in Newport they lost nineteen from disease, but only one man deserted. Returning to New York in spring 1777, they may have been part of the "Corps of Pioneers" that accompanied Sir William Howe's army during early summer New Jersey field operations. That Corps also took part in the landing at the head of the Chesapeake in late August 1777, which led to the capture of Philadelphia on September 26. When in garrison the Black Pioneers cut and hauled wood, helped maintain barracks, and built or upgraded fortifications, and other needed menial tasks. For instance, while in Philadelphia in March 1778 they were ordered to "Attend the Scavengers, Assist in Cleaning the Streets & Removing all Newsiances being thrown in the streets."

At least a portion of the Black Pioneers were with Sir Henry Clinton's columns during the June–July 1778 Monmouth campaign. Numbering forty-nine men and two women, they were listed under "Non-Combatants," while Captain Simon Fraser's 206-strong "Guides and Pioneers" were termed "Provincial Infantry." Still, according to June 23 orders at Crosswicks, New Jersey, the army was to march the next day in the same order as before, "all the pioneers to march in the Rare of the 2d Batln of Light Infantry [and] Pioneers of the Regts at the head of their Respective Brigades."

By September 1779 Captain Stewart's Pioneer company in New York numbered 107; in May 1780 at Charleston, South Carolina, he was noted as commanding three companies of Pioneers, with a total of 285 men and women (the source does separate the numbers), plus forty-five children. Following the 1780 Charleston siege Captain Stewart and his second in command remained in South Carolina to raise a new Loyalist regiment. The northern Pioneers returned to New York, on January 1, 1781, sending New Year greetings to Commander in Chief Sir Henry Clinton from "your Excellency's old Company of Black Pioneers." During the 1783 British withdrawal from New York City, a two-volume "Inspection Roll of Negroes" was compiled, listing Black evacuees; among them were twenty-two Black Pioneer veterans, with their wives and children, bound for Annapolis Royal, Nova Scotia, including: "Levitia, [age] 28, ordinary fellow . . . Formerly servant to Samuel LaGree, Santee river, South Carolina; left him in 1776"; "Bob Harrison, 21, likely fellow . . . Formerly servant to Benjamin Harrison, James River, Virginia; left him in 1779"; and, "Tom, 60, ordinary fellow . . . Formerly servant to Colonel Conner, Valley Forge, Pennsylvania; left him 1777."

A second, Southern, Black Pioneer unit was formed by British engineer James Moncrief. He was chief engineer at Savannah in 1780 and again during the 1780 Charleston siege. In 1782 he wrote of the "Negroes who have followed me on every service since the first period of my Arrival in the Province of Georgia." At Savannah Captain-Lieutenant Moncrief formed refugee slaves into a labor force to build fortifications; during the September–October 1779 siege these men were given firearms and joined British and Loyalist troops in defending the city. Reverting to military laborers, during the April–May 1780 Charleston siege, Major Moncrief's men, 154 in all, were assigned to the Royal Artillery, constructing batteries, manhandling cannon, and rebuilding earthworks, likely under enemy fire. The Southern Pioneers (including seventy-eight artificers or military craftsmen) remained in Charleston until the 1782 evacuation, when some 240 of them were transported to St. Lucia in the West Indies. There, along with seventy Black Dragoon veterans, they were formed into the armed Carolina Corps; in 1796 that corps was drafted into the 1st West India Regiment.

Sources: Benjamin A. Quarles, *The Negro in the American Revolution* (New York, London: W.W. Norton & Company, 1973), 134; Todd W. Braisted, "The Black Pioneers and Others: The Military Role of Black Loyalists in the American War for Independence," in John W. Pulis (ed.), *Moving On: Black Loyalists in the Afro-Atlantic World* (New York and London: Garland Publishing, 1999), 11–18, 20–21;. Anon., *A Military Dictionary, Explaining and Describing the Technical Terms, Phrases, Works, and Machines, used in the Science of War* (London: Printed for G. Robinson, and Fielding and Walker, in Paternoster-Row, 1778); General Orders, May 28, 1777, "'Necessarys . . . to be Properley Packd: & Slung in their Blanketts': Transcription of the 40th Regiment of Foot Order Book," (British Orderly Book [40th Regiment of Foot] April 20, 1777 to August 28, 1777, George Washington Papers, Library of Congress, Series 6B, vol. 1, reel 117), https://www.academia.edu/105693640/_Necessarys_to_be_Properley_Packd_and_Slung_in_their_Blanketts_Transcription_of_the_40th_Regiment_of_Foot_Order_Book; Anon., ed., *The Kemble Papers*, Collections of the New-York Historical Society for the Year 1883, two vols. (New York: Printed for the Society, 1884), vol. 1, 448, 451, 455, 466, 475, 489, 499; Paul

Leicester Ford, ed., *Orderly Book of the "Maryland loyalists regiment," June 18th, 1778, to October 12th, 1778. Including General Orders Issued by Sir Henry Clinton, Baron Wilhelm von Knyphausen, Sir William Erskine, Charles, Lord Cornwallis, General William Tryon and General Oliver De Lancey. Kept by Captain Caleb Jones* (Brooklyn, NY: Historical Printing Club, 1891), 19–21, https://www.loc.gov/resource/gdcmassbookdig.orderlybookofmar00mary/?st=gallery; Todd W. Braisted, James L. Kochan, Donald M. Londahl-Smidt, and Garry Wheeler Stone, eds., "Return of the Number of Men, Wagoners, Women & Children Victualled at Monmouth the 27 & 28th June 1778 inclusive" (Sir Henry Clinton Papers, vol. 36, no. 5, William L. Clements Library, the University of Michigan); "State of the Forces under . . . Sir Henry Clinton, 3 July 1778," (Library of Congress, Mss. Division: PRO CO 5:96), 77, https://www.academia.edu/36671248/CROWN_FORCES_28_JUNE_1778_Return_of_wagoners_women_and_children_with_British_German_and_Loyalist_Forces_at_Monmouth_Courthouse_New_Jersey); Alan Gilbert, *Black Patriots and Loyalists: Fighting for Emancipation in the War for Independence* (Chicago: University of Chicago Press, 2013), 121–22; Gary Sellick, "Black Men, Red Coats: The Carolina Corps, Race, and Society in the Revolutionary British Atlantic," Dissertation, University of South Carolina, 2018, 38–41, 49–51, 63–66, https://scholarcommons.sc.edu/etd/4932; "Black Pioneers New Year's Greetings," http://www.royalprovincial.com/military/rhist/blkpion/blklet3.htm; "Inspection Roll of Negroes Book No. 1," National Archives, https://catalog.archives.gov/id/17337716; "Inspection Roll of Negroes Book No. 2," National Archives, https://catalog.archives.gov/id/5890797.

1780, 6th Connecticut Regiment

The 6th Connecticut Regiment was one of the Continental Army's workhorse units; while portions of the organization were involved in various actions, the corps never fought in its entirety against the enemy. Instead, the majority of its soldiers' service was spent in garrison at various military posts in the Hudson Highlands, most notably at West Point, where for a portion of their time they worked on fortifications.

A distinctive item in the 6th Regiment's equipage was the caps they wore. General Washington made note of them in January 1781, writing the Board of War:

> We have so constantly experienced the want of Hats, than which no part of dress is more essential to the appearance of a soldier, that I have been endeavouring to find out a substitute for them, which could be procured among ourselves. I have seen none so likely to answer the purpose, and which at the same time of so military an air as a leather Cap which was procured in the year 1777 for the 6th. Connecticut Regt.

The caps were still in use mid-war; at Morristown, New Jersey, in December 1779 6th Connecticut private Samuel Woods was noted to have been issued for that year, "three shirts Two pair Linnen & One pair of Woollen Overhauls Three pair of Shoes One pr Stockings One Frock One Leather Capp One [page torn] One Vest & One Stock." Militia soldier Daniel Banks recalled the February 26, 1779, British Connecticut raid, "when [Major] Gen [William] Tryon attacked Horse Neck Colo. [Hezekiah] Holdridge [7th Connecticut Regiment] commanded the Regular Troops . . . he had two or three different companies of different Regts under his . . . command." Banks remembered "one company called the Leather Caps had in front of their caps G W . . . in large letters—this company was commanded by Capt [Asa] Lay of the Connecticut Line . . . Regiment . . . Commanded by Colo Meggs."

Return Jonathan Meigs became the regiment's second commander after its first colonel William Douglas became ill and died in May 1777; Meigs may have been responsible for introducing the leather headwear to the entire unit, not, as was usually done, for restricted use by specialist companies such as light infantry or grenadiers. Jeffrey Brace (aka Stiles) was a 6th Regiment soldier. Serving from May to December 1778 he would have been an eight-month volunteer or draftee. His former master recalled in 1820,

> he was the owner of a Negro slave called Jeffery Stiles. . . . He then well understood that Jeffery was enlisted in the army to obtain his freedom … [he] remembers that he saw Jeffery a number of times after his enlistment in a soldiers Uniform with a Leather Cap he further recollects that some time in the War . . . thinks it must be in the year 1780 he was in the State of New York near West Point— met a Seargeants Guard all in Uniform— among the Guard was Jeffery & conversed with him—I am now acquainted with a Colored man calling himself Jeffery Brace & know him to be the same person then known by Jeffery Stiles— Jeffery sometimes was necked named Pomp London.

Brace submitted an extensive pension application, but only in his published memoirs did he mention wearing the leather cap Meigs's regiment was noted for. Relating an incident he said occurred near Hackensack, New Jersey, Brace claimed to have killed a British light horseman and captured his horse. Being pursued, he mounted the horse and fled,

"New Constructed" or "new model" cartridge pouch, adopted by the Continental Army in 1778; sufficient supplies were not available to equip General George Washington's main army until 1780. A copy of captured British pouches, it carries twenty-nine paper cartridges in an interior wooden block. This artifact is marked to the 2nd Company, 6th Connecticut Regiment. (Troiani Collection)

but having no spurs, and not being so good a horseman they gained upon me. I looked forward and saw my Capt. in full view, almost a mile distant. This encouraged me, and the long shanked negro, soldier with a leather cap, mounted on an elegant english gelding light horse, made all whistle again. When I came in about twenty or thirty rods, I heard the Captain say, "there comes one of our leather caps, and it is Jeffrey—reserve your fire so as not to kill him"; however the men fired, and three balls cut my garments, one struck my coat sleeve, the next hit my bayonet belt, and the third went through the back side of my leather-cap. They were so close upon me, that the same fire killed four of the British and five horses—and wounded some more.

A brief passage in his memoir also mentions a skirmish at "Horseneck [modern-day Greenwich, Connecticut] where I had a ball pass through my knapsack."

Brace recorded his enslavement and wartime experiences in an extraordinary 1810 autobiography, as well as in his pension recollections. Both garble his military career, highlighting the problem of relying on unverified memories. Mr. Brace begins his 1810 work with an account of his natal land in Africa, thought to be modern-day Mali. He then describes his capture, ill-treatment, and eventual brief service as a British seaman during the Seven Years' War. Making landfall at Boston, Brace was sold to a man residing at Milford, Connecticut, near the Oyster River. From that time until the war's onset he was transferred by purchase six times and ill-treated by most of his owners. Because of his military service and a postwar state manumission law Jeffrey Brace gained his freedom, despite his former master's unwillingness to grant it; he moved to Vermont in 1784.

Sources: John U. Rees, *"They Were Good Soldiers": African-Americans Serving in the Continental Army, 1775–1783* (Warwick, UK: Helion & Company Limited, 2019), 63–65; Robert K. Wright Jr., *The Continental Army* (Washington, DC: Government Printing Office, 1983), 236–37; National Archives, Pension files (microfilm), reel 134, Daniel Banks (S9811); reel 2630, Samuel Wood (S44101); Rees, "'None of you know the hardships of A soldiers life . . .': Service of the Connecticut Regiments in Maj. Gen. Alexander McDougall's Division, 1777–1778," https://www.academia.edu/14059235/_None_of_you_know_the _hardships_of_A_soldiers_life_Service_of_the_Connecticut_Regiments _of_Maj_Gen_Alexander_McDougall_s_Division_1777_1778, Bibliography, tinyurl.com/CT-troops-77to79. Kari J. Winter (ed.), *The Blind African Slave, or Memoirs of Boyrereau Brinch, Nick-Named Jeffrey Brace, as told to Benjamin F. Prentiss* (Madison: University of Wisconsin Press, 2004), 56–57, 195–216; Benjamin F. Prentiss, *The Blind African Slave, or Memoirs of Boyrereau Brinch, Nick-Named Jeffrey Brace* (St. Albans, VT: Harry Whitney, 1810), https://docsouth .unc.edu/neh/brinch/brinch.html.

1781, Spartanburg Militia Soldier (South Carolina)

Spartanburg County lies in the far northwestern corner of South Carolina, just below modern-day Asheville, North Carolina. The county's militia regiment was formed in late 1775, and, following the 1776 Cherokee War, was divided into two regiments. Their militia soldiers participated in a number of actions, beginning in December 1775 and continuing until at least 1781.

As with Continental troops, militia soldiers were formed into companies, and their parent regiments, but instead of long-term enlistments, the men did duty by turns, often one month on, one month off. In case of an enemy incursion, they could be called out en masse to repel invaders. Militia organization varied state by state, but South Carolina's generally had ten companies per regiment. Company captains usually commanded about twenty to thirty men, sometimes less, and on campaign small companies were combined for more efficient command and control. As seen in the accompanying image, militia generally wore their own civilian clothing into service, ensuring it was suited to the rigors of whatever duties lay before them.

The different state militias were not always equal in fighting quality, but the South Carolina regiments, particularly in the West, were quite experienced, contending with Native American forces and Loyalist contingents. These skills were invaluable when the war's main theater moved south in 1779, and especially after the May 1780 fall of Charleston, when British forces gained control of the state. At times the Spartanburgers served out of state, seeing action in March 1779 at Rocky Comfort Creek, Georgia, and in June 1780 at Ramseur's Mill in North Carolina.

The most important battle they fought was in their home state at Cowpens, Brigadier General Daniel Morgan's small but far-reaching January 17, 1781, victory over British and Loyalist forces commanded by Lieutenant Colonel Banastre Tarleton. Preparing for action, Morgan faced Tarleton's forces with a first line of militia, supported further back by a second line of Continental troops. Colonel John Thomas Jr.'s and Lieutenant Colonel Benjamin Roebuck's two Spartanburg battalions (at least seven companies strong) were on the right of the first line. When British regiments advanced within musket range an eyewitness wrote, "the militia fired first. It was for a time, pop-pop-pop—then a whole volley." When the British were within "forty or fifty yards" the militia began firing battalion volleys, five in all, ravaging their opponents. Having done their best, the militia ran for the rear of the Continentals, as General Morgan had directed. After the Continentals' ensuing combat and victory, the re-formed Spartanburg battalions pursued the fleeing enemy on Morgan's right. South Carolina militiamen Aaron Guyton recalled: "We defeated, killed & took all except Tarleton & his light Horse prisoners." Nine days after the battle Daniel Morgan wrote, "I was desirous to have a stroke at Tarlton . . . . & I have Given him a devil of a Whiping."

Unlike most other states, South Carolina never officially approved the enlistment of African Americans as soldiers, but still they served, in Continental, state, and militia forces. Three are known to have been with the Spartanburg militia at different times during the conflict. Lemerick Farr was enslaved by Lieutenant Colonel William Farr of the 2nd Regiment, took part in the August 1780 Musgrove's Mill battle and possibly other actions; Michael French served some five months in the beginning of 1783; and Edward Harris was a "free Negro" who first enlisted in a South Carolina Continental regiment (a man of the same name served in the 1st Regiment from November 1775 to August 1778), before enrolling with the militia of Spartanburg. He claimed to have fought in several battles, notably Camden in 1780, and Cowpens in 1781.

Sources: "The Spartan Regiment of Militia," https://www.carolana.com/SC/Revolution/patriot_militia_sc_spartan_regiment.html; "The Known Battles & Skirmishes in South Carolina," https://www.carolana.com/SC/Revolution/SC_Revolutiary_War_Known_Battles_Skirmishes.htm; "South Carolinians Outside of South Carolina During the Revolution," https://www.carolana.com/SC/Revolution/sc_troops_militia_outside_sc.html; Lawrence E. Babits, *A Devil of a Whipping: The Battle of Cowpens* (Chapel Hill and London: University of North Carolina Press, 1998), 1, 31, 36, 38–39, 90–97, 196 (note 84); Aaron Guytin, pension deposition, October 1, 1833 (W21237), http://revwarapps.org/w21237.pdf; Michael C. Scoggins, "To Assist His Countrymen in Arms: Motivations and Incentives in African-American Revolutionary War Service," *American Revolution Magazine*, vol. 1, no. 2 (May 2009), 51; Bobby Gilmer Moss and Michael C. Scoggins, *African-American Patriots in the Southern Campaign of the American Revolution* (Blacksburg, SC: Scotia-Hibernia Press, 2004), 83, 92, 110.

1781, Batallón de Morenos Libres de La Habana (Havana Battalion of Free Blacks)

The 1762 British siege of Havana enhanced the martial reputation of the city's militias of color, which were separated into *pardo* (mulatto) and *moreno* (Black) companies. Spanish national soldiers and seamen comprised the backbone of the defenders, but they were outnumbered by the militia who were reinforced by several thousand free and enslaved volunteers armed with machetes and pikes. Prior to the siege the *pardo* companies were considered better soldiers, largely because they had more off-island military service, but the Cuban *morenos*' warlike skills came to the fore during the fight for their city.

Perhaps the most celebrated feat of the siege was accomplished by thirteen Black bondsmen, led by enslaved native African Andres Gutiérrez. On June 26 they ambushed an enemy party advancing through a wooded area toward the Morro fortress. Armed only with machetes against British muskets, Gutiérrez's men killed one, captured seven, and routed the remainder. Noting that this small success raised the morale of the Spanish troops and *gente del país* (people of the country), Governor Prado emancipated the involved slave-soldiers. He was also moved to form a hundred-strong company of enslaved men led by a white command staff: militia soldiers, not auxiliaries. Following the June 26 action, Gutiérrez was promoted from an enslaved volunteer to captain in Havana's company of free Blacks. One effect of his feat was expressed by a Morro defender, a Spanish seaman, who related that "those of broken color did not cease to beg for another sally, promising to win from the enemy their batteries and maybe even take more prisoners."

After the war three 800-man African infantry battalions were created, apportioned as follows: Havana hosted two battalions, one of *pardo* foot militia, the other of *moreno* light infantry, and the towns of Santiago and Bayamo formed between them a single *pardo* militia foot battalion. Also created was the Compana de Moreños Esclavas, a company of one hundred African slaves to work with the artillery. All battalions were open to volunteers; age limits were from sixteen to forty for the Havana companies, fifteen to forty-five years in outlying districts. Volunteers were likely sufficient to fill the Black companies, but any shortfall was made up by a draft.

Each *pardo* and *moreno* battalion had dual white and Black command staffs; a white officer—an adjutant major—was commander, most often a regular army sergeant. Supporting him were four adjutants and five *garzones*, the latter filling the same role as veteran sergeants and corporals in white battalions. The Black battalions' small white veteran cadre meant that more responsibility was placed on the volunteer officers than those in white units. Indicative of their color, the highest officer in Black battalions had the title of commander, rather than colonel, had no real authority over the white command staff, and stood with bare heads in the presence of white officers. One important military benefit accorded white, mulatto, and Black Cuban militia soldiers was the *fuero militar*, essentially the right to military rather than civil jurisdiction in legal cases. In 1780 Cuban militia officers were accorded *fuero* rights equal to Spanish officers, while enlisted men's rights exceeded those of militias on the Spanish mainland.

Having rendered assistance with shipments of arms and equipment since 1776, Spain entered America's War for Independence three years later. In 1779 and 1780 Louisiana governor and brigadier general Bernardo de Gálvez quickly moved to take control of the lower Mississippi and to capture British-held Mobile. In October 1780 the naval and military forces he intended to take Pensacola were scattered en route by a hurricane. Regrouping, Gálvez set out again in mid-February 1781. Among the 3,350 troops that landed west of the town in late March were some 170 New Orleans Black militia, and four Black Havana companies totaling 278 soldiers, including two grenadier companies (one *pardo*, one *moreno*, each with eighty-eight men), and two light infantry companies (*pardo* and *moreno*, at fifty-one men apiece).

The ensuing month-and-a-half siege was grueling and hard-fought, with several attacks on the approach by the British and their allied Native warriors, counter-trench raids, and intense cannonades. On April 19, 1781, a second Spanish-French fleet arrived with reinforcements, raising Gálvez's army to 7,500 soldiers, including roughly 750 French troops. The Spanish siegeworks were begun on April 28 in the face of heavy artillery fire; in front of Pensacola were three fortifications, in a line north to south; the Queen's and Prince of Wales redoubts, and the larger Fort George. May 8 began as another day of incessant bombardment, but at 9:30 a.m. a Spanish shell entered the Queen's redoubt magazine; the resulting destruction led to its quick capture and presaged the siege's end. On May 10, 1781, the Pensacola garrison lay down their arms in surrender.

The detailed actions of the Havana free Black soldiers in the siege are unknown, but they and the New Orleanians were in the thick of the action; among the seventy-four Spanish mortalities, the governor-general listed ten *moreno* and *pardo* soldiers killed. And Gálvez admired the Spanish Black militias, noting after his 1779 Mississippi campaign that the "company of free blacks and mulattoes . . . were always in the vanguard, both in simulated attacks and frontal assaults, always firing at the enemy, behaving with as much courage, humanity, and selflessness as the white [troops]."

Sources: Gonzalo M. Quintero Saravia, *Bernardo de Gálvez: Spanish Hero of the American Revolution* (Chapel Hill: University of North Carolina Press, 2018), 148–49, 157, 180–227, 218, 355, 453; Lawrence Kinnaird, ed., "The Revolutionary Period, 1765–1781," part 1 of, *Spain in the Mississippi Valley, 1765–1794: Annual Report of the American Historical Association for the Year 1945*, vol. 2 (Washington, DC: Government Printing Office, 1949), 421–23; Maury Baker and Margaret Bissler Haas, eds., "Bernardo de Gálvez's Combat Diary for the Battle of Pensacola, 1781," *Florida Historical Quarterly*, vol. 56, no. 2 (October 1977), 176–99; Elena A. Schneider, *The Occupation of Havana: War, Trade, and Slavery in the Atlantic World* (Chapel Hill: University of North Carolina Press, 2018), 296–97 (and note 46); John U. Rees, "'Some of the best soldiers in the world.': The Havana Battalions of Free Blacks and Mulattos, 1762–1781," https://www.academia.edu/105729245/_Some_of_the_best_soldiers_in_the_world_The_Havana_Battalions_of_Free_Blacks_and_Mulattos_1762_1781.

1781, Gaskins's Virginia Battalion

The Virginia Continental line was a hard-fighting organization, hounded by ill-luck. Having performed admirably in 1776, by 1777 many of the regiments had men sufficient to fill only two or three companies. Still, in autumn 1777 the Virginia troops fought well at Brandywine and Germantown, and detachments saw action at the Battle of Monmouth, in June 1778. Still severely understrength, that September the number of Virginia regiments was reduced from fifteen to eleven, and in May 1779 another consolidation occurred. In autumn 1779 the entire Virginia contingent (three regiments and three battalions) marched south to join the garrison of Charleston, South Carolina. In May 1780, after a grueling month-and-a-half siege, Charleston was captured by British forces. Colonel Abraham Buford's Virginia detachment was marching to join the garrison when the city fell. On May 29 Buford's men were attacked and decimated at the Waxhaws, by Loyalist British Legion troops. With the city's surrender and the Waxhaws' defeat, the greatest part of the Continental contingents of Virginia and the Carolinas, some 3,800 officers and enlisted soldiers, was lost.

Needing to reconstitute their military, Virginia resorted to conscription from the state's militia. The drafted men would serve eighteen months in newly constituted Continental regiments. The first levy took place in autumn 1780 at Chesterfield Court House. These men were destined for the 1st and 2nd Virginia Regiments, which served in Major General Nathanael Greene's army in the Carolinas, seeing action at Guilford Courthouse and later battles. A third organization, called by General Washington, the "2nd. Regmt. of Levies," and eventually known as Lieutenant Colonel Thomas Gaskins's Virginia Battalion, served in their home state that summer and autumn.

The battalion's formation was hurried and resources were lacking. Through most of the 1781 summer Gaskins's soldiers were poorly clothed, Colonel Christian Febiger complaining on June 30, "Lord have mercy upon us, a modest army of Women on examining Any Thing lower than the navel, would instantly take to their [door] Scrapers on the Appearance of so many naked Clubs. . . . The fact is the men are literally naked, shirts and Blankets excepted." Coats, gaitered overalls, hats, shirts, shoes, blankets, and cartridge pouches were desperately needed. Belatedly, by autumn 1781 the battalion attained some semblance of uniformity.

In February 1781 Major General the Marquis de Lafayette had marched south with three provisional battalions to augment Virginia's defenses. In mid-May the small army of Lieutenant General Charles, Lord Cornwallis, reached Petersburg, linking with British forces already there. Lafayette's army, reinforced in early June by Brigadier General Anthony Wayne's Pennsylvania battalions, now had to contend with a superior force. Thus began the cat-and-mouse summer 1781 Virginia campaign, setting the stage for the autumn Yorktown siege.

June was a month of march and countermarch, with each side looking for an opening to overwhelm or damage their opponent. As of the 25th, Lafayette's army consisted of 4,500 men, included 1,550 Continental troops, plus Gaskins's 425 men, who had arrived on the 19th. To oppose him, Cornwallis had approximately 6,500 effectives. On June 26 the Marquis's cavalry, with light infantry soldiers mounted behind, and supported by Virginia riflemen, attacked the Queen's Rangers at Spencer's Ordinary, inflicting an embarrassment, though not a defeat, on the Loyalist troops. In the beginning of July, Lord Cornwallis's army moved from Williamsburg to James Island, with a view to crossing the river. Awaiting such an opportunity, and hoping to overwhelm the British rear guard, Lafayette directed Wayne's three Pennsylvanian battalions and a small advance guard to attack. They fell into a British ambuscade, pitting 7,000 Crown troops against Wayne's 900; only luck and an unexpected Pennsylvanian bayonet charge allowed him to escape, though with heavy losses. After crossing to the south bank of the James River, Cornwallis's forces took post at Portsmouth, Virginia, before moving up the York River to Yorktown.

The two Virginia regiments that joined Major General Greene before March 1781 contained a number of Black soldiers, including some of the autumn 1780 Chesterfield levies (of 913 conscripted men, at least fifty-six—6.1 percent—were of African descent). A second draft was held in April 1781, of which Major General Friedrich Wilhelm de Steuben wrote, "in the whole only 450 are yet assembled"; all were destined to serve in Gaskins's Battalion. Similarly, the drafts that joined Gaskin also included African Americans. While full numbers are unknown, five Black veterans' pension applications show service under Gaskin in 1781: They were Francis Bundy, John Chavers, William Jackson, Bennett McKey, and William Wedgbare.

Lieutenant Colonel Gaskins's Battalion experienced a surplus of marching in summer 1781, but no large battles, only, as former private William Wedgbare noted, "various Skirmishes." Veteran William White recalled that the battalion was "attached to [Wayne's] forces as light infantry"; as such it must have been in the fore of many small skirmishes. At the Yorktown siege that autumn, the battalion was brigaded with Anthony Wayne's Pennsylvanians. Following Cornwallis's October 19, 1781, surrender, Gaskins's men marched to South Carolina, where the Virginians were combined into a single regiment under Colonel Thomas Posey for the last two years of the war.

Sources: Henry P. Johnston, *The Yorktown Campaign and the Surrender of Cornwallis 1781* (New York, 1881), 55; Harold E. Selesky, ed., *Encyclopedia of the American Revolution: Library of Military History*, two vols., 2nd Ed., vol. 2 (Charles Scribner's Sons, 2006), 1208; E. M. Sanchez-Saavedra, *A Guide to Virginia Military Organizations in the American Revolution, 1774–1787* (Richmond: Virginia State Library, 1978), 177–81; Carl P. Borick, *A Gallant Defense: The Siege of Charleston, 1780* (Columbia: University of South Carolina Press, 2012), 223, 237; John U. Rees, *"They Were Good Soldiers": African-Americans Serving in the Continental Army, 1775–1783* (Warwick, UK: Helion & Company Limited, 2019), 132–35; Richard C. Bush III, "The End Of Col. Gaskins's War May-October 1781," *Bulletin of the Northumberland County Historical Society*, vol. XXXIII (1996), 39–56, https://freepages.rootsweb.com/~breedlove/genealogy/Gaskins.html; William Wedgbare/Wedgroof, "5 ½ Feet High, a Free Mulatto, 19 Yrs. of Age," Pension No. W2292, National Archives; William White, Pension No. S1735, National Archives.

September 6, 1781, Defending Fort Griswold, Connecticut Militia

In August 1781 British commander in chief Sir Henry Clinton was hoping to attack the small French fleet stationed at Newport, Rhode Island. On August 28 Admiral Sir Samuel Hood's naval squadron arrived in New York from the West Indies; Hood brought with him eighteen ships of the line and transports carrying three British regiments. That morning General Clinton was elated, finally having the forces to attack Rhode Island, but late that night he was informed the French vessels had sailed off, destination unknown.

Admiral Hood and Rear Admiral Thomas Graves thought the French objective was Cuba, Florida, or Georgia. Clinton, fearing an attack on New York, convinced the two officers to provide troops and ships for another small operation intended to divert attention from the city. The new target would be New London, Connecticut, shipbuilding center and successful privateer port.

On August 30 General Clinton informed Connecticut-born, former Continental Army major general Benedict Arnold he had been chosen to command the expedition. Brigadier General Arnold was to "immediately have 1500 Men [readied] for a Descent upon New London"; his objective was "to bring off or destroy the prize vessels, traders, or privateers, together with naval and other stores, said to be collected . . . to a very large amount." Two days later the troops were assembled, including the British 38th, 40th, and 54th regiments, and the Loyalist American Legion, Loyal American Regiment, and New Jersey Volunteers, plus a detachment of German *jäger* (riflemen).

After Arnold's regiments landed, to allow naval access to the Thames River and Groton harbor, Fort Trumbull, on the western shore, and Fort Griswold, to the east, would have to be stormed and captured. The overall American commander was Lieutenant Colonel William Ledyard, with Captain William

Latham in charge of the garrison in Griswold and Captain Adam Shapley at Fort Trumbull. Each fort was manned by a single fifty-man artillery company, plus any militia called out in time of trouble.

Just after midnight on September 6, 1781, Colonel Ledyard was awakened by a courier with the message that British forces "would soon pay him a visit if the wind was favorable the next morning." Orderly Sergeant Rufus Avery, on duty at Fort Griswold, recalled that "about three o'clock in the morning as soon as I had daylight so as to see the fleet, it appeared a short distance below the lighthouse . . . thirty-two vessels in number,—ships, brigs, schooners, and sloops."

The alarm was soon sounded, militia began coming in, and many families evacuated the area. Captain Latham ordered his slave Lambert to take his wife and children to safety. Lambert did as he was told, then returned to fight at Fort Griswold, where he was killed.

About 8:30 a.m. boats began landing British troops to the west of the Thames River. By 11:30 opposition on the west side had been overcome, Fort Trumbull taken, and British troops were advancing toward New London, but Arnold admitted that "the Enemy's ships would escape unless we could possess ourselves of Fort Griswold."

After landing the British western column, the ships' boats began disembarking the 40th and 54th regiments, New Jersey Volunteers, forty *jäger*, and two cannon (950 total) on the eastern shore. That was accomplished by 10:30. Tasked solely with capturing Fort Griswold, their commander, Lieutenant Colonel Edmund Eyre, moved forward. Delayed by poor roads, rough terrain, and intermittent skirmishing, Eyre's men took two hours to near the fort. Shortly afterward, the *jäger* moved to block any reinforcements reaching Colonel Ledyard

Circa 1900 view of the ruins of Fort Griswold, before restoration (Ulbrich Collection)

in Griswold. The New Jersey Loyalists having gone astray, Colonel Eyre now had only 750 men to assault, "a strong work flanked every where, with a rampart 20 feet thick, and some places 16 feet high, strongly frazed . . . defended by many cannon" and with a garrison of unknown size. Receiving a preemptory order to take the fort, at the same time that Colonel Ledyard refused to surrender, Eyre decided to attack.

Inside Fort Griswold, Ledyard, with about 180 militia and seaman, armed with muskets and sixteen-foot-long pikes, awaited the onslaught. A little after 1:00 p.m., the British moved forward, advancing in three columns, hitting the north, south, and east ramparts simultaneously. Eyre's southern column stalled; to the east Major William Montgomery's 40th Regiment continued to charge "under a shower of grape shot and musquetry." The 40th entered the fort first, but as Major Montgomery mounted a gun embrasure, he was killed by a pike-wielding defender. Two other breaches were soon made, 54th lieutenant Hugh Colvill recalling that the "besieged . . . made every effort in their power to repulse us, with long lances and small arms. . . but at last British bravery succeeded, and we got upon the [pickets], and in at the embrasures." In the resulting melee Colonel Ledyard was killed while trying to end the fighting. The Fort was taken.

The Fort's garrison contained unknown numbers of Black militia and seamen; free Black Jordan Freeman, Ledyard's orderly who died in the battle, had been credited with killing Colonel Montgomery, but that has since been questioned. Still, when the British left, they carried with them captured free Black Shoreman Stanton. And militia veteran Jason Stanton later recalled of the battle's aftermath, "The dead all lay as they were slain except a row drawn with their heads against the Barracks—Colonel Ledyard was drawn up against the North End of the Barrack—between two negroes, one on each side of him."

Sources: Harold E. Selesky, ed., *Encyclopedia of the American Revolution: Library of Military History*, 2nd Ed., two vols. (New York and London: Charles Scribner's Sons, 2006), vol. 1, 26–30; Matthew E. Reardon, "The Traitor's Homecoming: Benedict Arnold's Raid on New London, Connecticut, September 4–13, 1781," 396 pages (author's draft, October 19, 2021); Benjamin Quarles, *The Negro in the American Revolution* (New York, London: W.W. Norton & Company, 1973), 76.

1781–1782, Rhode Island Regiment

In February 1781 the remaining two companies of the segregated 1st Rhode Island joined the 2nd Regiment at "Rhode Island Village" in the Hudson highlands, thus forming the conjoined Rhode Island Regiment. When all the 1st Regiment private soldiers arrived they were formed into two segregated companies, the 6th and 8th. At the same time the Rhode Island Regiment was seeking new recruits, with Lieutenant Colonel Jeremiah Olney supervising. Olney noted, "Negroes will not

be received, nor any but able-bodied effective men." When looking for recruits in March 1782, Olney again stipulated in a newspaper advertisement, "it has been found, from long and fatal Experience, that Indians, Negroes and Mulattoes (and from a total Want of Perserverance, and Fortitude to bear the various Fatigues incident to an Army) cannot answer the public Service; they will therefore not on any Account be received." The service of African Americans throughout the war showed

this to be untrue, but Olney's disallowance was likely due to the inordinately high number of Black Rhode Island soldiers who died from smallpox and other diseases during the 1781–1782 winter. It must be noted that Lieutenant Colonel Olney also barred "Foreigners" from service partly due to their being unable to withstand "uncommon Fatigues in the Field."

In April 1781 a small Rhode Island detachment was posted at Pines Bridge guarding a crossing over the Croton River. On May 14, De Lancey's Loyalist militia attacked, killing Colonel Christopher Greene, Major Ebenezer Flagg, and six enlisted men. Colonel Greene was assaulted and mortally wounded inside his quarters, defended only by several Black soldier-servants, while the detachments camped outside the house fled. In addition, five enlisted men were wounded, and three sub-alterns, one surgeon, and thirty-four men missing. Many historians and others have written of this incident as if the entire

Excavated soldier's coat and waistcoat pewter buttons, 1781–1783 Rhode Island Regiment. The large button was found near Saratoga, New York, the smaller one in Virginia. (Troiani Collection)

Continental enlisted contingent involved in the action, and all those wounded or killed, were African American Rhode Islanders. In truth, one of the dead was a Massachusetts enlisted soldier and seven New Hampshire enlisted men were among the missing. Add to that, the Rhode Island force comprised both white and Black rank and file. Four of the five dead enlisted Rhode Islanders were Black. Two other Black Rhode Islanders were mortally wounded and one of the other two wounded men was Black, while ten of the twenty-seven men missing or captured were soldiers of color. Of the thirty-six Rhode Island casualties incurred, seventeen were men of color; more Black than white Rhode Islanders died in the affair.

The Rhode Island Regiment marched to Virginia with the combined Franco-American army at summer's end to confront Lord Cornwallis at Yorktown, passing through Philadelphia en route. (In June 1781 they had been issued the distinctive leather caps, hunting shirts, and overalls.) Also at Yorktown were three Rhode Island soldiers (two Black) selected to join the Corps of Sappers and Miners, and one lieutenant, two non-commissioned officers, and nineteen privates (including seven Black soldiers) detached from the Rhode Island Regiment to serve with Colonel Alexander Scammel's Light Infantry Battalion, formed in late May 1781. Following the British capitulation at Yorktown, the Rhode Islanders endured several months of rampaging illness while forming part of the Philadelphia garrison. In June 1782 the regiment joined the grand army at West Point and took part in the encampment and field maneuvers at Verplank's Point that autumn.

Ordered to join the Northern Department, the Rhode Islanders spent the winter at Saratoga, New York, and in February 1783 portions of five Rhode Island companies, with both Black and white soldiers, took part with New York troops in an ill-fated expedition against British-held Fort Oswego. In freezing temperatures and deep snow, the men marched toward their target. The indigenous guides lost their way, and eventually the commander determined to turn back. New York sergeant Immanuel Doke recalled: "After it was found out that we were misled fires were built to warm us, when it was ascertained a great number were frozen considerably." On the return trip they took shelter in the ruins of "Fort Stanwix our provisions were nearly all exhausted & the last five days before we arrived . . . we had no provision, except dead horse flesh, or something of that kind." Rhode Island veteran Prince Vaughan noted, "he enlisted in the Black Regiment . . . in . . . March 1778 . . . was in the Oswego expedition under the command of Colonel Willet when he had all his toes frozen on his right foot, and his left foot partially frozen. . . . He was honorably discharged by Captain William Allen at Albany in the year 1783."

In February 1783 the regiment was reorganized into a six-company Rhode Island Battalion. Four of the companies consisted of white soldiers, a fifth company had only African American musicians and privates, while the sixth was integrated. In June all but the 1781 three-years men were discharged and the battalion reformed with two companies. The Rhode Island Detachment was one of the last Continental units discharged. Containing only two companies, the 1st Company was segregated white, while the 2nd was integrated. The combined companies had ninety-one musicians and private soldiers as of December 25, 1783; soldiers of color (consisting of twelve Blacks, four mulattoes, seven Indians, and two mustees) comprised 27.47 percent of the whole. The Detachment left camp at Saratoga in late December, and did not reach Rhode Island until mid-January 1784.

Sources: Daniel M. Popek, *They ". . . fought bravely, but were unfortunate": The True Story of Rhode Island's "Black Regiment" and the Failure of Segregation in Rhode Island's Continental Line, 1777–1783* (Bloomington, IN: AuthorHouse, 2015), 270–84, 317, 318, 347, 356, 421–32, 442–53, 496–98, 513–54, 590–604, 606–7; John M. McDonald Papers, 1844–1850 (oral history), Hufeland Collection, Manuscript Books No. 1, Westchester County Historical Society, 69–70, 74–76, 184, 205–6, 209, 291; National Archives, Pension files (microfilm), reel 2455, Prince Vaughan (S42603); John U. Rees, "'We began a smart fire with our Artillery & our small armes': African and Native Americans in the Rhode Island Regiments, 1775–1783," https://www.academia.edu/112997530/_We_began_a_smart_fire_with_our_Artillery_and_our_small_armes_African_and_Native_Americans_in_the_Rhode_Island_Regiments_1775_1783.

1781–1782, Drummer, Hessen-Hanau Artillery Company

On January 15, 1776, a representative of Frederick II, landgrave of Hessen-Kassel, signed a treaty to hire out 12,000 troops to augment British forces fighting in North America. By the war's end perhaps 20,000 of Frederick's soldiers had served on that continent. Being the largest contingent, all German soldiers who fought in the eight-year war were usually called Hessians, but similar treaties were made with the principalities of Hessen-Hanau, Braunschweig, Anhalt-Zerbst, Ansbach-Bayreuth, and Waldeck.

In early September 1776 Captain Georg Pausch of the Hessen-Hanau Artillery Company made landfall in Canada; he and his men soon joined British forces preparing to invade New York state. In 1782—after fighting a naval battle on Lake Champlain in autumn 1776 and in the 1777 Saratoga campaign, during which he was captured and was three years a prisoner—Captain Pausch found himself free, on Long Island, New York, with most of his company. He wrote Hessen-Hanau ruler Count William on June 6, 1781, from near Brooklyn:

> Almost all the Hessen-Kassel regiments and grenadier battalions have taken on Negroes as drummers, pipers, and pack servants. . . . I have followed this practice and at little cost have engaged three drummers for the artillery company . . . as well as a hunting-horn player for the Jaeger Corps, and sent a commission to a good friend in Virginia for a pack servant and twelve artillery servants, each between fourteen and eighteen years of age and well-developed. I hope most humbly, if this local recruiting is not disapproved there, to have . . . fulfilled Your Serene Highness's most gracious intention, as these blacks passed muster as musicians and servants in all of the regiments and have served well. It is possible . . . to fill the whole regiment, in time, with similar blacks. The artillery and pack servants would always be available to support the . . . musicians and to replace their losses. . . . The three drummers for the Artillery Company were initially supplied with complete uniforms; with a uniform hat for daily use, but during a grand parade with a white band, whose top is covered with crimson taffeta and tied above in the fashion of a ribbon . . . on the left side are two red and white inter-mixed feathers about six inches high, before which lies a cockade of blue, white, and red silk tape, in whose center is a silver-washed button. . . . During the present heat and in order to save the uniforms . . . they wear long white linen breeches [gaitered overalls], similar vests, and a very short white linen coat.

The mentioned artillery drummers were Neckern Heckward, John Louis, and William Johns.

Captain Pausch also notes that the "Brunswick Dragoon Regiment has filled its needs with black drummers, which were however, a present to Major General [Friedrich] von Riedesel from Brigadier General [Benedict] Arnold."

As the captain writes, by 1777, and especially as military operations centered in the South, German regiments began taking on Black men, many formerly enslaved. Some served as musicians, but many more were "*Knecht* (servants or laborers) . . . *Packknechte* (sumpters, packhands [packhorse drivers]) and *Wagenknechte* (carters, teamsters)." Historian George Fenwick Jones notes that at least eighty-three African drummers and three fifers served in German corps. He continues,

> it is not always possible to ascertain what duties the *Knecht* performed. No doubt, in time of need, such as while preparing for Count D'Estaing's attack on Savannah, all hands pitched in to dig trenches. The "Moor" John Jack replaced Christoph Schmidt as *Packknecht* on 1 March 1780; and the drummer John Hunter was reassigned as *Wagenknecht* on 16 April 1783 after more than three years as a drummer. Sam of Virginia enlisted for the first time, at the age of fourteen, as a drummer; but three years later, having increased in age and size, he reenlisted in the same regiment as a *Knecht*.

When several Hessian companies were captured on board the ships *Molly* and *Triton* in 1779, three men of African descent were removed and taken away, despite the protests of at least one officer. And following capture at Yorktown in 1781, two Blacks, Jean Rode and Thomas, were taken from the Regiment Erbprinz. In 1783 and 1784 200 or more Black men, women, and children, at least eighty originating in South Carolina, accompanied regiments back to Germany.

Sources: George Fenwick Jones, "The Black Hessians: Negroes Recruited by the Hessians in South Carolina and Other Colonies," *South Carolina Historical Magazine*, vol. 83, no. 4, 1982, 287–302; Friederike Baer, *Hessians: German Soldiers in the American Revolutionary War* (New York: Oxford University Press, 2022), 12–13, 96–97, 379–83; Bruce E. Burgoyne, ed., *Georg Pausch's Journal and Reports of the Campaign in America* (Bowie, MD: Heritage Books, 1996), 28, 111–12;. Maria I. Diedrich, "From American Slaves to Hessian Subjects: Silenced Black Narratives of the American Revolution," in Mischa Honeck, Martin Klimke, and Anna Kuhlmann, eds., *Germany and the Black Diaspora: Point of Contact, 1250–1914* (New York and Oxford: Berghahn Books, 2013), 93–111.

1782, 1st Massachusetts Regiment

By 1782 some proportion of serving Continental soldiers had been in the army for six or seven years, and Commander in Chief George Washington thought they deserved some recognition for their sacrifice. Army orders at Newburgh, New York, August 7, 1782, directed:

> Honorary Badges of distinction are to be conferred on the veteran Non commissioned officers and soldiers of the army who have served more than three years with bravery, fidelity and good conduct; for this purpose a narrow piece of white cloath of an angular form is to be fixed to the left arm on the uniform Coat. Non commissioned officers and soldiers who have served with equal reputation more than six years are to be distinguished by two pieces of cloth set in parellel to each other in a similar form; should any who are not entitled to these honors have the insolence to assume the badges of them they shall be severely punished. On the other hand it is expected those gallant men who are thus designated will on all occasions be treated with particular confidence and consideration.

Four days later a clarification was issued:

> In order to prevent misapplication of the honorary badges of distinction . . . in consequence of long and faithful service . . . the general thinks proper to inform the army that they are only attainable by an uninterrupted series of faithful and honorable services. A soldier who has once retired from the field of glory forfeits all pretentions to precedence from former services; and a man who has deservedly met an ignominious punishmt. or degredation cannot be admitted a Candadate for any honorary distinction, unless he shall have wiped away the stain his reputation has suffered by some very brilliant achievement, or by serving with reputation after his disgrace the number of years which entitle other men to that indulgence.

The directive continued, "The badges . . . are to be of the same colour with the facings of the corps they belong to and not white in every instance as directed in the orders of the 7th. instant."

It was not enough that a soldier had a desire to remain in service, they had to survive the vagaries of everyday military life; hard labor, poor food, rough lodgings, and grueling marches were more often experienced than battlefield dangers. York Ruggles was one of those soldiers. Noted as having been born in Africa, he enlisted in Colonel Joseph Vose's 1st Massachusetts Regiment in May 1777 and was discharged in 1783. Other 1st Massachusetts Black soldiers were eligible. Cato Griger enlisted for three years on January 20, 1778, and joined Vose's regiment at Valley Forge. Griger reenlisted when that term expired, and served to the war's end, when "he was regularly discharged in the rear of Newburgh in New York after a service of more than five years. . . . [He] did not suppose his discharge was of any value and did not take any precautions to preserve it. . . . He believes it was lost & destroyed by his children with other papers of no value." Depositions in his pension claim he was indigenous Lenni Lenape (Delaware), but a descriptive roster notes him having black hair and a black complexion, meaning he was possibly mixed African-Indian, or using a period term, a "mustee." In another unit, John Van Huff, "a Man of Coler," first joined Colonel Goose Van Schaick's 1776 New York regiment for ten months. In June 1777 Van Huff enlisted in the 1st Massachusetts for the war, fought the same year in the Saratoga battles (in his words "the taking of Burgoin"), and at Monmouth in June 1778.

Primus Coburn, 1st Massachusetts veteran and "free man of Colour," claimed to have been eligible for a three-year service stripe, but existing records indicate otherwise. He seems to have first served in 1780 in the 2nd Regiment as a six-month levy under the name Primus Cobus, the year he claimed first service in his pension. He went on to join Colonel Vose's 1st Regiment on July 15, 1781. Having served six months in 1780 and then enlisted for three years the following July, this begs the question as to whether the badge of distinction requires continuous, unbroken service ("an uninterrupted series of faithful and honorable services") for eligibility. In any event Mr. Coburn recalled "he was authorized . . . at the time of discharge to wear as a badge of honor, on the left arm, something resembling a 'V.'" (For a period image of a Continental Army veteran's stripe, see the soldier grouping at the far right of Pierre L'Enfant's 1782 painting of West Point and its surroundings.)

Whatever the case, Primus Coburn served honorably, having been "slightly wounded in the leg at a place called "Morris sina' [Morrisania] below 'Kings ferry' on the North river, while on picket guard." He also claimed that when British major John André was hanged for espionage on October 2, 1780, "he was present when the Regiment was drawn up and surrounded him at his execution."

Sources: *Massachusetts Soldiers and Sailors of the Revolutionary War*, (Boston: Wright & Potter Printing Co., 1897), vol. 3, 693, vol. 6 (1899), 867, vol. 13 (1905), 656, vol. 16 (1907), 285, 286–87. Compiled Service Records of Soldiers Who Served in the American Army During the Revolutionary War (National Archives Microfilm Publication M881), Record Group 93 (Massachusetts), First Massachusetts Regiment, Cato Greger and John Vanhuff, Second Massachusetts Regiment, Primus Cobus; National Archives, Revolutionary War Pension and Bounty-Land Warrant Application Files (National Archives Microfilm Publication M804), Records of the Department of Veterans Affairs, Record Group 15, Washington, DC, reel 594, Obed Coffin (W14569), reel 589, Primus/Primes Coburn (S34703), reel 1135, Cato Griger (W2731), reel 2447, John Van Huff (S42575); John Hannigan email to the author, August 1 and 2, 2023; Library of Congress, Panoramic view of West Point, New York showing American encampments on the Hudson River (pencilled on back: "Encampment of the Revolutionary Army on the Hudson River."), Pierre Charles L'Enfant, 1754–1825, artist, watercolor created after August 1782, Call Number: DRWG 1 - L'Enfant, no. 1 (F size) [P&P], Repository: Library of Congress Prints and Photographs Division, Washington, DC (available online); See also, R. Scott Stephenson, Philip C. Mead, Mark A. Turdo, Matthew Skic, *Among His Troops: Washington's War Tent in a Newly Discovered Watercolor* (Philadelphia: Museum of the American Revolution, 2019), 65.

1782, Charleston, South Carolina, Black Dragoons

On March 16, 1776, Sir William Howe, North American commander in chief, stated that,

> being desirous that the Provincial Forces should be put on the most respectable Footing, and according to his first Intention be composed of His Majesty's Loyal American Subjects, has directed that all Negroes, Molattoes, and other Improper Persons who have been admitted into these Corps be immediately discharged; the Inspector Genl. of Provincial Corps [former British captain Alexander Innes] will receive particular Orders on this Subject to Prevent such Abuses in future.

Historian Todd Braisted notes it is impossible to determine how many Black Loyalists were then serving, but a man named Mungo Dick was enlisted in a Provincial independent company, and freeman John Thompson was with the King's American Regiment. The Ethiopian Regiment, then serving in Virginia, was, due to Howe's stricture, disbanded upon reaching New York, but the unarmed Black Pioneers continued in service.

The commander in chief's ban could only be maintained in units on the official Provincial Establishment, but as the conflict wore on Black men again began to serve. One estimate claims that perhaps a dozen Black soldiers served under arms in Major John Butler's Corps of Rangers, but only two are certainly known, African-born Richard Pierpoint and Thomas Tinbrook. African Americans continued to serve as armed soldiers in Loyalist militia and irregular corps. Perhaps the best known was a band of "refugees" commanded by "Colonel Tye." Titus, or Tye, is known to have run away from his Shrewsbury, New Jersey, master in November 1775, reputedly going on to serve in the Ethiopian Regiment. He later led a group of Black and white Loyalists operating from the fortified Sandy Hook lighthouse. Tye and his men (known as the "Black Brigade") harassed local Whigs from early 1779 until his death from wounds in autumn 1780. Tye's "Brigade" disintegrated after his death. but Loyalist African American partisans, with their white counterparts, continued to operate along the New Jersey coast well into 1782. The Loyalist Refugee Volunteers, another integrated corps, operated in northern New Jersey beginning in 1780; their best-known action was the defeat of Brigadier General Anthony Wayne's Pennsylvania troops when they attacked the Volunteers' Bull's Ferry blockhouse in July 1780.

In 1781 Benjamin Thompson, undersecretary for America under British secretary of state Lord Germain, requested command of the newly forming King's American Dragoons. Thompson left to join his regiment at New York in autumn 1781, his ship instead making landfall at Charleston, South Carolina. Being at loose ends, in December Lieutenant Colonel Thompson was asked by Lieutenant General Alexander Leslie to take the local cavalry in hand and mold them into a force to be reckoned with. He assembled horse soldiers from several Loyalist corps, including the British Legion and Queen's Rangers, at his "Cavalry Camp Advanced Post," four miles outside the city. With them, too, was "a Seapoy Troop (*Gens de Couleers*)," commanded by Captain March (possibly March Kingston). Thompson gave that sobriquet to the Independent Troop of Black Dragoons (aka the Black Pioneer Troop), a unit of some thirty to fifty horsemen, all Black, with a mostly Black command staff. The Troop was Loyalist militia cavalry, clothed in spare British Legion coats and helmets. With the training provided by Lieutenant Colonel Thompson, Captain March's men gained both discipline and expertise.

Two days in February 1782 proved the efficacy of Thompson's training. On the 24th his massed horsemen, operating with infantry support, surprised 500 militia and state troops at Wambaw Bridge; the Loyalist horse charged, upon which the "the enemy fired their pistols, broke in confusion, and were pursued with great slaughter." The following day at Tidyman's Plantation, two miles farther on, Thompson's cavalry attacked a combined force commanded by Lieutenant Colonel Francis Marion, once again routing the Whigs and capturing tentage and other abandoned equipment. Several soldiers mentioned the Black Dragoons in their diaries, including various accounts of a skirmish in April 1782; Pennsylvania lieutenant John Bell Tilden noted, "April 21. This morning Capt. [Ferdinand O'] Neil of ye [Lee's] Partizan Legion, commanding thirty dragoons, fell in with one of ye British negro Captains and his Troop, when he charged and put them to flight. On his return he met with a large body of ye British horse, who proved too much for him; his men all got off except five or six. Two officers and twenty men came in from the British with their arms." Captain Walter Finney described the occasion as "Captn. Neel Dissecting a Negroe Captn. Nam'd Smart, and some of his Affrican Banditty." According to one source Smart was a white captain who commanded the Dragoons when they were out in strength. If taken Black troopers could expect no mercy; South Carolina governor John Mathews wrote that when captured, "they must be tried by negro law; and if found guilty executed."

In November 1782 Delaware sergeant major William Seymour wrote: "The British deserters come in now every day, and may be averaged at thirty per week, and numbers more would come off, but are prevented by the Negro Horse, as they are kept constantly patrolling for that purpose. They all give an account that the British are for evacuating the town. Some are bound for [St.] Augustine, some for the Island of Jamaica, some for Halifax, Nova Scotia, and some for Europe." In December 1782 the Black Dragoons troop emigrated from Charleston to Jamaica.

Sources: Todd W. Braisted, "The Black Pioneers and Others: The Military Role of Black Loyalists in the American War for Independence," in John W. Pulis, ed., *Moving On: Black Loyalists in the Afro-Atlantic World* (New York and London: Garland Publishing, 1999), 4, 18–25; Michael S. Adelberg, *The American Revolution in Monmouth County: The Theatre of Spoil and Destruction* (Charleston and London: History Press, 2010), 84–90; William Smy, *An Annotated Roll of Butler's Rangers 1777–1784 with Documentary Sources* (St. Catherine's, ON: 2004), 84 (cited in Stuart Salmon, "The Loyalist Regiments of the American Revolutionary War 1775–1783," Dissertation, University of Stirling, 2009, 329, https://dspace.stir.ac.uk/bitstream/1893/2514/4/The-Loyalist-Regiments-of-the-American-Revolution-Final.pdf); David and Peter Meyler, *A Stolen Life: Searching for Richard Pierpoint* (Toronto: Natural Heritage Press, 1999); Braisted, "'Such

Above: Royal Provincials pewter coat button issued after 1780 to most Loyalist units lacking their own distinctive uniform button (Troiani Collection)

as are absolutely Free': Benjamin Thompson's Black Dragoons," *Journal of the American Revolution* (online), February 23, 2021, https://allthingsliberty.com/2021/02/such-as-are-absolutely-free-benjamin-thompsons-black-dragoons/?fbclid=IwAR3t9gG1a1Q-U1r43RQpvfUVwX3GAdSKSjyJwkLUwOk4XcK0d-06_sEu30E); Joseph Lee Boyle, ed., "The Revolutionary War Diaries of Captain Walter Finney," *South Carolina Historical Magazine*, vol. 98, no. 2 (April 1997), 137, 146; William McDowell, "Journal of Lieut. William McDowell of the First Penn'a. Regiment, in the Southern Campaign, 1781-1782," in William Henry Egle, ed., *Journals and Diaries of the War of the Revolution, with Lists of Officers and Soldiers, 1775–1783* (Harrisburg, PA: E. K. Meyers, State Printer, 1893), 320; John Bell Tilden Phelps, "Extracts from the Journal of Lieutenant John Bell Tilden, Second Pennsylvania Line, 1781–1782," *Pennsylvania Magazine of History and Biography*, vol. 19, no. 2 (1895), 225; William Seymour, "A Journal of the Southern Expedition, 1780–1783," *Papers of the Historical Society of Delaware*, vol. 15 (Wilmington: Historical Society of Delaware, 1896), 35, 40–41; Gary Sellick, "Black Men, Red Coats: The Carolina Corps, Race, and Society in the Revolutionary British Atlantic," Dissertation, University of South Carolina, 2018, 33–35, https://scholarcommons.sc.edu/etd/4932; "Claims and Memorials Memorial of March Kingston of South Carolina," Great Britain, Public Record Office, Audit Office, Class 13, Volume 130, folio 293, http://www.royalprovincial.com/military/mems/sc/clmkingston.htm; "Black Dragoons Abstract of Pay," Great Britain, Public Record Office, Treasury Office, Class 50, Volume 2, folio 372, http://www.royalprovincial.com/military/rhist/scmil/scmpay.htm.

4. *"If we mean to be what we ought to be."*[1]

Interwar Years through the War of 1812 (1791–1815)

British and Canadian Soldiers

John Ellis notes that during the Napoleonic era the Black man was largely seen by Britons

> as a passive non-combatant witness to the worst excesses of Republican brutality, [which] gave the British public a character that owed all his woes to France, whilst in contrast his present and future liberation had been ensured by a benevolent Britain . . . [instead of Blacks] in the British Army . . . [who] like William Afflick [formerly of St. Kitts, 1801–1819 10th Hussar Regiment trumpeter, and veteran of the Peninsular War and Waterloo] [were] disturbingly efficient combat soldiers, the responsibility of whose woes could be placed firmly on Britain's involvement in slavery, and who had repeatedly asserted their "right" to freedom by their own skill at arms.[2]

British army 1790s Black regiments were born of revolution, in a revolutionary era. The War for American Independence lit the spark, followed by the 1789 French Revolution, and the 1791 slave rebellion in French Saint-Domingue that, after much blood and suffering, led to Haitian independence in 1804. As a result of France's political turmoil and during the Saint-Domingue upheavals, the Caribbean was the scene of unrest and, with war declared in 1793, for Great Britain fear of French incursions on their West Indies possessions. Adding to slave-nations' unease, in September 1793 French commissioners Léger Félicité Sonthonax and Étienne Polverel, on their own, abolished slavery on Saint-Domingue, largely to secure the assistance of people of color in the new war and to restore peace to the island.[3] Four months later, the French government went a step further, decreeing that

> the National Convention declares the abolition of Negro slavery in all the colonies; in consequence it decrees that all men, without distinction of color, residing in the colonies are French citizens and will enjoy all the rights assured by the constitution. It asks the Committee of Public Safety to make a report as soon as possible on the measures that should be taken to assure the execution of the present decree.[4]

Whereas the 1789 Revolution was a threat to monarchy, the February 1794 decree jeopardized slave-nations' economic stability and increased the fear of slave insurrections. (One belated backlash was Napoleon Bonaparte's "Law of 30 Floréal Year X" [May 20, 1802], which led to the reinstatement of slavery and the slave trade in France's colonial possessions, and, eventually, a June 1802 return to the monarchical law banning "Blacks and coloureds entering the territory of the Republic without authorization.")[5]

The Franco-British war lasted from 1793 to 1815, barring a single year of peace in 1802. As a result of the widespread conflict, concurrent manpower shortages (in 1793 the British Army comprised just under 40,000 soldiers), and recent defeats in the Caribbean,[6] in December 1794 Lieutenant General Sir John Vaughan wrote the home secretary,

> I am of the opinion that a corps of one thousand Men, composed of blacks and Mulattoes, and commanded by British Officers would render more essential service in the Country [*sic*, the West Indies] than treble the number of Europeans who are unaccustomed to the Climate. And as the Enemy have adopted this measure to recruit their Armies [the French on Guadeloupe had some 4,000 to 5,000 "blacks under arms"], I think we should pursue a similar plan to meet them on equal terms.[7]

Such had been suggested before in the West Indies; in 1788 British captain John Gosling proposed a single permanent regiment composed of free men of color, to be armed in time of war, and during peace serving as either infantry or a labor corps. Vaughan continued planning for his proposed Black corps, stipulating the regiments would be patterned on British regimental organization, and the men composed of "the ablest and most robust Negroes." Any slaves purchased to serve as soldiers would be given the British government as "Grants or Gifts," and any shortfall bolstered by offering "a modest Bounty" to free Blacks. An alternative plan called for purchasing Africans off newly arrived slave ships. Eventually, a large proportion of West India soldiers were recent captives from Africa; Roger Buckley contends that in the late eighteenth and early nineteenth centuries, "the British government was itself, perhaps, the largest individual buyer of slaves," acquiring some 13,400 enslaved Africans for the regiments. Philip Morgan and Andrew O'Shaughnessy state that "the West India Regiments . . . formed the largest slave army of any European power between 1794 and 1833." Buckley notes, "between

West India Regiments*

Regiment No.	Date Formed	Original	Joined By
1st	April 24, 1795	Whyte's Regiment of Foot	Carolina Corps/ Royal Rangers, 1796
2nd	April 24, 1795	Myer's Regiment of Foot	St. Vincent Rangers, 1795
3rd	May 20, 1795	Keppel's Regiment of Foot	
4th	May 20, 1795	Nicoll's Regiment of Foot	
5th	May 20, 1795	Howe's Regiment of Foot	
6th	September 1, 1795	Whitelocke's Regiment of Foot	
7th	September 15, 1795	Lewe's Regiment of Foot	9th, 10th, and 12th W.I. Regiments, 1802
8th	September 15, 1795	Skerrett's Regiment of Foot (broken up 1802, replaced by 11th West India Regiment)	Loyal Dominica Rangers, 1798
9th	August 1798	Trinidad Rangers or Drault's (Guadeloupe, disbanded 1802)	
10th	Unknown	Soter's Island Rangers (Martinique, disbanded 1802)	
11th	Unknown	South American Rangers (Demerara, renamed the 8th, 1802)	
12th	Unknown	O'Meara's Rangers (island unknown, disbanded 1802)	

*St. George's Caye Archaeology Project Report 1, July 12–19, 2010, http://www.stgeorgescayebelize.org/uploads/9/6/7/0/9670208/sgc_july_28.pdf; chart compiled from René Chartrand and Paul Chappell, *British Forces in the West Indies, 1793–1815* (London: Osprey, 1996) and *The 1st. Battalion West India Regiment* (Williams, 2008). See also, Buckley, *Slaves in Red Coats*, 14–16, and René Chartrand, "Black Corps in the British West Indies, 1793–1815," *Journal of the Society for Army Historical Research*, vol. 76, no. 308 (1998), 248–52.

March 1798 and January 1805 the Windward and Leeward Islands Command alone . . . purchased . . . well over four thousand slaves . . . for those West India Regiments serving within its theatre of operations." By the end of 1805 a total of 5,204 enslaved Africans had been purchased for that purpose.[8]

Individual Black soldiers also served in predominantly white British regiments. One such was George Rose, born enslaved in Jamaica, a private soldier in the 73rd Regiment, who fought in Germany and the Netherlands, 1813–1814, and in 1815 at Quatre Bra and Waterloo, where he was wounded in the right arm.[9] Others fought with British regular regiments in North America. Drummer John Wise carried out the tradition of 29th Regiment Black drummers, enlisting at fourteen years of age in 1809, and serving

four years and six months in the [Spanish] Peninsula, seven months in Gibraltar, two years and one month in North America, and eight years seven months in the Mauritius. Was present at the battles of Rolica, Vimiera, Talavera and Albuera, and also at the capture of the Ponotscot [Penobscot] Territory, United States, North America, in the expedition under the command of Lt. Gen. Sir John Sherbroke in 1814.[10]

The 1814 Penobscot expedition ended in a battle at Hampden, Maine, and resulted in British possession of the Massachusetts district north of the Penobscot River until the war's conclusion. Upon being discharged in 1835 Rose's papers read in part, "his conduct has always been that of an excellent soldier, always efficient, seldom in hospital, trustworthy and strictly sober."[11] Private Edward Baptist was a bandsman in the 1st Battalion, 44th Regiment, which fought at the battles of Bladensburg, North Point, and New Orleans, and at the burning of Washington, DC. While in Louisiana Baptist was listed as a private soldier in the Fourth Company, possibly meaning that he carried a musket when not playing in the band. Also present before New Orleans were two mulatto privates with the 43rd Regiment, Charles Arundell and Gibeon Lippett.[12]

In Canada Peter Zamphier was discharged on May 19, 1819, having served almost twenty years as a drummer in the 49th Regiment. "He received a pension of 9 pence a day, and a grant of 100 acres behind Perth in Upper Canada," but had to quit the land after three months due to "old wounds" which had reopened. The 49th Foot had been deployed to Canada in 1802 and remained until the late 1830s. When his daughter was baptized in August 1813, John Baptiste Gaspard was identified as a "*nègre*" and soldier in the 89th Regiment. A single company of the regiment's second battalion, then serving on the Spanish Peninsula, embarked for Canada in summer 1812; they went on to fight at Black Rock, Crysler's Farm, Buffalo, Longwood, Lundy's Lane, and Fort Erie. Another baptismal record listed William Feeler, "a black man," as a private soldier in the Corps of Provincial Royal Artillery Drivers.[13]

One Canadian regiment, eventually on the Royal establishment, included Black soldiers, most serving as pioneers, one for each company, as well as some musicians. The King's New Brunswick Regiment, first formed in 1793, was disbanded and then reinstituted as the New Brunswick Fencibles in 1803. In September 1810 the unit was added to the British Army and renamed the 104th Regiment of Foot. Recruits were garnered in Canada and the United Kingdom, and, while predominantly white, at least sixteen men of color joined the New Brunswick Fencibles, continuing into the 104th. All or most of them became pioneers, a small armed labor force in every foot regiment. Pioneer troops built roads, bridges, and fortifications, and were often at the fore when attacking fortified posts. Besides muskets, their tools consisted of axes, fascine knives, saws, shovels, spades, and pickaxes. Four 104th Black soldiers are known by name; two early enlistees were Henry McEvoy and Richard Houldin. McEvoy seems to have served only in 1804, while Houldin joined the same year and remained until November 1814, when he transferred to the 10th Royal Veterans Battalion. Charles Falkner enlisted as a private in 1804, becoming a horn-player sometime before he joined a Fencible regiment in June 1812.

Henry (Harry) Grant joined in 1808 and prior to February 1813 was a bass drummer in the 104th regimental band.[14]

One all-Black Canadian Provincial unit was formed in 1812, titled "Captain Runchey's Company of Coloured Men" or the "Coloured Corps." First proposed by Butler's Rangers Black veteran Richard Pierpont, the Corps was composed of free Blacks and indentured servants enlisted in July to serve for the war. It was first commanded by Lincoln militia captain Robert Runchey, a much-disliked officer, but the unit survived his leadership and went on to fight in several actions, including Queenston Heights (October 13, 1812), Fort George (May 27, 1813), and Stoney Creek (June 6, 1813). At Queenston Heights the Colored Corps was thirty-eight men strong; that winter Sergeant William Thompson and thirteen York militia Black soldiers voluntarily transferred to the Corps, but at Fort George in May 1813 only twenty-seven men took part in the battle. Too small to serve effectively as a fighting unit, in December 1813 the Colored Corps veterans joined the Corps of Provincial Artificers, attached to the Royal Engineers, posted at Fort Mississauga. A similar unit, formed in Nova Scotia, was the "Coloured Company" of the Halifax militia, described by the governor as "fine young men, equal in every respect to the White Militia, both in Discipline and Appearance [and] of their loyalty and steady attachment to the Parent State there can be no doubt."[15]

Black men served in other Canadian provincial and militia units. Hero Richardson, residing in Montreal, "a negro native of Green Island [a village near Troy, New York]," enlisted in Lieutenant Colonel Charles Michel de Salaberry's Corps of Canadian Voltigeurs when he was seventeen, signing on "*et même Six mois après les guerre s'il en est requis*" (and even for six months after the war if needed). Black farmers John Dolphin and Henry Thomson enlisted in the Voltigeurs together, on February 16, 1813. Dolphin's enlistment paper indicates he was thirty-one years old, but at his death in 1819 he was said to be fifty-six, meaning he was fifty in 1813, far older than the age thirty-five recruitment bar. Dolphin was 5 foot 7 inches tall, complexion "*noire nègre*" (negro black), hair "*de laine*" (wooly), eyes "*noir*." Thomsen was 5'4" in height and thirty-five years old. Two Black men, former raftsmen, enlisted in Salaberry's Voltigeurs in December 1812; Castor Jay was a thirty-one-year-old "person of color," while Thomas Cockburn was a twenty-eight-years old "*nègro*." It is likely some or all these men fought at the October 26, 1813, Chateauguay battle which, along with the battle at Crysler's Farm, turned back the American invasion along the St. Lawrence River that autumn. Numbers of Black men also served in the Canadian Select Embodied Militia and other part-time units.[16]

Federal Regiments and State Militias

President James Madison signed a formal declaration of war on June 18, 1812.[17] Up to that point the U.S. Army was an all-white organization, mimicking the May 8, 1792, Militia Act, which for the first time at the federal level barred Black Americans from state militia service.

[Article] I. Be it enacted by the Senate and House of Representatives of the United States of America, in Congress assembled, That each and every free able-bodied white male citizen of the respective States, resident therein, who is or shall be of age of eighteen years, and under the age of forty-five years (except as is herein after excepted) shall severally and respectively be enrolled in the militia, by the Captain or Commanding Officer of the company, within whose bounds such citizen shall reside, and that within twelve months after the passing of this Act.[18]

The 1792 law, which said nothing about federal soldiers, was either adopted by the U.S. Army or mirrored already existing, perhaps uncodified, strictures. May 1792 recruiting orders for the captain of a federal light horse troop included the stipulation that "no negro [enslaved person], mulatto [free black], or Indian, [is] to be recruited." Four years later instructions for Captain William Preston, 4th Sub Legion under Major General Anthony Wayne, contained that same exact phrase. Just prior to the turn of the century, two other documents mention denying Black enlistment: the U.S. Army 1798 *Rules and Regulations Respecting the Recruiting Service* state: "Negroes mulattoes or Indians are not to be inlisted. Natives of fair conduct and character are to be preferred; but foreigners of good reputation for sobriety and honesty may also be enlisted." And in September 1799 Colonel William Bentley, 7th U.S. Infantry, reminded Inspector General Alexander Hamilton, "our recruiting instructions forbids recruiting Mulatto's." Federal military legislation does not contain racial terms; the April 30, 1790, "act for regulating the Military Establishment of the United States" merely states, "the non-commissioned officers and privates . . . shall, at the time of their enlistments . . . be able bodied men, not under five feet six inches in height, without shoes; nor under the age of eighteen, nor above the age of forty-six years." That was amended in 1802 to include "able-bodied citizen[s] of the United States"; the 1802 law superseded previous legislation and seems to have opened the door to Black enlistment, up to and including the War of 1812. Not until December 1814 do we have a law that, in a roundabout manner, refers to Black enlistment; the "act making further provisions for filling the ranks of the army of the United States" stated, "every commissioned officer who shall be employed in the recruiting service . . . is, authorized to enlist into the army of the United States, any free, effective, able-bodied man, between the ages of eighteen and fifty years." As men of color had been serving in U.S. regiments since at least 1812, and likely before, that legislation was merely codifying already in place recruiting procedures.[19]

Black civilians contributed to the war effort when they could. In 1814 the British fleet off the Atlantic coast and in the Chesapeake raided at will, and coastal cities tried to augment their defenses. The August 17, 1814 *New-York Evening Post* contained this notice:

The free colored people of the 9th ward, are requested to meet on Thursday evening the 17th inst. At 7 o'clock, at the house of Peter Stephens, near 3-mile stone, on the Harlem Road, for the purpose of tendering their services to the committee of defence, in the erection of the fortifications at Brooklyn Heights.

Cato Alexander

That was likely one of a series of similar meetings, as evidenced by a story in the August 24 *New-York Herald.*

Patriotism of the Africans. This morning between 800 and 1000 of the hardy and patriotic sons of Africa, accompanied by a delightful band of music and appropriate flags, crossed the ferry at Catharine slip, to work on the fortifications at Brooklyn heights. These men, knowing the value of freedom, are anxious to defend it, and too much praise cannot be bestowed on them for their voluntary exertion. [20]

Two days later Black Revolutionary veteran James Forten took part in a meeting in Philadelphia "to make arrangements for . . . defence of a cause that is common to all without distinction." Forten, an activist in the causes of equality and abolition, along with Reverends Richard Allen and Absolom Jones called for "the aid of the people of color in erecting suitable defenses." To support the effort, James Forten at his own expense offered to provide canvas and his employees' labor to construct sandbags. Mr. Forten partnered in leading a Committee of Defense to broadcast the appeal, at the same time asking "those gentlemen that have men of colour in their employment [to allow] them to join their brethren in this laudable undertaking." On September 21, 1814, over 1,000 Black Philadelphians joined white citizens and marched south to build fortifications on the Schuylkill River's west bank. Forty-eight-year-old James Forten participated along with twenty of his men, working mostly at the Gray's Ferry crossing.[21]

Records of Black soldiers in the U.S. Army and state militias, 1812–1814, have yet to be properly gleaned, but a brief study of print and manuscript sources reveal some. Some are known to be of African descent, others are possibly men of color due to their name and/or personal description. One or several men named Africa Peterson were in the Massachusetts militia, separate entries noting service with Thomas's and Sweet's regiments, as well as Captain Duston's company. Records show that in two cases Mr. Peterson also had a connection to the names Benjamin Peterson and Thomas Smith, either nom de plumes or perhaps the names of masters. Virginian George Graves signed on with the 14th Regiment at Alexandria in August 1814. That October he was "left sick at Greenbush [eastern shore Virginia] . . . Jany 31/[18]15, Nurse in Gen'l Hosp'l." Graves was noted to have dark eyes, black hair, and a dark complexion; those attributes and the fact he was serving as a nurse may indicate he was a Black man. John Lyndes was another soldier whose ethnicity is uncertain. A twenty-one-year-old Connecticut farmer, he had black eyes, black hair, and dark complexion. He enlisted in July 1812 at Hartford, was "wounded through the right arm in action at Stony Creek, June 6/13, and taken prisoner"; exchanged at Chazy, New York, in May 1814, he was discharged at Fort Columbus, Governor's Island, New York, on September 19, 1815.[22]

Jacob Dexter was a private in the 25th Regiment, Captain Daniel Ketcham's company. Dexter, a "colored man," enlisted March 18, 1814, at Windsor, Connecticut, and was "wounded in the battle of Chippewa, July 5/[18]14." Mulatto Judith Lines was originally from Connecticut, but moved with her husband John and family to Vermont in 1793. John had served with the 5th Connecticut Regiment during the War of the Revolution, and Judith had been with him at camp for one summer, where she contracted smallpox. In a March 1837 deposition Judith testified, "my youngest son died of a wound recd. in the last war, his name was Benjamin, the wound was recd. at the Battle of Chippewa." No military records have been found for Benjamin, but he may have enlisted under another name. William Lynes (aka Lines) enlisted in the 30th U.S. Regiment in April 1814 at Burlington, Vermont, age unknown. Under the entry for William Lines he is described as a "Mullatto."[23] William had a varied service record, being

tried by Court-Martial at Plattsburg, July 24/[18]14. [for] Deserting at Plattsburg, July 11/[18]14. [and sentenced to] Hard labor during [his] term of enlistment . . . [noted as] absent in Navy since Sept. 6/14 [likely served as a marine with the Lake Champlain fleet during the Battle of Plattsburgh] . . . absent in State prison (counterfeit money) since Nov. 13/[18]14 . . . Deserted at Burlington, Feb. 28/[18]15 . . . Returned from desertion, April 19/[18]15, [was] confined and deserted from the guard House at Burlington, April 30/[18]15.[24]

There is, however, no evidence connecting Benjamin Lines with William Lynes.

The presence of Black men in the ranks irked some. South Carolinian George Izard began his army career as a lieutenant of engineers in June 1794. From Plattsburgh on July 3, 1814, as major general and commander of the "Northern Frontier of the United States," Izard wrote Secretary of War John Armstrong:

There was, some years ago, a regulation of our service, prohibiting the enlistment of negroes and people of colour. I have not heard of it being enforced. Among the New England recruits there have lately been brought hither a number of these people, to the great annoyance of the officers and soldiers here. The latter object to doing duty with them. The Inspector General is now organizing them as a sort of pioneer corps. Shall they be retained and mustered in that capacity?[25]

Gene Smith notes that a company of Black Massachusetts recruits arrived at Plattsburgh expecting to serve under arms, but that the white officers refused to command them; they were then formed into a segregated labor corps for building needed fortifications.[26]

The service record for Vermonter Richard Boyington indicates a deliberate plan to cull Black soldiers from the postwar U.S. Army. Boyington was sixteen when he enlisted in the 4th Infantry Regiment on June 25, 1812. He was "Discharged at Philadelphia, May 18/[18]15." Colonel Henry Atkinson, a North Carolinian, noted that Boyington, "belonged to the 11th U.S. Infy in Aug 1813 when I took him as a servant at Burlington, Vt. — In the following winter he was transferred to the 4 U.S. Infy." Atkinson then wrote, "Discharged under an order from the War Dept. directing all soldiers of color should be discharged."[27]

In 1824 and 1825 former Continental Army major general the Marquis de Lafayette returned to the United States. In Louisiana he met with a group of African American veterans who fought at the Battle of New Orleans. Their commander, John Mercier, addressed Lafayette, saying in part, "the Corps of men of Colour who so eminently contributed to the defense of this Country . . . felt that they should first offer to one of the Heroes of the American Independence, their tribute of respect and admiration."[28] The April 19, 1825, *Courier of New Orleans* recorded:

The General received the men of colour with demonstrations of esteem and affection, and said to them: "Gentlemen, I have often during the War of Independence, seen African blood shed with honor in our ranks for the cause of the United States. I have learnt with the liveliest interest . . . what a glorious use you made of your arms for the defense of Louisiana. I cherish the sentiments of gratitude for your services, and of admiration for your valor. Accept those also of my personal friendship, and of the pleasure I shall always experience in meeting with you again." The General then kindly shook hands with them all, and thanked the Governor for the opportunity he had given him to become acquainted with them.[29]

Thirty-six years later some of their descendants would take part in another conflict that would threaten to permanently split the country apart. (Note: The War of 1812 artwork section contains detailed information on the three all-Black units that were formed in 1815—one U.S. regiment and two Louisiana battalions.)

1812–1815, Seaman, U.S. Navy

In his book *Boarders Away*, artist and historian William Gilkerson writes of the June 1813 sea-duel between HMS *Shannon*, Captain Philip Broke, and USS *Chesapeake*, Captain James Lawrence. While preparing for battle Broke told his men, "you will let them know today that there are Englishmen in the *Shannon* who still know how to fight." An advocate for boarding the enemy, Broke then advised, "kill the men and the ship is yours. . . . Don't hit them about the head, for they have steel caps on, but give it them through the body."

The only clue the pictured seaman is American lay in the iron and leather boarding helmet he wears (this example with bearskin side-whisker chin-strap), an innovation used only in the U.S. Navy, circa 1800–1837. Except for that detail, the image could depict a British sailor or one from a number of European countries. The common and able-bodied seamen who worked the ships had no formal uniform, barring the double-breasted sailor's jacket, which, though extremely practical, was not required apparel.

Black seamen crewed European naval and merchant ships in increasing numbers since the sixteenth century, mirroring the growth of slavery and the Africa-trade. During the Seven Years' War free Blacks served in the Royal Navy, while enslaved men were impressed or joined of their own volition to escape bondage. In October 1762 Vice-Admiral Alexander Colville took aboard HMS *Northumberland* several slaves to replace "thirty of her best Seamen [dead] by a Malignant Fever." He informed the admiralty secretary, "these Negroe Slaves shared the same Fate with such freeborn White Men, as we could pick up at a very critical time." Slaves belonging to ship's officers also augmented the crew; abolitionist Olaudah Equiano, who purchased his freedom in 1766, at one time belonged to British lieutenant Michael Pascal. He was in several naval actions, and at the sieges of Louisbourg and Havana. While aboard the ship *Roebuck*, Equiano helped work the vessel, at sail and in combat. Jeffrey Brace, who was manumitted after service as a Continental soldier in the War of the Revolution, belonged to a ship's captain, and also served as a seaman, seeing action in the Seven Years' War off the American coast and Cuba.

Crewing naval and trade shipping went hand in hand, the same men often serving on both at different times. During intercontinental conflicts, as in the War of the American Revolution and War of 1812, merchant shipping suffered from blockades and predatory enemy vessels, leading to unemployed seamen who then joined fighting ships. The choice then was whether to sign with the nation's navy or with privately financed letter-of-marque (privateer) vessels.

During 1768 London political unrest, an eyewitness related that the most notorious rioters were multiethnic American seamen, "wretches of a mongrel descent," the "immediate sons of Jamaica, or African Blacks by Asiatic Mulatoes." Among those thousands of "wretches" was fourteen-year-old free Black Philadelphian James Forten, who signed aboard Stephen Decatur Sr.'s letter-of-marque *Royal Louis*, a twenty-two-gun ship with a crew of 200. The *Royal Louis* returned to Philadelphia following a successful voyage and, after refitting, went to sea again. On this trip the *Louis* was captured; Forten was incarcerated on the prison ship *Jersey* as inmate 4120. Freed after seven months, he walked home barefoot from northern New Jersey. In after-years he became a successful businessman and prominent Philadelphian. In 1777, on the Piscataqua River between Maine and New Hampshire, Cato Carlile and Scipio Africanus enlisted for service under Captain John Paul Jones. And in October 1779 Captain Abraham Whipple requested that two British seamen, John Onion, a Black, and William Bartlett, American Indian, be released from captivity to serve aboard the Continental frigate *Providence*; Whipple noted that since they fought against America, once captured they should be grateful to fight for her. They were only two of the many men of color who manned British vessels. One source claims that by the end of the eighteenth century Black seamen formed 25 percent of the men who crewed ships of the Royal Navy.

Two anecdotes about the War of 1812 provide a good idea of numbers of Black seamen on American ships. Mr. Lewis Allen recalled that after Commodore Stephen Decatur Jr.'s USS *United States* brought the defeated HMS *Macedonian* into New York, in January 1813, the city gave Decatur a feast,

shortly after [that] they gave a dinner to the crew. . . . One third of the crew were colored, mulattoes, and full blacks. They walked side by side with the white sailors. . . . Some gentlemen seeing the negro element expressed surprise . . . and enquired if the men were good for anything in a fight. The Commodore replied, "They are as brave men as ever fired a gun. There are no stouter hearts in the service."

The following year an eyewitness saw the crew of the USS *Constitution* as they were being taken by wagon from a Massachusetts port "to man the American ships on Lake Ontario." "The crew consisted of three or four hundred sailors . . . nearly or quite half . . . was composed of colored men, and most of them distinctly Negroes. Their relations and intercourse with the white sailors seemed perfectly equal and harmonious."

Despite prewar attempts to reduce their enlistment, some 19,000 Black men served in the Union Navy (1861–1865), as pilots, sailors, landsmen, and cooks, on some ships representing 15 to 80 percent of the crew.

Sources: William Gilkerson, *Boarders Away, With Steel-Edged Weapons and Polearms* (Lincoln, RI: Andrew Mowbray, 1991), 7–8, 104–6, illustrations facing pages 50 and 51; Elena A. Schneider, *The Occupation of Havana: War, Trade, and Slavery in the Atlantic World* (Chapel Hill: University of North Carolina Press, 2018), 79, 238 (note 37); Maria Alessandra Bollettino, "Slavery, War, and Britain's Atlantic Empire: Black Soldiers, Sailors, and Rebels in the Seven Years' War, Dissertation, University of Texas at Austin, December 2009, 165–67, https://repositories.lib.utexas.edu/handle/2152/ETD -UT-2009-12-543; Olaudah Equiano, *The Interesting Narrative and Other Writings* (New York and London: Penguin Books, 2003), 68–94; Douglas R. Egerton, *Death or Liberty: African Americans and Revolutionary America* (Oxford and New York: Oxford University Press, 2009), 15–16; Kari J. Winter (ed.), *The Blind African Slave, or Memoirs of Boyrereau Brinch, Nick-Named Jeffrey Brace, as told to Benjamin F. Prentiss* (Madison: University of Wisconsin Press, 2004), 27–30; Peter Linebaugh and Marcus Rediker, *The Many-Headed Hydra: Sailors, Slaves, Commoners, and the Hidden History of the Revolutionary Atlantic* (Boston: Beacon Press, 2013), 221; Julie Winch, *A Gentleman of Color: The Life of James Forten* (Oxford and New York: Oxford University Press, 2002), 29–52; Adam E. Zielinski, "James Forten, Revolutionary: Forgotten No More," June 13, 2023, *Journal of the American Revolution* (online), https://allthingsliberty.com/2023/06/ james-forten-revolutionary-forgotten-no-more/; Benjamin A. Quarles, *The Negro in the American Revolution* (New York, London: W.W. Norton & Company, 1973), 83–93, 152–56; Jordan Dean, "British Sailors and Revolutionary Culture in the 'Age of Revolution,'" Dissertation, University of Hertfordshire, 2014, 24; Paul Gilroy, *The Black Atlantic: Modernity and Double Consciousness* (London, 1993), 13; Benson J. Lossing, *The American Historical Record, and Repertory of Notes and Queries* (Philadelphia: Chase & Town, Publishers, 1872), 114–15, 224–25; Matthew Brenckle, "A Marblehead Escape," April 2, 1814, https://ussconstitutionmuseum.org/2014/04/02/ a-marblehead-escape/#:~:text=So%2C%20instead%20of%20 risking%20a,whole%20countryside%20followed%20the%20 chase; Michael Shawn Davis, "'Many of them are among my best men': The United States Navy Looks at Its African American Crewmen, 1755–1955," Dissertation, University of Kansas, 2011), 36–38; John U. Rees, "'They stripped to the waist & fought like devils': Black Sailors in British and American Sea Service (1754–1865)," https://www.academia .edu/113016514/_They_stripped_to_the_waist_and_fought _like_devils_British_and_American_Sea_Service_1754 _1865_.

1813–1814, 104th Regiment of Foot

President James Madison signed a formal declaration of war on June 18, 1812. Following major U.S. losses early-on, the first substantial field battle occurred on October 13 on the Niagara River frontier. Over a thousand American troops crossed the river and attacked at Queenston Heights. Among the defenders was a company of thirty-eight Black Canadians called "Captain Runchey's Company of Coloured Men" or the "Coloured Corps." Consisting of free Blacks and indentured servants enlisted in July to serve for the war, they fought again at Fort George and lesser actions. In December 1813 Colored Corps veterans joined the Corps of Provincial Artificers, attached to the Royal Engineers.

One Canadian regiment, eventually on the Royal establishment, had a Black presence. First formed in 1793 as the King's New Brunswick Regiment, it was disbanded after the 1802 Treaty of Amiens; in 1803 it was reinstituted as the New Brunswick Fencibles. In response to officers' requests, in September 1810 the unit was added to the British Army and renamed the 104th Regiment of Foot. Recruits were garnered in Canada and the United Kingdom, and, while predominantly white, at least sixteen men of color joined the New Brunswick Fencibles, continuing into the 104th. All or most of them became pioneers, a small armed labor force in every foot regiment. Pioneer troops built roads, bridges, and fortifications, and were often at the fore when attacking fortified posts. Besides muskets, their tools consisted of axes, fascine knives, saws, shovels, spades, and pickaxes. Four 104th Black soldiers are known by name; two early enlistees were Henry McEvoy and Richard Houldin. McEvoy seems to have served only in 1804, while Houldin joined the same year and remained until November 1814, when he transferred to the 10th Royal Veterans Battalion. Charles Falkner enlisted as a private in 1804, becoming a horn-player sometime before he joined a Fencible regiment in June 1812. Henry (Harry) Grant joined in 1808 and prior to February 1813 was a bass drummer in the 104th regimental band.

At the beginning of the conflict, the 104th Foot was stationed in dispersed New Brunswick and Nova Scotia. In early February 1813, the regiment was ordered overland to Upper Canada via Québec City. Four companies remained in place; the other six, on snowshoes, with sledges for bulky equipment, left one day apart, beginning with the grenadier company on February 16, and ending with the light company on the 21st. The march was about 700 miles, in the dead of winter. Through at least one severe snowstorm, and temperatures as low as minus 16 Fahrenheit, the lead company took fifty-three days to reach Kingston (via Québec City and Montreal). Two men (possibly five others) died of the cold, and more suffered from frostbite. In spring 1813 two of three companies still in New Brunswick took ship and sailed up the St. Lawrence River; only one company went on to Kingston, the other stayed first at Québec City, and moved to Three Rivers in December 1813.

The 104th Regiment initially joined the garrison at the Lake Ontario port of Kingston, as well as nearby Points Henry and Frederick, guarding the St. Lawrence River entrance. In late May four companies took part in a failed raid on the American Sackets Harbor naval base, where 104th soldiers suffered significant casualties. Early in June the 104th Regiment went by boat to the west end of Lake Ontario, prior to a move against American forces on the Niagara frontier.

On June 24 the 104th flank companies helped defeat an American raiding force at Beaver Dams. On October 3, 1813, the entire regiment departed by batteau, suffering a cold, wet five-day journey before they disembarked and rejoined the garrison at and near Kingston. On other fronts fighting continued, including the November 1, 1813, British victory at Crysler's Farm and the mid-December capture of Forts George and Niagara.

In mid-June 1814, at Kingston, the entire regiment was assigned to work on completing a 104-gun ship-of-the-line, later named the HMS *St. Lawrence*; in early July the Americans had, once again, crossed the Niagara into Canada, this time well trained and better led. The 104th flank companies rushed to the frontier, while the regiment's main body garrisoned Fort Wellington, at Prescott on the St. Lawrence River. On July 25 the grenadier and light companies were present at the Lundy Lane battle, but experienced no combat. Following that bloody but inconclusive action, British lieutenant general Gordon Drummond reorganized his Right Division, placing Lieutenant Colonel William Drummond of the 104th in command of a flank battalion, including his own two companies.

At July's end word was received that Major General Jacob Brown's American Left Division had removed to Fort Erie. Lieutenant General Drummond's forces marched south and began a siege that lasted forty-eight days. On the night of August 15–16, the British attacked the fort. The 104th Regiment flank companies were with the main assault column under Lieutenant Colonel Drummond; they captured the fort's northeast bastion, then, after the powder magazine exploded, were forced to retreat with great loss. The siege was abandoned on September 21.

The 104th flank companies saw action one last time at Cook's Mills, October 19, 1814, a British defeat, and the final battle of the war on Canadian soil. The flank companies were withdrawn and landed at Kingston on October 26. The 104th Regiment continued in service until May 1817, when it was disbanded.

Sources: George F. G. Stanley, *The War of 1812: Land Operations* (Toronto: Macmillan of Canada, 1983), 4, 121–31, 216–21; "Captain Runchey's Company of Coloured Men," https://en.wikipedia.org/wiki/Captain_Runchey%27s_Company_of_Coloured_Men; Gareth Newfield, "The Coloured Corps: Black Canadians and the War of 1812," https://www.thecanadianencyclopedia.ca/en/article/the-coloured-corps-african-canadians-and-the-war-of-1812; John R. Grodzinski, *The 104th (New Brunswick) Regiment of Foot in the War of 1812* (Fredericton, NB: Goose Lane Editions, 2014), 20–22, 24 (Blacks), 25, 36–40; Frank Mackey, *Done with Slavery: The Black Fact in Montreal, 1760–1840* (Montreal: McGill-Queen's University Press, 2010), 203–5; See also, Don Troiani, Earl J. Coates, and James L. Kochan, *Don Troiani's Soldiers in America, 1754–1865* (Mechanicsburg, PA: Stackpole Books, 1998), 100, 103.

Above: Enlisted soldier's cast pewter button, 104th Regiment of Foot (Brian Rollason Collection)

1814–1816, British Colonial Marines

Early in 1814, because of enslaved American Blacks, earlier friendly reception for invading British forces, Colonial Secretary for War and the Colonies Henry, Earl Bathurst, ordered Sir Alexander Cochrane to offer entire families their freedom. To advertise that, Cochrane disseminated this notice:

By the Honorable Sir Alexander Cochrane, K.B.

Vice Admiral of the Red, and Commander in Chief of His Majesty's Ships and Vessels, upon the North American Station, &c. &c. &c.

A Proclamation
This is therefore to Give Notice,
    That all those who may be disposed to emigrate from the United States will, with their Families, be received on board of His Majesty's Ships or Vessels of War, or at the Military Posts that may be established, upon or near the Coast of the United States, when they will have their choice of either entering into His Majesty's Sea or Land Forces, or being sent as FREE Settlers to the British possessions in North America or the West Indies, where they will meet with all due encouragement.
    GIVEN under my Hand at Bermuda, this 2nd day of April, 1814.

Alexander Cochrane.
By Command of the Vice Admiral, William Balhetchett.
GOD SAVE THE KING

In 1813 commander of the North American Naval Station, Admiral John Warren, gave his subordinate Vice Admiral George Cockburn the task of making the Chesapeake Bay a safe-haven for British naval forces. One of Cockburn's tools was terror, burning and shelling anything on shore that had a whiff of any military connotation. But enslaved Africans flocked to his ships and landing parties, providing pilots and guides, and asking for freedom. Cochrane's 1814 Proclamation was intended to make the most of those runaways, and Cockburn was asked to forward it in a particular manner. Beginning with Black volunteers already serving with the fleet, all formerly enslaved in the American South, on May 14, 1814, he created a force of Colonial Marines. While serving in the British West Indies in 1808, Cockburn was responsible for creating the first Corps of Colonial Marines, recruited with enslaved men, as were the twelve West Indian Regiments formed between 1795 and 1798. The original Corps was formed to defend Marie Galante island against the French; the slaves who volunteered demanded they not be returned to their owners. That Corps, commanded by Royal Marine officers, served only in the Caribbean, and was disbanded in October 1810; seventy men were dispersed among the region's naval squadron, twenty-five more to a battery on the Saintes, with fifty garrisoning Marie Galante. Each man continued to be listed on ship's muster rolls as "Colonial Marine" until mid-1815. Regarding both Colonial Marine establishments, the 1807 Mutiny Act emancipated all slaves serving with the British Army, meaning that any afterward enlisted were immediately free.

Oval brass shoulder-belt plate with the anchor device of the British Royal Marines, circa 1795–1815 (Troiani Collection)

Admiral Cockburn chose Tangier Island in the Chesapeake as his base, a location that new Marine recruits and refugees would know of and easily find. Enlisted men first came from Maryland and Virginia, but as naval operations branched south to Cumberland Island, many Georgia volunteers were accepted. Noncommissioned officers for the new unit were taken from the best of the early volunteers. The British government's original instructions were to enlist all Black volunteers into existing West India regiments, but the Americans balked. Instead, these Colonial Marines remained a Black American corps with a largely Black American command staff, barring white commissioned officers.

The 1814 Colonial Marines saw wide service in numerous small actions in the role of light troops, scouts, and guides; postwar, comparing them with white troops, Admiral Cockburn described the Black Marines as "infinitely more dreaded." Their first action was on May 30, at the Pungoteague Creek in Virginia, assisting in taking an artillery battery. Captain James Ross of the HMS *Albion* called the Corps "a most excellent specimen of what they are likely to be. Their conduct was marked by great spirit and vivacity, and perfect obedience." Seeing one of their own killed, "did not daunt or check the others, but on the contrary animated them to seek revenge"; following their Chesapeake exploits the admiral noted his Black Marines had refrained from "improper outrages" and performed "unexpectedly well."

Their raids in the Chesapeake region are too numerous to mention, but at the Battle of Bladensburg and burning of Washington the Corps lost one killed and three wounded. On September 3, 1814, three veteran Royal Marine companies combined with the three Colonial companies to form the 3rd Battalion Royal and Colonial Marines; as such they fought at the September 12 battle of North Point, outside Baltimore, Maryland. That autumn the Black Marines numbered some 200 men and, despite losses from disease over the winter, in the first months of 1815 two more companies were raised in Georgia. While there they helped guide about 1,500 Georgia slaves to freedom. After further service in Florida, early in 1815 the Royal Marine companies were sent back to England, and six Black Marine companies, plus a Royal Marine staff company, were formed into 3rd Battalion Colonial Marines. Still refusing to join one of the West Indies regiments, the Black Marines were disbanded in Trinidad in August 1816, where their descendants, known as "Merikens," remain to this day.

Sources: "Corps of Colonial Marines," https://en.wikipedia.org/wiki/Corps_of_Colonial _Marines; John McNish Weiss, "The Corps of Colonial Marines: Black Freedom Fighters of the War of 1812," https://web.archive.org/web/20180208143724/http:// www.mcnishandweiss.co.uk/history/colonialmarines.html and https://web.archive.org/ web/20171008165503/http://www.mcnishandweiss.co.uk/history/sources.html, expansion of Weiss's earlier article, "The Corps of Colonial Marines 1814–16: A Summary," *Immigrants & Minorities: Historical Studies in Ethnicity, Migration and Diaspora,* vol. 15, No. 1 (1996), 80–90; David Lambert, "'[A] Mere Cloak for their Proud Contempt and Antipathy towards the African Race': Imagining Britain's West India Regiments in the Caribbean, 1795–1838," *Journal of Imperial and Commonwealth History,* vol. 46, no. 4 (2018), 627–50; Omar Shareef Price, "Away to Freedom: African American Soldiers and the War of 1812," Dissertation, University of Louisville, 2011, 16–17, 23–25, https://ir.library .louisville.edu/cgi/viewcontent.cgi?article=2152&context=etd.

September 13–14, 1814, Fort McHenry, Private William Williams, 38th U.S. Regiment

The May 14, 1814, Baltimore *American & Commercial Advertiser* contained the following notice:

News from France

The [ship] *Fair American* has arrived from Liverpool, at New York; also, the *Ida* from France at Boston—They both bring late and important news of the great contest in France, which has seemingly taken a decisive turn against the *Emperor* Napoleon—Both Bordeaux and Paris are taken by the Allies, and the *Imperial* Court has fled, perhaps never to return—[Secretary of State for Foreign Affairs Robert Stewart, Viscount] Castlereagh's gold has overcome Bonaparte's steel.

By the time this was published it was already old news, Napoleon Bonaparte having abdicated on April 6, 1814. This victory allowed the British government to order sixteen veteran regiments to Canada, while six others were allotted for seaborne operations aimed at the United States's eastern and southern coasts.

That same issue of the *American & Commercial Advertiser* published on its last page a runaway advertisement:

Forty Dollars Reward

For apprehending and securing in jail so that I get him again, Negro Frederick

Sometimes calls himself Frederick Hall, a bright mulatto; straight and well made; 21 years old; 5 feet 7 or 8 inches high, with a short chub nose and so fair as to show freckles, he has no scars or marks of any kind that is recollected: his clothing when he left home, two months since, was home made cotton shirts, jacket and Pantaloons of cotton and yarn twilled, all white. It is probable he may be in Baltimore, having a relation there, a house servant to a Mr. Williams, by the name of Frank who is also a mulatto, but not so fair as Frederick.

Benjamin Oden

Prince George's County, May 12th.

Frederick had been living as a slave at Oden's Bellefields Plantation at Croom, a village in Prince George's County, Maryland, probably for most or all of his life. Passing himself off as a free man, he enlisted on April 14 as William Williams in the 38th U.S. Regiment and received a fifty-dollar bounty for doing so. He was signed on by Ensign John Martin who did not check Williams's credentials; being a slave according to Federal law he "could make no valid contract with the government."

The 38th Regiment was first raised on January 29, 1813, and spent much of its existence doing garrison duty in the Baltimore area. On June 26, 1814, Private Williams was with the regiment when it marched to support Commodore Joshua Barney's "mosquito fleet" gunboats in a clash with the Royal Navy at St. Leonard's Creek, Maryland. The regiment experienced no combat then, and at the August 24 Battle of Bladensburg was little engaged and had no losses. Following that action British forces advanced to Washington and, in retaliation for the torching of York, Ontario, Canada, burned the White House and other government buildings.

Baltimore City, a haven for American privateers and merchant vessels, was the next target. Fort McHenry, on the Patapsco River, protected the harbor, but additional fortifications had to be constructed to cover eastern land approaches, with civilians, seamen, and enslaved men as laborers. On the morning of September 12, 1814, British major general Robert Ross landed at North Point with 3,700 veteran regulars and armed seamen, plus 1,000 marines. They were checked, first in open battle by Maryland forces, then at newly built fortifications nearer the city. With the land attack stalled, Vice Admiral Sir Alexander Cochrane determined to destroy Fort McHenry.

With the impending British threat to Baltimore, the 38th U.S. Regiment joined the Fort McHenry garrison, working to strengthen existing defenses, and building some anew. Cochrane's vessels were in position shortly after dawn on September 13. Over the next twenty-seven hours they unleashed a rain of shells; just after 2:00 p.m. the fort was battered, with four dead and fourteen wounded, plus a soldier's wife cut in two. The bombardment continued after the bomb vessels and rocket ship moved nearer the fort. The soldiers of the 38th took shelter in a dry ditch surrounding McHenry; at some point William Williams was "severely wounded, having his leg blown off by a cannon ball." He was taken to the garrison hospital and then into Baltimore, where he died in November.

That night a British joint land and sea assault was planned. In the pouring rain the troops waited; about 11:00 p.m. the bombardment intensified, supporting the naval attack on Fort McHenry. Soon Cochrane received word that the shipborne assault had failed, leading to cancellation of the land offensive. At 7:00 a.m. on the 14th, British naval fire ceased and Admiral Cochrane's fleet began to withdraw. The city was saved.

Learning of William Williams's (aka Frederick's) death, Benjamin Oden petitioned the government for William's land bounty, but the case was dismissed, "inasmuch as a slave cannot possess or acquire title to real estate by the laws of the land, in his own right, no right can be set up by the master as his representative."

Sources: *American & Commercial Advertiser* (Baltimore), May 14, 1814, 2, 4; John R. Elting, *Amateurs to Arms!: A Military History of the War of 1812* (Chapel Hill, NC: Algonquin Books of Chapel Hill,1991), 178, 207–43; "William Williams," https://userpages.umbc.edu/~jamie/html/william_williams_and_the_battl.html; "A Black Soldier Defends Fort McHenry," Library Field Guide No. 1, Fort McHenry National Monument and Historic Shrine Maryland, National Park Service U.S. Department of the Interior; "Negro Frederick, alias William Williams, 38th U.S. Infantry at Fort McHenry, Sept. 1814," https://maryland1812.com/2011/04/10/negro-frederick-alias-william-williams-38th-u-s-infantry-at-fort-mchenry-sept-1814/; John C. Frederiksen, *The United States Army in the War of 1812* (Jefferson, NC, and London: McFarland & Co., Publishers, 2009), 270–71.

Left: Model 1795 U.S. infantry flintlock musket, manufactured at Harpers Ferry Arsenal. Also made at Springfield Arsenal, the Model 1795 comprised the largest proportion of firearms issued to regular U.S. troops during the War of 1812. (Troiani Collection)

1814–1815, New Orleans Campaign, Major Louis D'Aquin's 2nd (Louisiana) Battalion of Free Men of Color

On September 21, 1814, Major General Andrew Jackson issued a proclamation from Mobile, Alabama, "to the Free Colored Inhabitants of Louisiana . . . As sons of freedom" to "defend our most inestimable blessing." As the general noted, "through a mistaken policy, you have heretofore been deprived of a participation in the glorious struggle for national rights in which our country is engaged. This no longer shall exist." He continued:

> To every noble-hearted, generous freeman of color, volunteering to serve during the present contest with Great Britain, and no longer, there will be paid the same bounty, in money and lands, now received by the white soldiers of the United States. . . . The non-commissioned officers and privates will also be entitled to the same monthly pay and daily rations, and clothes, furnished to any American soldier. . . . Due regard will be paid to the feelings of freemen soldiers. You will not, by being associated with white men in the same corps, be exposed to improper comparisons or unjust sarcasm. As a distinct, independent battalion . . . pursuing the path of glory, you will, undivided, receive the applause and gratitude of your countrymen.

On December 18, the general made a second address to the New Orleans "men of Color." The following February Jackson confessed to President James Monroe that his appeal was partly due to

> great fears . . . lest the free persons of colour should unite themselves to the enemy . . . and become the means of stirring up insurrection among the slaves. . . . We must either have this part of the population in our own ranks or find it in the ranks of the enemy.

Major Pierre Lacoste's 1st (Louisiana) Battalion of Free Men of Color was formed the mid-October following the first appeal; Lacoste and Colonel Michael Fortier, senior officers of the Black battalions, both white men, had served in the militia under the old Spanish regime, and Lacoste's Battalion was centered around Spanish-descended Black Louisianans.

With surplus "sons of freedom" wishing to serve, D'Aquin's 2nd Battalion of Free Men of Color was organized in December, on or before Jackson's New Orleans address. The 2nd Battalion (sometimes termed the "*Bataillion* of St. Domingo") was largely recruited by Second Major Joseph Savary; Savary was a light-skinned former colonel of a French mulatto regiment that fought Haitian rebels on Saint-Domingue. The 2nd Battalion was nominally led by white Creole Major Louis D'Aquin, but Savary commanded in the field (Lacoste's second major, Vincent Populus, was also Black). D'Aquin's men were largely Saint-Domingue immigrants with military experience, and, as with Lacoste's Battalion, at least some company officers were of African descent.

Having been appointed Seventh Military District commander, General Jackson arrived in New Orleans on December 1, 1814. His immediate duty was to review his available forces and prepare defenses against an attempt on the city. The British moved north, but on December 13–14 were diverted from moving via Lake Pontchartrain, deciding instead to advance up the Mississippi. On December 14 Lacoste's Battalion was mustered into federal service; D'Aquin's corps followed on the 19th. On December 17 Lacoste's men moved south to Chef Menteur, between Lakes Borgne and Pontchartrain, then moved back to "ligne Jackson" (the Chalmette/Rodriguez canal defense line) on the 26th, where they were reunited with D'Aquin. British forces camped at the Villeré plantation on the evening of December 23, seven miles south of New Orleans. The Americans, including D'Aquin's soldiers, attacked that night; the action cost the British 267 casualties and delayed their advance several days; General Jackson praised the battalion afterward, stating, "Savary's volunteers led by him under the command of Major Daquin manifested great bravery."

Following a December 28 probing action and January 1 artillery bombardment and sortie (before which, to celebrate the New Year, Lacoste's battalion band played "Yankee Doodle" and "The Marseillaise"), the British attacked on the 8th in force. The 1st and 2nd Free Battalions were in the center of the American works with, respectively, 280 and 150 men. Not being at a point of attack, they took little part in the main action, but that afternoon some of D'Aquin's men sallied out to eliminate British marksmen preventing removal of wounded soldiers.

The New Orleans battle was a decisive defeat for the British, with their commander Lieutenant General Sir Edward Pakenham and 700 other ranks killed, 1,400 wounded, and 500 captured. Unbeknownst to the combatants, the Treaty of Ghent, ending the war, was signed on December 24, 1814.

In March 1815 Joseph Savary, still in federal service, sent a petition to General Jackson on behalf of the "*Volontaire* officers of Colour of the *Bataillion* of St. Domingo":

> As we hope shortly to enjoy the benefit of peace after a hard & short Campaign, they humbly beseech his excellency to take in consideration [that they will] . . . as soon as the laws of this state will take their ordinary courses, [be] exposed to the most humiliating vexations. If it pleases your excellency to grant to each of the supplicants . . . a protection which will put them beyond a prejudice which always existed in this country . . . This act of Justice will save them from future insult.

> As far as is known, Jackson never answered their plea.

Sources: Donald K. Midkiff, "Recognition and Acceptance: An Examination of the Louisiana Volunteer Battalions on Line Jackson," Thesis, University of New Orleans, May 2020, 1–3 (incl. note 1) 5–8, 12, 13–15, 17–18, 20–21, 23, 24–31, https://scholarworks.uno.edu/cgi/viewcontent.cgi?article=3906&context=td; Roland C. McConnell, *Negro Troops in Antebellum Louisiana: A History of the Battalion of Free Men of Color* (Baton Rouge: Louisiana State University Press, 1968), 53, 66–72, 84; "Major D'Aquin's Battalion of Free Men of Color," https://en.wikipedia.org/wiki/Major_D%27Aquin%27s_Battalion_of_Free_Men_of_Color#CITEREFAslakson2014; "General Washington and General [Andrew] Jackson, on Negro Soldiers" (Philadelphia: Henry Carey Baird, 1863), 7–8, https://www.loc.gov/resource/rbaapc.02500/?st=gallery; "War of 1812 Louisiana Militia Muster Rolls," incl. foreword, http://geauxguardmuseums.com/wp-content/uploads/2022/12/2013.005.070_war_of_1812_muster_rolls_finding_aid.pdf; Andrew Jackson to James Monroe, February 13, 1815, https://www.loc.gov/resource/maj.01032_0187_0194); Jerome Greene, "The New Orleans Campaign of 1814–1815 in Relation to the Chalmette Battlefield," 34, 40–41, 44–49, 62–63, 72–75, 112–13, 126–28, 138–39, 155, 158 (note 37), https://www.nps.gov/parkhistory/online_books/jela/lost_riverfront/Part_1.pdf; Charles E. Kinzer, "The Band of Music of the First Battalion of Free Men of Color and the Siege of New Orleans, 1814–1815," *American Music*, vol. 10, no. 3 (1992), 348–69.

1814–1815, New Orleans Campaign, 1st West Indian Regiment

Near the end of the War of the American Revolution, British forces relinquished one seaport after another, and white and Black refugees left with them. Black evacuees included men, women, and children of color (free and enslaved) with British and Loyalist military units, thousands of enslaved people belonging to white Loyalists, small numbers of unattached freed slaves and free Blacks, and, at New York, escaped Blacks seeking freedom. By far the greatest portion of those Black emigrants were enslaved people, either Loyalist-owned or sequestered from rebellious Americans.

When American Loyalist corps were disbanded, some of their Black retainers—men, women, and children—were listed in the two-volume "Book of Negroes," a compilation of 2,997 Black refugees who left New York City in June 1783. Black members of British and German regiments (musicians and support personnel) remained with those organizations and went uncounted. South Carolina hosted a substantial contingent of Black "Loyalists," meaning those of African descent who found it in their interest to side with Crown forces for an assurance of safe haven and possible (though unpromised) freedom; unfortunately, most were left behind in 1782.

The men of two Loyalist organizations were evacuated to the British West Indies. The largest was the Southern contingent of the Black Pioneers; created by engineer Colonel John Moncrief in late 1778, they served in the 1779 Savannah and 1780 Charleston sieges. The Pioneers continued in service until the December 1782 evacuation of South Carolina. The Black Dragoons was an all–African American cavalry unit of some fifty men, formed in late 1781. It was one of only two armed Black corps that served on the mainland, the other being the 1775–1776 Ethiopian Regiment. When the British left Charleston in autumn and early winter 1782, they took with them about 300 men of both units; landing in Grenada, they were formed into a single organization called the Carolina Corps.

On April 24, 1795, the 1st West India Regiment was authorized and entered the British military establishment and pay. By March 1796 the greater part of the Black Royal Rangers (raised for the French war) and Carolina Corps had been drafted into the 1st West India; the following March the remaining two companies of the Carolina Corps joined.

Between 1797 and 1814 the 1st West India took part in numerous actions and operations, but two just before the War of 1812 were the most significant. At the 1809 capture of Martinique they received kudos: "From the day of the regiment landing, to that of the enemy's surrender, it served with the greatest credit under all the disadvantages to which a West India regiment is exposed. The hard and severe work is generally performed by them, which the European soldiers could not undergo from the climate." In 1810 the flank companies helped in capturing Guadeloupe; because of these operations, "the words 'Martinique' and 'Guadaloupe' were inscribed on the colours of the regiment, 'as a mark of royal favour and approbation of its gallant conduct at the capture of those islands.'"

In late November 1814, the 1st West India joined the expedition to take New Orleans, Louisiana, arriving at the entrance of Lake Borgne on December 10. The base camp was on shelterless Pea Island, sixty miles from where the fleet lay at anchor. Beginning there, the West Indian soldiers "suffered in consequence of the severe cold, a thing with which they were totally unacquainted, and against which they were ill provided." Early on, some "fell fast asleep, and perished before morning."

After passage above the city via Lake Pontchartrain was found unviable, Major General John Keane determined to advance to the Mississippi and attack upriver. Major General Sir Edward Pakenham having arrived, he decided on a reconnaissance-in-force for December 28; the West Indians advanced along the river in the rear of Keane's column, but had no direct part in the fighting.

Gaining reinforcements, Pakenham set January 8 for the final assault on the American Rodriguez Canal/Chalmette fortifications. Early in the morning of the 8th, two attack columns advanced, hitting the American center and center-left; they were repulsed, taking heavy losses. The reserve First Brigade, including the 1st West India (minus two companies), moved to support them, but fell back along with the retreating columns.

One hundred 1st Regiment soldiers (likely the grenadier company) formed with several light companies to cover the right attack column's flank; on the left, next to the river, were 100 more 1st West Indians (light infantry), with the 7th, 43rd, and 93rd light companies. Unable to see what was occurring to their right, they advanced along the river, where they took a small advanced redoubt but, getting no further, withdrew.

With General Pakenham dead, and over two thousand killed and wounded, on January 17, British forces began retiring toward the coast. By their early February embarkation, the 1st West India Regiment had gone from a December strength of 713 rank and file to 634; losses in the January 8 action were five killed, twenty-three wounded, and one missing.

Francis Castly and John Dorset enlisted in the 1st Regiment at Dominica in 1806, and both were discharged in 1843; Mr. Castly noted having served "at the capture of Guadeloupe and Martinique and was with his corps in America." John Dorset had been "present at the capture of Guadeloupe (twice) and wounded through the body, was also with his corps at New Orleans."

Enlisted soldier's brass shoulder-belt plate, 1st West India Regiment (Brian Rollason Collection)

Right: British "India" pattern flintlock musket, with a thirty-nine-inch barrel; this example is marked to the 9th Company, 1st West India Regiment. The standard arm of the British Army in the Napoleonic era. (Troiani Collection)

Sources: Sylvia R. Frey, *Water from the Rock: Black Resistance in a Revolutionary Age* (Princeton: Princeton University Press, 1991), 172; John W. Pulis, "Bridging Troubled Waters: Moses Baker, George Liele, and the African Diaspora to Jamaica," in John W. Pulis, (ed.), *Moving On: Black Loyalists in the Afro-Atlantic World* (New York and London: Garland Publishing, 1999), xx, 183–86; "Inspection Roll of Negroes Book No. 1," National Archives, https://catalog.archives.gov/id/17337716; "Inspection Roll of Negroes Book No. 2," National Archives, https://catalog.archives.gov/id/5890797; Gary Sellick, "Black Men, Red Coats: The Carolina Corps, Race, and Society in the Revolutionary British Atlantic," Dissertation, University of South Carolina, 2018, 16–17, 33–35, 38–49, 58–59, 71–73, 85, 94, https://scholarcommons.sc.edu/etd/4932; For a discussion of wartime Black soldiers in the British West Indies see Albert W. Haarmann, "Jamaican Provincial Corps, 1780–1783," *Journal of the Society for Army Historical Research*, vol. 48, no. 193 (Spring 1970), 8–13; A. B. Ellis, *First West India Regiment* (London: Chapman and Hall, 1885), 78, 97–99, 103–15, 118–59; Jerome Greene, "The New Orleans Campaign of 1814–1815 in Relation to the Chalmette Battlefield," 86–87, 90–93, 132–39, 146–54, 158–59, 167–68, https://www.nps.gov/parkhistory/online_books/jela/lost_riverfront/Part_1.pdf; Timothy James Lockley, "The West India Regiments and the War of 1812," *Journal of the Early Republic* (in press), 2–4, 15–19, https://wrap.warwick.ac.uk/170927/1/WRAP-West-India-Regiments-War-1812-22.pdf; Robin Reilly, *The British at the Gates: The New Orleans Campaign in the War of 1812* (New York: G.P. Putnam's Sons, 1974), 226–27; Richard W. Dixon, "The 1815 Battle of New Orleans—A Physical Geographic Analysis," in Douglas R. Caldwell, Judy Ehlen, Russell S. Harmon, eds., *Studies in Military Geography and Geology* (Dordrecht, Boston, and London: Kluwer Academic Publishers, 2004), 152–53, https://archive.org/details/springer_10.1007-978-1-4020-3105-2/page/n155/mode/2up; John U. Rees, "'Distinguished and gallant conduct' Formation of the West India Regiments, and War of 1812 Service (1794–1815)," https://www.academia.edu/112999449/_Distinguished_and_gallant_conduct_Formation_of_the_West_India_Regiments_and_War_of_1812_Service_1794_1815_.

1814–1815, New Orleans Campaign, Drummer Jordan Noble, 7th U.S. Infantry Regiment

In the late nineteenth century, veteran Jordan Noble responded to a query from New Orleans *Picayune* editor Edward Wharton; his statement was printed in the October 12, 1881, edition:

in comply with your request and wish . . . I was born in . . . Georgia, October 14 ____ Came to New Orleans in . . . 1812 was enlisted as Drummer in the 7th Reg. U.S. Army in 1813, Major ____ Commanding and served under him until December 23rd 1814 When Major [illegible] of the 44th Regiment took command and led us against the British in the Battle of the 23rd of December 1814 and commanded our Regiment at Camp Jackson until the British retired from New Orleans, January 12th 1815 . . .

I was a volunteer in Florida in 1836 in the first Louisiana Brigade under General P[ersifor].F[razer]. Smith and in Mexico in General P.F. Smith's Brigade, General Z. Taylor in 1841 [*sic*, 1846]. Colonel J.B. Walton, 1st Louisiana Regiment in Company H. Captain J.M. Vandegrift.

I also served in U.S.A[rmy]. As Captain of Company C. in [unclear] Louisiana Volunteer 1863 . . . From all of which I was honorably discharged.

Yours Respectfully
Jordan B[ankston]. Noble

Much has been written about Jordan Noble, including a children's book, but no definitive well-researched recounting has been published; because of that, some aspects of his life remain uncertain. The best biography (unsourced) is filmmaker Jerry Brock's, which appeared in the Winter 2015 issue of *64 Parishes* magazine.

Even the beginning of Mr. Noble's life is uncertain; in four documents he gave four birthdates, ranging from 1796 to 1804. His natal year is usually given as 1800, with a birthdate of October 14, which would make him fourteen years old in December 1814 (or eighteen if born in 1796). He was born into enslavement in Georgia; he and his mother Judie (or Judith), then thirty years old, were sold in autumn 1813 to John Brandt of East Baton Rouge and later purchased on June 2, 1814, by John Noble, a North Carolinian and captain in the 7th U.S. Regiment. Jordan later recounted that he and his mother then lived in the Old Spanish Barracks in New Orleans, where a portion of the 7th Regiment was quartered.

Jordan Noble was taken into the regiment as a drummer; being enslaved his pay would have belonged to Captain Noble. The captain was wounded in the December 23, 1814, American night attack on the British at the Villeré plantation. John Noble died in 1817; before that he sold Jordan and his mother to Alexander White, retired 12th U.S. Regiment lieutenant colonel and, in 1823, they were purchased by John Reed. We do not know when Jordan Noble obtained his freedom, but by 1861 he was no longer enslaved.

As he asserts, it is likely Mr. Noble served in Florida and the 1840s Mexican War. He mentions P. F. Smith, certainly

Persifor Frazer Smith, who was a colonel of Louisiana Volunteers in 1836, and under Major General Zachary Taylor, at the battle of Monterrey commanded a brigade which included Captain Albert Blanchard's Louisiana Volunteer Company. Noble's claim regarding Civil War service rings true, as well; the 1st and 2nd Louisiana Native Guards, including Black company officers, were in the Port Hudson battle, May 27, 1863. In mid-June 1865 Private S. H. Smothers, former Ohio teacher, was en route to Texas with the 45th U.S. Colored Troops of the 25th Corps. Smothers visited Jordan Noble during a one-day stop at New Orleans; among other things, he noted that Mr. Noble was publisher of the "'Black Republican' newspaper, No. 6, Carondolet street." Noble also told him,

in the present war he went out as a Captain in one of the regiments of the Louisiana Native Guards. There were two of these regiments, both of which were raised in New Orleans, composed of free colored men, and the line officers were all colored men. They took a prominent part in the battle of Port Hudson, but soon after . . . when they had been in service only three months, the prejudice among the white officers against the colored officer became so strong that . . . to avoid having their commissions taken from them, [they] resigned.

Drummer Noble had two harrowing experiences in the 1814–1815 New Orleans campaign; the December 23, 1814 night attack must have overwhelmed the senses of a young man in his first combat, but one contemporary noted, "the battle of the eight of Jany was won on the 23d of Dec'r."

Historian Jerome Greene notes the position of the 7th U.S. Regiment and adjacent units in the fortified line during the January 8 New Orleans battle: "At the extreme right [next to the Mississippi River] were nearly 40 members of Beale's New Orleans volunteer company of riflemen. [To their left] Between Batteries No. 1 and 3 stood about 440 members of the Seventh Infantry." This was the point of assault by the British 43rd, 7th, and 1st West India light companies; while they took a small redoubt in front of the line, their attack failed under withering fire from American artillery and infantry.

Jordan Noble's duties during the battle are unclear; he would have drummed "Beat to Arms" for the men to form, and repeated the cease fire signal ("the first part of the general") at the end of the action. In between, he was likely busy carrying away wounded or bringing up water, when not observing the action.

Sources: "Letter, Jordan B. Noble to Edward C. Wharton," https://louisianadigitallibrary.org/islandora/object/tahil-aaw%3A544; Freddi Evans, *The Battle of New Orleans: The Drummer's Story* (Mount Pleasant, SC: Arcadia Publishing, 2005); Jerry Brock, "Jordan Noble: Drummer, Soldier, Statesman: The Incredible Life of a Marching Music Pioneer," https://64parishes.org/jordan-noble#:~:text=Jordan%20Bankston%20Noble%20was,of%20the%20War%20of%201812; F. B. Heitman, *Historical Register of the United States Army, from Its Organization, September 29, 1789, to September 29, 1889* (Washington, DC: National Tribune, 1890), 601; Stephen A. Carney, *"Gateway South": The Campaign for Monterrey (The U.S. Army Campaigns of the Mexican War)* (Washington, DC: Government Printing Office, 2005), https://history.army.mil/brochures/the%20campaign%20for%20monterrey/the%20campaign%20for%20monterrey.htm#gate; William A. Dobak, *Freedom by the Sword: The U.S. Colored Troops, 1862–1867* (New York: Skyhorse Publishing, 2013), 104–8; Edwin S. Redkey. ed., *A Grand Army of Black Men: Letters from African-American Soldiers in the Union Army, 1861–1865* (Cambridge, UK: Cambridge University Press, 1992), 196–97; Jerome Greene, "The New Orleans Campaign of 1814–1815 in Relation to the Chalmette Battlefield," 20, 27–28, 40–50, 63, 73–74, 111–12, 126, 128, 132–39, 147–52, 169–71, https://www.nps.gov/parkhistory/online_books/jela/lost_riverfront/Part_1.pdf; Charles Stewart Ashworth. *A New, Useful and Complete System of Drum Beating Including the Reveille, the Troop, Retreat, Officers Calls, Signals, Salutes and the Whole of the Camp Duty as Practiced at Head Quarters, Washington City, Intended Particularly for the United States Army and Navy* (Boston: Graupner and Price, 1812), 8; "Jordan Noble Drum," Historic New Orleans Collection, https://www.hnoc.org/jordan-noble-drum.

1814–1815, New Orleans Campaign, 5th West Indian Regiment

Seventeenth- and eighteenth-century European colonial powers often armed slaves in periods of dire need, usually without manumitting them. Even British South Carolina, with its great fear of slave rebellions, armed enslaved men. Historian Maria Bollettino shares:

> "A General Return of the Officers and Men in the Charles Town Regiment of Foot" reveals that Colonel Othniel Beale commanded five militia companies in 1756, which together consisted of 744 effective private men, 137 alarm men, and 608 slaves. Each militia company enrolled between 100 and 150 enslaved black men alongside an only slightly higher number of white militiamen. Moreover, it is likely that black slaves . . . often outnumbered white privates, as fewer white men joined their companies at musters than were enumerated on the rolls.

To augment the defenders during the 1762 Havana siege, enslaved Cubans were armed with pikes and machetes; in several instances small groups of slaves fought particularly well, were freed in consequence, and joined the Havana free black militia company.

In the War of the American Revolution several states, particularly Connecticut, allowed owners to enlist their slaves in the state's Continental regiments. There are solid indications that the 755 men of General George Washington's main army listed in the August 1778 "Return of the Negroes" were all enslaved. At the same time British West Indian governments balked at arming slaves; in extremis, in 1782, Jamaica finally agreed to organize the Jamaica Rangers, but with free Black and mulatto recruits.

Between 1784 and 1795 several British West Indies independent Black corps were formed, some of which were drafted into the twelve West India regiments. The 1790s French wars strained Britain's ability to defend their West Indies possessions; in 1795 eight West India regiments were formed and joined the British establishment. In 1798 four more were added.

Enslaved men, in the main direct from Africa—"New Negroes"—were used to fill out the new units. Historians Philip D. Morgan and Andrew O'Shaughnessy state that "the West India Regiments . . . formed the largest slave army of any European power between 1794 and 1833." Historian Robert Buckley notes, "between March 1798 and January 1805 the Windward and Leeward Islands Command alone . . . purchased . . . well over four thousand slaves . . . for those West India Regiments serving within its theatre of operations." By the end of 1805 a total of 5,204 enslaved Africans had been purchased for that purpose.

A brief from Commander in Chief of the West Indies Sir Ralph Abercromby, January 26, 1797, titled, "Instructions to Major Genl Hunter, for Guidance in the Purchase and Approval of Blacks and Coloured People for the West India Regts," laid the groundwork for staffing the new Black corps.

Recruits were to be age eighteen to thirty years and none "to be received with a Family or follower." Article Four stipulated,

> the Blacks &ca of the West Indies Regiments are to be upon all points, upon the same footing with the Soldiers of the Regular Regiments, and if their behaviour is deserving, they will be entitled to a Pension equal to Chelsea, when disabled in the Service, by Wounds or Age.

Under "Prices":

> For each Recruit who is particularly fit for service; from his Age, Stature, and Character, making him a proper subject for a Flank Company–Seventy Pounds S[ter]lg.
> For those of an Inferior Description—Sixty—d[itt] o—or five or six more, according to Quality.
> For those which are bought from the African Ships Fifty Pounds Slg. with a Latitude of five or six Pounds for very fine well made Men.

The 5th West India Regiment was formed in 1795. From 1798 to 1807 it recruited 710 "New Negros" (Africans), eighty-eight Creole (West Indies) Blacks, seven "East Indians" ("lascars," seamen from the Indian subcontinent), and seven from Europe.

The 5th West India Regiment was not a standout, but as reliable as its brother units and inured to hardship. Little is known of its pre-1814 service, but that year it was assigned to the New Orleans expedition. The fleet arrived at the inlet to Lake Bourgne on December 10, landing the troops on an open island sixty miles up the lake, suffering early on from cold, frosty nights. The weather turned milder but still wet in the new year. British forces moved overland from the lake to the Mississippi River and, after several encounters with American forces, were set to attack their fortifications at the Rodriguez Canal/Chalmette line.

At daylight on January 8, the two main British assault columns moved forward in the face of overwhelming artillery

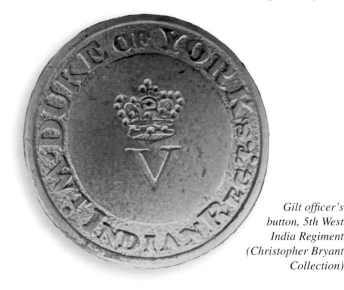

Gilt officer's button, 5th West India Regiment (Christopher Bryant Collection)

and musket fire. On the British far right the 5th West India, some 450 strong, began before daylight, to "endeavour by a small circuit to reach the left flank of the Enemy's position . . . and if circumstances actually permit, to penetrate his Rear." The West Indians moved through a cypress swamp, ankle- or knee-deep in water and mud, against the extended American line. Opposing them were Brigadier General John Coffee's 2,500 Tennessee riflemen, behind fortifications with a clear field of fire. Given the failure of the main assaults, in impossible circumstances, the 5th West India carried out their orders as best they could, then withdrew.

Leaving the Louisiana coast in early February 1815, the 1st and 5th West India Regiments were slated to land in Florida, to make "an inroad in the back of Georgia." The 5th Regiment disembarked, but word of the war's end arrived and terminated military operations.

Sources: Maria Alessandra Bollettino, "Slavery, War, and Britain's Atlantic Empire: Black Soldiers, Sailors, and Rebels in the Seven Years' War," Dissertation, University of Texas at Austin, December 2009, 37–38, 47–48, https://repositories.lib.utexas.edu/handle/2152/ETD-UT-2009-12-543; Albert W. Haarmann, "Jamaican Provincial Corps, 1780–1783," *Journal of the Society for Army Historical Research*, vol. 48, no. 193 (Spring 1970), 8–13: See also Maria Alessandro Bollettino, Matthew P. Dziennik, and Simon P. Newman, "'All spirited likely young lads': Free Men of Colour, the Defence of Jamaica, and Subjecthood During the American War for Independence" (manuscript version), published in *Slavery and Abolition*, vol. 41, no 2 (2020), 187–211; René Chartrand and Paul Chappell, *British Forces in the West Indies, 1793–1815* (London: Osprey Publishing, 1996); Philip D. Morgan and Andrew O'Shaughnessy, "Arming Slaves in the American Revolution," in Christopher Leslie Brown and Philip D. Morgan, eds., *Arming Slaves, from Classical Times to the Modern Age* (New Haven and London: Yale University Press, 2006), 180; Roger N. Buckley, "Slave or Freedmen: The Question of the Legal Status of the British West India Soldier, 1795–1807," *Caribbean Studies*, vol. 17, nos. 3/4 (1977), 91–92, 97, 107–8; Tim Lockley, "Creating the West India Regiments" (2017), Sir Ralph Abercromby to Major General [?] Hunter, January 26, 1797, "Heads of Instructions to Major Genl Hunter, for Guidance in the Purchase and Approval of Blacks and Coloured People for the West India Regts," https://www.bl.uk/west-india-regiment/articles/creating-the-west-india-regiments; Timothy James Lockley, "The West India Regiments and the War of 1812," submitted to *Journal of the Early Republic* (in press), 17–21, https://wrap.warwick.ac.uk/170927/1/WRAP-West-India-Regiments-War-1812-22.pdf; Jerome Greene, "The New Orleans Campaign of 1814–1815 in Relation to the Chalmette Battlefield," 78, 96–97, https://www.nps.gov/parkhistory/online_books/jela/lost_riverfront/Part_1.pdf; Richard W. Dixon, "The 1815 Battle of New Orleans—A Physical Geographic Analysis," in Douglas R. Caldwell, Judy Ehlen, Russell S. Harmon, eds., *Studies in Military Geography and Geology* (Dordrecht, Boston, and London: Kluwer Academic Publishers, 2004), 152–53, https://archive.org/details/springer_10.1007-978-1-4020-3105-2/page/n155/mode/2up; John U. Rees, "'Distinguished and gallant conduct': Formation of the West India Regiments, and War of 1812 Service (1794–1815)," https://www.academia.edu/112999449/_Distinguished_and_gallant_conduct_Formation_of_the_West_India_Regiments_and_War_of_1812_Service_1794_1815_).

1815, 2nd West Indian Regiment

In the early 1820s Jamaican J. A. Stewart wrote of public disgust upon viewing white soldiers, deserters, "pinioned and in a miserable plight"; the reason for the civilians' distress was the "novel and revolting" sight of them being guarded by formerly enslaved Black soldiers of the 2nd West India Regiment.

The February 1793 French declaration of war on Great Britain showed the need for additional soldiers to defend the Crown's Caribbean possessions. British West India island governments grudgingly accepted the eight 1795 West India regiments as a stopgap against enemy invasion, but by 1798 the French naval threat had diminished, four more Black regiments were being organized, and the enlistment of "New Negroes," government-purchased newly captured Africans, was becoming common. By the end of 1801, 3,033 enslaved Africans had been enlisted.

That same year island assemblies were arguing that West India Black soldiers were covered by local slave laws, not military jurisprudence. Brigadier General Thomas Hislop noted that if Black soldiers

> are amenable to the Slave Laws, and therefore subject to every degradation, that the unfortunate Slave is doomed to endure. . . . How then could . . . a West India Soldier . . . with safety perform his Duty? For instance, if a white Man insults him on his Post, or attempts to act contrary to the orders he has received, he could not resist him, and if even struck, or any attempt was made to disarm him, he could not oppose with the firmness his duty as a Soldier would demand, and for the neglect of which, the Law . . . would award him a severe punishment.

If the colonial interpretation was supported by British law it would lead to the crippling or dissolution of the West India regiments. Despite legal opinions supporting Black soldiers being treated as slaves—the first from the St. Vincent's Attorney General Gloster (January 10, 1799), then three more opinions from law officers of the Crown (March 11, 1799, March 11, 1801, December 14, 1801)—the army continued treating Black soldiers as they would enlisted whites. The British government in fact, if not law, was committed to a policy of equality among Black and white soldiers, and insisted that West India regiments receive equal "attention and favor." West Indies commander in chief Sir Ralph Abercromby extended those policies in January 1797, declaring all West India soldiers no longer fit for service would be free upon discharge and, by extension, eligible for a pension. But it was not until late 1807 that a new clause in the Mutiny Act declared free all Blacks in the king's service.

The 2nd West India Regiment formed in late April 1795. First stationed on Martinique, in September it moved to the island of St. Vincent where the St. Vincent Rangers was drafted into it; initially comprising only "15 sergeants, 9 drummers, and 84 rank and file," the merging added 247 men. The year after their formation the 2nd West India soldiers fought their first action, against rebelling St. Vincent Caribs, a mixed group of indigenous people and escaped slaves. On January 8, 1796, they covered the retreat of the overwhelmed British 40th and 54th Regiments; taking a defensive position twelve miles from Kingston, the 2nd Regiment had lost 152 men, more than three-quarters of those who went into action.

Following threats of a French invasion in 1804 and 1805, in 1807 the regiment was concentrated at Fort Augusta, near Kingston. All West India regiments received government-purchased slaves as recruits; on May 27, 1808, thirty-three drafts, "natives of Chama and Cormantine, on the Gold Coast," mutinied while drilling, killing two officers before being subdued with seventeen mutineers dead. After a trial and subsequent executions, the major general commanding at Jamaica "to shew his undiminished confidence, ordered the 2nd West India to furnish the daily guard at his residence in the neighbourhood of Kingston."

In December 1814, hoping to prevent reinforcements being sent to New Orleans, a British expedition set out to attack the coast of Georgia; the HMS *Rota* carried 200 men of the 2nd West India light infantry and grenadier companies. Those companies, in conjunction with two marine battalions, quickly seized Cumberland Island on January 10, 1815. The following day they crossed to the mainland, took Fort Peter, then advanced up the St. Mary's River, toward the town of the same name. The attacking column was led by the 2nd West India flank companies. Royal Marine private John Miller wrote his brother, "the black regiment employed on this service acted with great gallantry. Blacky had *no idea of giving quarters;* and was with difficulty restrained from putting *the prisoners to death*. The Yankee riflemen fired at our men in ambush; blacky, on the impulse of the moment, left the ranks and pursued them into the woods, fighting like heroes." Assisted by British gunboats, St. Mary's was captured, "the enemy continuing their retreat to Savannah. In this affair, the [British] troops were employed without rest or intermission for 22 hours." Crown forces occupied St. Mary's until February when, reduced by illness and in the face of advancing Americans, they abandoned the post. The 2nd West India companies set sail for the Bahamas on March 13, 1815.

Two men born in America joined the 2nd Regiment on February 25, 1815; they likely left local plantation owners with the same last name. April Bailey was twenty-five years old and died May 8, 1815. Richard Butler, age thirty, served till discharged on July 31, 1831. When the British left Cumberland Island in March 1815, they took with them 1,500 former slaves.

Sources: David Lambert, "'[A] Mere Cloak for their Proud Contempt and Antipathy towards the African Race': Imagining Britain's West India Regiments in the Caribbean, 1795–1838," *Journal of Imperial and Commonwealth History*, vol. 46, no. 4 (2018), 628; Roger N. Buckley, "Slave or Freedmen: The Question of the Legal Status of the British West India Soldier, 1795–1807," *Caribbean Studies*, vol. 17, nos. 3/4 (1977), 86–89, 91–98, 107, 110–11; J. E. Caulfield, *100 Years' History of the 2nd West India Regiment, 1795 to 1898* (London, UK: Forster Groom & Co., 1900), 5–6, 8–9, 11–14, 16, 18–20, 22–34, https://play.google.com/books/reader?id=o0a-BAAAQBAJ&hl=en_IE; Timothy James Lockley, "The West India Regiments and the War of 1812," submitted to *Journal of the Early Republic* (in press), 6, 9–10, 15, 18–20, https://wrap.warwick.ac.uk/170927/1/WRAP-West-India-Regiments-War-1812-22.pdf; John D. Ellis, "'The King's Men' II: Afro-American Soldiers of the Second West India Regiment," https://www.academia.edu/42641762/_The_Kings_Men_II_Afro_American_Soldiers_of_the_Second_West_India_Regiment; John U. Rees, "'Distinguished and gallant conduct': Formation of the West India Regiments, and War of 1812 Service (1794–1815)," https://www.academia.edu/112944449/_Distinguished_and_gallant_conduct_Formation_of_the_West_India_Regiments_and_War_of_1812_Service_1794_1815_.

1814–1815, 26th U.S. Infantry Regiment, 2nd Battalion

The 26th U.S. Regiment began as a hard-luck unit. Formed in Ohio in January 1813 and dissolved in May 1814, it experienced chronic manpower shortages throughout. In the same month the early 26th Regiment was struck off the rolls, the 48th U.S. Regiment, raised in Vermont, was renumbered as the 26th; after enlisting sufficient men, the unit was rearmed with rifles. With portions spread from western Pennsylvania into New York, one company took part in the late summer defense of Fort Erie, while a hundred-man detachment fought at the September 11, 1814, battle of Plattsburgh.

A second battalion of the new regiment was formed in the latter half of 1814. Philadelphian and adjutant general of the army Colonel William Duane wrote Secretary of War John Armstrong on July 12 concerning the possibility of raising battalions composed of free Black men, with white field and company officers. Duane noted, "there are many thousands of free people of color in this state who would make as good soldiers as any in the world." Receiving the letter three days later, Armstrong quickly sent a reply, stating that raising African American troops en masse,

has been much under my consideration, and I have been attempting to sound the depths and shoals of southern prejudice in relation to it. How long shall even history and experience go for nothing! No service in Europe rejects black or coloured men. The nations of Asia and Africa are all such. Our Navy has no scruples of this kind, and yet *we* are more squeamish and stand on the complexion of our rank and file, meagre as it is. We must get over this nonsense, and much more than this, if we mean to be what we ought to be.

A week later Duane relayed his plan for a "Corps of Coloured men" to various people, among them Thomas Jefferson. In his missive Duane insisted on African American noncommissioned officers and, eventually, commissioned officers. In early August 1814, Armstrong authorized and funded Duane's plan. On August 24 British forces burned the White House and other government buildings, resulting in the destruction of many War Department papers, including a preponderance of the evidence of the Pennsylvania Black battalion. That loss left the impression, almost to the present day, that Colonel Duane's idea was never realized.

In late summer 1814, recruiting broadsides broadcast the formation of a second battalion of the 26th U.S. Regiment, "Armed as Riflemen" and commanded by Colonel Isaac Clark, the hero of Bennington in 1777. By mid-September 1814, recruiters had raised 150 African Americans; shortly thereafter that number was almost doubled. When the British attacked Baltimore, instigating worries about Philadelphia, some early recruits joined scouting parties traveling as far south as Maryland, while a large portion of the 26th garrisoned Fort Mifflin on the Delaware River. The new secretary of war, James Monroe, desperate for men and mindful that African Americans had served as soldiers in the Continental Army, allowed the 26th Regiment Black battalion to continue recruiting and training. Remarkably, agreeable with Duane's original plan, the battalion did appoint African American corporals and sergeants. Some 26th U.S. Black recruits were sent north in small groups; in early February 1815, the entire battalion was ordered to Plattsburgh, and were soon on their way. When word of a peace treaty arrived, the battalion was recalled to Philadelphia and mustered out in early-summer 1815.

The 26th Regiment Black battalion's story survives in scattered documents, miscellaneous recollections, and pension records. In 1847 John Greenleaf Whittier, citing Black Americans' military contributions, wrote that "a battalion of colored troops was . . . organized in the city [of Philadelphia], under an officer of the United States army; and they were on the point of marching to the frontier, when peace was proclaimed." In 1856 a participant in a newspaper debate concerning the last military unit to have crossed the frozen Delaware River, claimed it was the "colored soldiers" of the 26th during the winter of 1814–1815. Twenty years later a newspaper article stated that "citizens living in 1814 agree that there was an organization of black troops in Philadelphia that year, and one of them . . . remembers having several times seen the colored soldiers march to Christ Church to attend religious services."

The new 26th, including its Black battalion, was intended to be a model rifle unit. African American musician and 26th veteran Robert Peterson, remembered "the . . . Regiment was principally composed of colored persons" and "was organized as mounted riflemen." With John Armstrong's prodding, the Black 26th was clothed and partially equipped as such. Evidence suggests that Philadelphia 26th recruits were issued rifle frocks, half boots, gray trousers, gray fatigue jackets with rifle buttons, and later in the fall, rifle coatees, although they may have only drilled with standard infantry muskets, not rifles. They were likely issued the new "Glengarry" knapsack, then being manufactured in great numbers at Philadelphia.

As with the 1778–1780 segregated 1st Rhode Island Regiment, the federally authorized 26th Regiment Black battalion served as a precedent that nineteenth-century American white supremacists did not wish to proclaim or propagate. The 1814 burning of Washington served to destroy some evidence of the battalion, and, in the midst of the 1820 Missouri Crisis, Secretary of War John Calhoun tried to ensure it would never again happen, issuing orders that "no negro or mulatto will be received as a recruit of the army."

Sources: National Archives, Records of the Office of the Secretary of War, 1791–1947 (Record Group 107, M221), reel 61, William Duane to John Armstrong, July 12, 1814, Armstrong to Duane, July 15, 1814; "Selections from the Duane Papers," *Historical Magazine*, vol. IV, Second Series (Morrisania, NY.: Henry B. Dawson, 1868), 63; John Greenleaf Whittier, "The Black Men of the Revolution and the War of 1812," *National Era*, July 22, 1847, Washington, DC; John C. Fredriksen, *The United States Army in the War of 1812* (Jefferson, NC, and London: McFarland & Company, Publishers, 2009), 257–58; Jack D. Foner, *Blacks and the Military in American History: A New Perspective* (New York and Washington: Praeger Publishers, 1974), 27. (History and research courtesy of Matthew C. White.)

Above: U.S. Model 1803 flintlock rifle, Harpers Ferry Arsenal. The weapon featured a half-stock, with a brass-covered patch box. (Troiani Collection)

5. *"Our Lives for Liberty"*[1]

American Civil War Era (1842–1865)

In August 1857, on the twenty-third anniversary of emancipation in the British West Indies, abolitionist and journalist Frederick Douglass gave a speech titled "If there is no struggle, there is no progress."[2] He said, in part,

let me give you a word of the philosophy of reform. The whole history of the progress of human liberty shows that all concessions yet made to her august claims have been born of earnest struggle. The conflict has been exciting, agitating, all-absorbing, and for the time being, putting all other tumults to silence. It must do this or it does nothing. If there is no struggle there is no progress. Those who profess to favor freedom and yet deprecate agitation are men who want crops without plowing up the ground; they want rain without thunder and lightning. They want the ocean without the awful roar of its many waters. This struggle may be a moral one, or it may be a physical one, and it may be both moral and physical, but it must be a struggle. Power concedes nothing without a demand. It never did and it never will.[3]

Douglass's statement speaks to the strife of antebellum America, from the 1820 Missouri Crisis, through Nat Turner's 1831 rebellion, to "Bleeding Kansas" in the late 1850s.[4]

The struggle at hand was against Southern enslavement of people of African descent, and with internecine warfare in Kansas and John Brown's October 1859 Harpers Ferry raid and ensuing martyrdom as catalysts, matters came to a head with Abraham Lincoln's election as president in 1860. On April 12, 1861, South Carolina forces fired on the Union garrison of Fort Sumter in Charleston harbor; three days later President Lincoln issued a call for 75,000 ninety-day state volunteers to quell the insurrection.[5]

During the war's first two years the Federal government had no interest in forming Black regiments, partly because there was no wish to tie the issue of slavery and abolition to their goals in the conflict. Another was that officials and the high command were following legislation or army orders implemented over the previous seventy years. The ban on Black soldiers in Federal regiments is tied to the ascent of Southern commanders before, and especially after the War of 1812. Toward the end of that conflict, with James Monroe as secretary of war, and men such as South Carolinian George Izard in high command and Virginian Winfield Scott a rising star, there seems to have been a sub-rosa movement to cull Black men from the army. Oddly enough, one piece of evidence was included in a private soldier's enlistment record, where colonel and North Carolinian Henry Atkinson noted, "discharged under an order from the War Dept. directing all soldiers of color should be discharged." That can be paired with Major General Izard's July 1814 letter to Secretary of War Armstrong concerning some newly arrived Black recruits; Izard posed a quasi-question, noting that "there was, some years ago, a regulation of our service, prohibiting the enlistment of negroes and people of colour. I have not heard of it being enforced." In 1817 President Monroe appointed South Carolinian John C. Calhoun as secretary of war, a position he occupied until 1825. Calhoun had a profound impact on the U.S. Army, including a comprehensive reorganization and the creation of the West Point Military Academy.[6] Concurrent with the Missouri Compromise, Calhoun implemented a ban on Black soldiers, not via federal law but in a mundane general order regarding army recruiting:

Adjutant and Inspector General's Office, February 18, 1820
General Order,
No Negro or Mulatto will be received as a recruit of the army; and the bounty, clothing, and expense of enlisting minors, who are discharged by the civil authority, for want of the written consent of parents or guardians, will be charged to the officers who make such enlistments.
By order,
D[aniel]. Parker
Adj. & Ins. Gen.[7]

One year later the 1821 *General regulations for the Army; or, Military Institutes*, authored by Winfield Scott, restricted enlistment to "all free white male persons." That stricture explains why no Blacks served as soldiers in U.S. regiments during the war with Mexico.[8]

During the War of 1812 the country's mainstay was its regular regiments, but in the 1860s Civil War the Federal army was small and the conflict's main burden was placed on state volunteer regiments, which operated under the 1795 militia law. In 1861, before the organization of Black regiments, men of color wished to serve en masse but were denied. A convocation at Boston's Twelfth Baptist Church resolved that Massachusetts people of color were "ready to stand by and defend the Government with 'our lives, our fortunes, and our sacred honor,'" and Black militias were forming in many cities, including Cincinnati, New York, Philadelphia, and Providence. In Washington, DC, Jacob Dodson, companion of John C. Fremont on three western explorations, in April 1861 volunteered "300 reliable colored free citizens" for defense. Still, during the conflict's first year, and despite Frederick Douglass's

August 1861 call to "Let the slaves and free colored people be called into service," they were refused. In response to Dodson's offer Secretary of War Simon Cameron stated, "I have to say that this Department has no intention to call into the service of the Government any colored soldiers."[9]

A few Black men did manage to enlist in white regiments, some of whom may have carried arms, but most serving in noncombat roles; these included Philadelphian George Stevens who enlisted in 1861 as cook to the colonel of 26th Pennsylvania Volunteers, and William Johnson, 8th Connecticut Regiment, who served in North Carolina in 1862, possibly as an arms-bearing soldier. In 1862 H. Ford Douglas enlisted in the 95th Illinois Volunteers, a unit he helped organize. He served for ten months, during which he wrote Congressman Owen Lovejoy, "Although I am respected by my own regiment and treated kindly by those who know me, still there are those in other regiments . . . who have no regard for my feelings simply because I have the hated blood coursing in my veins." Another who enlisted early was sixty-five-year-old Nicholas Biddle of Pottsville, Pennsylvania, who joined a local artillery company and was struck by a stone thrown during their march through Baltimore, on the way to the nation's capital. Other men signed on later; Crowder Edgar Patience (or Pacien) enlisted at Plymouth, North Carolina, in April 1864 as a cook with the 103rd Pennsylvania Volunteer Regiment.[10]

Indianan Richard McDaniel, a soldier of the 14th Rhode Island Heavy Artillery in June 1865, wrote of his early experience:

In the year 1861 . . . I was one among the first of my township to rally to the stand and offer my services; but what was the reply of Capt. Menray, of Knightstown, Ind.? His answer to me was, "Stand back, my young fellow; I will give you a berth of cooking for my mess or attending my horse." . . . [As the company marched off] The last word I heard [was] from a particular friend—as I thought . . . [who] shook his head and bellowed back at me . . . "Why, you niggers are the cause of my having to leave my home. If it had not been for the negroes this war would never have been."[11]

What was likely a prevailing early-war attitude was echoed by a Cincinnati policeman who, in dispersing a group of Black men calling for the opportunity to serve under arms, retorted, "We want you d---d niggers to keep out of this! This is a white man's war."[12]

While Southerners openly avowed that their secession and bid for independence centered on slavery, Abraham Lincoln's primary goal was to restore the Union, all other aims serving that higher purpose. Still, he recognized that the American Experiment had been blighted by African enslavement since the country's founding, famously declaiming in June 1858, "'a house divided against itself cannot stand.' I believe this government cannot endure, permanently half slave and half free." Once Lincoln enacted partial emancipation on January 1, 1863, he was committed to that cause, writing in August 1864: "If they stake their lives for us they must be prompted by the strongest motive—even the promise of freedom. And the

promise being made, must be kept." He continued, "There have been men who have proposed to me to return to slavery the black warriors of [the battles of] Port Hudson & Olustee. I should be damned in time & in eternity for so doing. The world shall know that I will keep my faith to friends & enemies, come what will."[13]

From 1861 into 1862 President Lincoln was unwilling to enlist men of color, but a few individuals pushed the issue and took the initiative, forming Black regiments with or without Federal permission. The earliest was abolitionist Major General David Hunter, who in March 1862 began forming escaped slaves into companies, and eventually a battalion-size unit. Unfortunately, his zeal led him to onerous methods of impressing unwilling Black men; his effort misfired, but eventually led to the formation of four South Carolina Black regiments. Controversial Kansas free-stater and senator James Lane took the lead in the West. Having secured the Federal appointment as commissioner of recruiting in the just established Department of Kansas, Lane was commissioned to raise one or more brigades of volunteers.[14] His appointment coincided with the passage of the July 17, 1862, congressional amendment to the Militia Act which authorized "persons of African descent" to enter

the service of the United States, for the purpose of constructing entrenchments, or performing camp service, or any other labor, or any military or naval service for which they may be found competent . . . [they] shall be enrolled and organized under such regulations, not inconsistent with the Constitution and laws, as the President may prescribe.[15]

Just after he began recruiting James Lane wrote Secretary of War Stanton: "Recruiting opens up beautifully. Good for four regiments of whites and two of blacks." This was not what the government wanted to hear, but while commander in chief Major General Henry Halleck responded that Lane's actions were "without authority of law," in August the Adjutant General's office wired that the "negro regiments will under no circumstances be paid bounty and premium," thus implying their enlistment could continue. In any case, Commissioner Lane continued recruiting Blacks, possibly with President Lincoln's tacit approval. Still understrength that October, the 1st Kansas Regiment (Colored) was ordered to string a telegraph line from Fort Scott to Fort Leavenworth, which Major General Samuel Curtis objected to, the men being promised service as soldiers; Curtis's chief-of-staff replied, "they would, I think, commence the construction of this telegraph willingly if they could be mustered, in the hope that a time would come when they might fight." On October 26, 1863, they had their chance, when Captain Richard Ward and 224 1st Kansas soldiers were sent on a mission to find a force of Confederate irregulars, "some 700 or 800 men, all splendidly mounted." Discovering the enemy on an island in the Osage River, there began the two-day Island Mound action during which the Kansans gained the upper hand. On October 29 they "moved forward to the attack and drove the enemy from position to position until they had been driven some four miles . . . the enemy shouting to the boys 'come on, you d---d niggers,' and the boys politely requesting them to wait for them, as they were not mounted." Later that day the Confederates seeing Black skirmishers outside the Kansas camp, "charged with a yell. . . . The boys took the double-quick over the mound in order to gain a small ravine on the north side," but the Kansas soldiers were caught by the horsemen. Captain Ward noted, "I have witnessed some hard fights, but I never saw a braver sight than that handful . . . fighting 117 men who were all around and in amongst them. Not one surrendered or gave up his weapon. At this juncture [Captain Andrew] Armstrong came . . . yelling to his men to follow him, and cursing them for not going faster when they were already on the keen jump." More Kansans joined the fray, attacking from several directions, and the Southerners were routed. Lieutenant Richard Hinton wrote of the Black soldiers, "the men fought like tigers and the main difficulty was to hold them well in hand." The 1st Kansas lost eight killed and eleven wounded, while Confederate casualties were estimated as fifteen dead and the same number wounded. This small victory, the first substantial action of the war fought by Black troops, occurred before the Kansans had been accepted into Federal service; on January 13, 1863, the 1st Kansas Regiment (Colored), still understrength, was finally mustered into the Union Army.[16]

Having petitioned the Federal government, on January 26, 1863, Massachusetts governor John Andrew received permission to enlist three-year volunteers in regiments containing "persons of African descent, organized into separate corps." In March 1863 Governor Andrew had assured businessman George Downing that the Black soldiers of Massachusetts "in respect to pay, equipments, bounty, or aid and protection . . . will be precisely the same, in every particular, as that of any and all other volunteers." Unfortunately, the aforementioned July 1862 Militia Act stipulated "that persons of African descent, who under this law shall be employed, shall receive ten dollars per month and one ration, three dollars of which monthly pay may be in clothing." Thus, Black soldiers from 1862 to 1865 were paid ten dollars monthly, minus a three-dollar clothing allowance, while white soldiers received thirteen dollars with no deductions. Besides vociferous protests, many soldiers of color refused their pay, including those in the 54th and 55th Massachusetts regiments. Governor Andrew's statement was based on Secretary of War Stanton's August 1862 assurance that Black soldiers should "receive the same pay and rations as are allowed by law to volunteers in the service." Northern and other free Black soldiers finally received their due with the passage of a June 1864 military appropriations bill equalizing pay, including arrears retroactive to the date of enlistment. The retroactive pay pertained only to soldiers who had been free at the war's beginning. In a ruling that applied only to the South Carolina freedmen regiments, Stanton's statement was finally upheld in March 1865. Other freedmen soldiers were not included, but their cases were afterward considered on an individual basis, and at least some got their due.[17]

Following enactment of the Emancipation Proclamation on January 1, 1863, the Federal government prepared to raise Black regiments. The first formal government effort was implemented by Adjutant General Lorenzo Thomas, who was sent west along the Mississippi to, among other duties,

ascertain what military officers are willing to take command of colored troops; ascertain their qualifications for that purpose, and if troops can be raised and organized you will, so far as can be done without prejudice to the service, relieve officers and privates from the service in which they are engaged, to receive commissions such as they may be qualified to exercise in the organization of brigades, regiments, and companies of colored troops. You are authorized in this connection to issue in the name of this Department letters of appointment for field and company officers, and to organize such troops for military service to the utmost extent to which they can be obtained in accordance with the rules and regulations of the service.[18]

From May to December 1863 Brigadier General Thomas organized eighteen Black infantry regiments, nine artillery units, and one regiment of cavalry.[19]

On May 22, 1863, the War Department issued General Order 143 authorizing the raising of Black regiments, and setting out some basic regulations. To facilitate formation of the new United States Colored Troops (U.S.C.T.) regiments, beginning in 1863 eighteen depots were built to receive and train Black recruits; the first, Camp William Penn, was established west of Philadelphia, Pennsylvania, in late May 1863. Others soon followed, including Camp Casey in Arlington, Virginia, and eight sites in Kentucky, with Camp Nelson being the best known.[20]

Despite the best intentions, training Union Black regiments was haphazard, and very much depended on available time, the quality of a regiment's officers, and whether they were present in sufficient numbers. Colonel Thomas Higginson's 1st South Carolina (Colored) and the two Massachusetts regiments were fortunate in having a dedicated command corps, but in general U.S.C.T. officers were a mixed group. There were many empathetic U.S.C.T. officers, but quite a few, kind or not, viewed their black subordinates as childlike; a less commendable minority thought of them as savage children and treated them accordingly.[21] Some of the latter were described by a soldier in the 43rd U.S.C.T., a Pennsylvania regiment. The 43rd was a veteran of the July 30, 1864, Battle of the Crater, where its soldiers captured an enemy battle flag, and recaptured the national colors of another Union regiment. The anonymous "Private" wrote from Bermuda Hundred, December 23, 1864:

The conduct of the officers toward the soldiers is good only at times. . . . [Some] strike the men with their swords, and jog and punch them in their side to show them how to drill. . . . I do not think it is right that soldiers should be cuffed and knocked around so by their officers, especially as we colored soldiers are. It is not consistent with either the laws of nature or of humanity, and is a base and cowardly act to do so. Some of these men who do these base things are not overgifted with spunk. If I understand military tactics aright, it says no officer has a right to strike or misuse a private in any way. I know it is inconsistent with military rules. . . . Our officers must stop beating their men across the head and back with their swords, or I fear there will be trouble with some of us. There are men in this regiment who were born free, and have been brought up as well as any officer in the 43d, and will not stand being punched with swords and driven around like a dog. . . . Such is the usage we get for our conduct as soldiers and men. Some of our friends have attempted to write you concerning our marching, hardships, trials . . . &c., but they don't let you know how we are treated. . . . Our friends should arouse themselves, and be ready to do something for those who are down in Dixie suffering and fighting for the Union, and get no thanks but—"No negro shall be a citizen of the United States."[22]

During the war Black officers also served, but they remained a distinct minority. Major General Nathaniel Banks objected to the Louisiana regiments under his command having Black commissioned officers; since this pertained only to the Black Native Guards regiments, the commanding general engaged in an effort to purge those units of one major (Francis Dumas, one of only two Black men to make that rank during the war) and seventy-five company officers. Colonel Nathan Daniels of the 2nd Native Guards protested the convening of a board "to examine into the capacity, propriety of conduct and efficiency" of seven of his Black officers.[23] The board found three men unsuited to retain command. William Dobak writes:

Despite [Daniels's] objection, the three deficient officers were discharged on 24 February 1863 and the other four submitted their resignations nine days later. Most of the rest of the regiment's original company officers were gone by late summer. Just seven held on into the next year, the last of them [first lieutenant and quartermaster Charles Sauvenet] mustering out of service on 18 July 1865, well after the Confederate surrender. By that time, all of the original company officers of the other two regiments had long since resigned or suffered discharge or dismissal.[24]

On April 9, 1863, Colonel Daniels led 180 soldiers of his regiment in an attack on Pascagoula, Mississippi, west of Mobile Bay. In his report he commended five Black officers, stating they were "constantly in the thickest of the fight . . . their unflinching bravery and admirable handling of their commands contributed to the success of the attack." In total, the Native Guards and its descendant units had seventy-nine officers, most being discharged or retiring before the end of the war; the 104th Regiment U.S.C.T. had a Black major and captain, the Independent Battery U.S.C. Light Artillery a Black captain and two lieutenants, and the 54th and 55th Massachusetts each had three Black lieutenants, plus surgeons and chaplains.[25]

In general, field experience seems to have been the best, and often only, instructor. In November 1863 forty-five soldiers of the 6th Mississippi (African Descent) had just returned from duty escorting wagons, where they had been attacked by sixty Southern cavalry, the regimental adjutant noting, "The men behaved well, returning the enemy's fire briskly and finely routing them." That despite their continual work on the Natchez fortifications having kept them from any military training. Optimally, military discipline began when companies were formally mustered into service. Writing in September 1863, Colonel James Alexander of the 1st Alabama (African Descent) noted they only managed "a few days' drill," at Corinth, Mississippi, in May, after which they began the daily rounds of guard, picket, and other duties, "in all of which they have been doing a heavy duty ever since."[26] The 8th Regiment U.S.C.T., raised at Camp William Penn, was authorized on September 22, 1863, and mustered in early December. They entered the mismanaged February 20, 1864, Olustee battle with little practical training; Lieutenant Oliver Norton of the 8th wrote:

Military men say it takes veteran troops to maneuver under fire, but our regiment with knapsacks on and unloaded pieces, after a run of half a mile, formed a line under the most destructive fire I ever knew. We were not more than two hundred yards from the enemy, concealed in pits and behind trees, and what did the regiment do? At first they were stunned, bewildered, and knew not what to do. They curled to the ground, and as men fell around them they seemed terribly scared, but gradually they recovered their senses and commenced firing. And here was the great trouble—they could not use their arms to advantage. We have had very little practice in firing, and, though they could stand and be killed, they could not kill a concealed enemy fast enough to satisfy my feelings.[27]

After additional experience, that autumn the 8th Regiment was transferred to Virginia, where it performed well.

Colonel Thomas Higginson, Massachusetts colonel of a Black South Carolina Regiment, wrote postwar that he and his men had fought "with ropes around our necks," referring to their uncertain fate if captured. Atrocities did occur, both small—in May 1864 while shadowing supply trains belonging to the Army of the Potomac, a Virginia cavalryman wrote, "we captured three negro soldiers the first we had seen. They were taken out on the road side and shot, & their bodies left there"—and large, most notably the Confederate capture of Fort Pillow, whose 500-man garrison included some 300 men of the 2nd and 6th U.S.C. Artillery. In the aftermath of the assault, about 255 men were killed, two-thirds of whom were Black soldiers.[28] Eyewitness William Ferguson wrote afterward:

Around on every side horrible testimony to the truth . . . could be seen. Bodies with gaping wounds, . . . some with skulls beaten through, others with hideous wounds as if their bowels had been ripped open with bowie-knives, plainly told that but little quarter was shown. . . .

Strewn from the fort to the river bank, in the ravines and hollows, behind logs and under the brush where they had crept for protection from the assassins who pursued them, we found bodies bayoneted, beaten, and shot to death, showing how cold-blooded and persistent was the slaughter. . . . Of course, when a work is carried by assault there will always be more or less bloodshed, even when all resistance has ceased; but here there were unmistakable evidences of a massacre carried on long after any resistance could have been offered, with a cold-blooded barbarity and perseverance which nothing can palliate.[29]

By November 1862 Confederate officials were discussing the fate of Black soldiers, with the commander at Savannah reporting the capture of four "negroes in federal uniforms with arms (muskets) in their hands." Wishing to inflict "swift and terrible punishment" to deter others, he contacted Secretary of War James Seddon, who replied that "summary execution" was proper, leaving it to his subordinate's "discretion."[30] In Louisiana in September 1862, Confederate officer Frank Powers wrote his commander:

A Squad of Negroes . . . (In arms) were captured at Jackson. . . . The morning after the affair . . . Col Griffith and myself ordered the Negroes [being on foot, to move off] Several hours in advance of the com[man]d—So as to arrive in camp at the proper time—Finding the Guard took the rong road . . . [we] rose in advance . . . to notify them of the fact & order them back—On the rout back four of the Negroes attemted to escape. I ordered the Guard to shoot them down. in the confusion the other Negroes attemted to escape likewise—I then ordered every one shot, and with my Six Shooter I assisted. . . . I believe few of ascaped most of them being Killed instantly.[31]

After reviewing this letter, Confederate colonel John L. Logan wrote General Stephen D. Lee, commander of cavalry of the Department of Mississippi: "My own opinion, is that the negroes were summarily disposed of."[32]

In the war's later years, it was more common for Black soldiers to be kept as prisoners, but some were sent into slavery. The most egregious case was that of 1st Arkansas Regiment (African Descent) private Samuel Anderson, captured in Louisiana at "the Mound Plantation" in May 1863. Three officers and eighty enlisted men were taken; the fate of forty-two rank and file is unknown. Private Anderson was claimed by a Texas captain, who took him home as a slave to Hill County, north of Waco; Anderson finally escaped in 1867. Black soldiers could be forgiven if they themselves gave no quarter. In the aftermath of the Red River campaign, at the April 30, 1864, Jenkins Ferry rearguard action, the 2nd Kansas (Colored) charged and captured several artillery pieces; a Confederate officer stated that three of his men were "killed by negroes after they had surrendered."[33] A 29th Iowa soldier wrote his brother,

our white negro officers and the negroes want to kill every wounded reb they come to and will do it if we did

not watch them . . . one of our boys seen a little negro pounding a wounded reb in the head with the butt of his gun and asked him what he was doing: the negro replied he is not dead yet! . . . it looks hard but the rebs cannot blame the negroes for it when they are guilty of the same trick both to the whites and negroes.[34]

Before we close, one subject and another regiment need to be examined. One prevailing myth of the 1861–1865 American Civil War is the existence of Confederate Black soldiers. A detailed discussion is far beyond the purview of this study, but suffice it to say that any "evidence" is based on the known presence of enslaved Black servants and laborers with campaigning Confederate forces, at fortified posts, and in other situations throughout the war. Some enslaved servants are known to have been armed, but they were not considered soldiers by their serving owners nor by Southern commanders. The first serious Southern plan to use Black men as soldiers came in January 1864 when Major General Patrick Cleburne proposed that slaves be enlisted in return for their manumission. His plan was suppressed by the government, not to be revealed until 1890. Ten months later President Jefferson Davis asked the Confederate Congress to enlist 40,000 enslaved men for noncombat roles, with the proviso they might in future be used as soldiers. In March 1865, only weeks from defeat, the Confederacy moved to emancipate some slaves that they may serve under arms, but the action was far too late.[35]

In 1861 an entire battalion comprising free men of color had been offered for Confederate service, but they were refused the opportunity. Louisiana was the only state that allowed free Blacks to serve in the militia; emulating their forebears who served during the 1814–1815 New Orleans campaign, *after* the capture of Fort Sumter, "free people of color" in and near New Orleans responded to Governor Thomas Moore's call for troops and formed the Native Guards militia, with white field officers and Black company commanders. In September 1861 the Louisiana Black battalion requested that they be assigned to guard Union prisoners, but Confederate general David Twiggs denied them. In January 1862 the state legislature passed a new militia law, amended to read that only "free white males capable of bearing arms" were eligible for service, leading to the Native Guards disbanding when the law went into effect on February 15. By month's end Admiral David Farragut's Union fleet was off the Mississippi coast, threatening invasion, and Governor Moore reconstituted the Guards to defend the city; Inspector General Maurice Grivot noted that Moore was "relying implicitly upon the loyalty of the free colored to protect their homes, property, and Southern rights from the pollution of a ruthless invader." On March 18 Farragut's ships began moving up the Mississippi River and, after capturing Forts St. Philip and Jackson, steamed toward New Orleans, which surrendered on April 26, 1862.[36]

Left behind as Confederate forces withdrew north, the Native Guards were dispersed once again, one day before the city's surrender. Major General Benjamin Butler commanded the Union forces occupying New Orleans; early in the Union tenancy four Guards officers visited Butler to learn the status of their battalion; General Butler told Secretary of War Edwin Stanton of the interview, noting, "in color, nay, also in conduct, they had much more the appearance of white gentlemen than some of those who have favored me with their presence claiming to be the 'chivalry of the South.'" Despite their good impression, Butler declined their offer of service, writing, among other things, that people of African descent had "a great horror of firearms, sometimes ludicrous in the extreme," and claiming the Black West India regiments performed badly in 1814 and 1815, thus handicapping British efforts to take New Orleans. Eventually, needing forces to defend the city, General Butler relented, on August 22, 1862, asking that "all the members of the Native Guards . . . and all other free colored citizens" enlist. The response was such that several weeks later the general claimed he would soon have "a regiment, 1,000 strong, of Native Guards (colored), the darkest of whom will be about the complexion of the late [Daniel] Webster." In truth, only 108 former Guards had joined, the rest being former slaves, Secretary of the Treasury Salmon Chase noting that, "the boldest and finest fugitives have enlisted." The 1st Louisiana Native Guard Regiment entered Federal service on September 27, 1862. The 2nd and 3rd Regiments were formed in October and November 1862, and the 4th entered service in February 1863. That spring three regiments were at Baton Rouge with the 1st Division, 19th Corps under Major General Nathaniel Banks, while the 2nd Native Guards was split, with seven companies on Ship Island and three at Fort Pike, on Lake Pontchartrain. On May 27 the 1st and 3rd Native Guards took part in assaults on Port Hudson, north of Baton Rouge, suffering severely. Not long after, General Banks redesignated the regiments as the 1st, 2nd, 3rd, and 4th Corps d'Afrique Infantry. In 1864, after the U.S. Colored Troops organization was instituted, they were renamed the 73rd through 76th Regiments U.S.C.T.[37]

In total, 178,975 men of color served in Black Union regiments (seven cavalry, "more than a dozen" artillery, and at least 124 infantry), the largest proportion being freedmen (formerly enslaved), and most originating in Confederate slave states.[38]

Recruited In	Union Black Soldiers, 1862–1865[39]
Northern Free States	32,671
Union Slave States	41,729
Confederate States	98,594

Add to those almost 18,000 Black sailors in the Union Navy; of those whose origin is known, 11,000 were from slave states, as opposed to 4,000 from free states.[40]

William Dobak notes that three years after the first Union black regiments were formed,

the U.S. Colored Troops managed to field more than 101,000 officers and enlisted men on average during the spring of 1865—nearly 15 percent of the Union's total land force as the fighting drew to a close. Far from performing only garrison duty, as the president and Congress first imagined they would, black soldiers' service included every kind of operation that Union armies undertook during the war: offensive and defensive battles, sieges, riverine and coastal expeditions, and cavalry raids. The fluid nature of the war that both sides conducted and the vast and varied country that they fought over guaranteed something more active than garrison duty.[41]

1862–1863, 1st South Carolina Regiment (African Descent) (33rd U.S. Colored Regiment)

On February 18, 1820, in the midst of the Missouri Crisis when disunion seemed a real possibility, at the behest of South Carolinian and secretary of war John Calhoun, Adjutant General Daniel Parker issued an order banning "Negro or mulatto" men from serving in the U.S. Army. One year later General Regulations of 1821 limited enlistment to "all free white male persons." That order stood until 1862.

The 1st South Carolina Regiment (African Descent) arguably shares the honor of being the first post-1821 U.S. Black unit with the 1st Louisiana Native Guard and 1st Kansas Regiment (Colored). Colonel Thomas Higginson, avid abolitionist, John Brown acquaintance, and 1st South Carolina (A.D.) commander, discounted the 1st Native Guards, writing, they

> scarcely belong to the same class . . . being recruited from the free colored population . . . "The darkest of them," said General Butler, "were about the complexion of the late Mr. [Daniel] Webster." . . . The First South Carolina . . . contained scarcely a freeman, had not one mulatto in ten, and a far smaller proportion who could read or write when they enlisted. The only contemporary regiment of a similar character was "The First Kansas Colored," which began recruiting a little earlier, though it was not mustered in—the usual basis for military seniority—till later. These were the only colored regiments recruited during . . . 1862. The Second South Carolina and the Fifty-Fourth Massachusetts followed early in 1863.

In truth, when the 1st Louisiana was recruited from the free-Black Confederate Native Guard, slightly more than a hundred privates consented to join; the remaining enlisted men were former slaves.

The 1st South Carolina (A.D.) survived an earlier, unsuccessful attempt in organizing them. Major General David Hunter was well aware of abolitionist firebrand James Lane who, despite government policy and orders to the contrary, in 1862 began arming freed slaves in Kansas, a process that would eventually come to fruition as the 1st Kansas Regiment (Colored). Assigned to command the Southern District in March 1862, Hunter began forming escaped slaves into companies. His recruiting methods eventually proved onerous, with white soldiers making sweeps through occupied land and impressing Blacks, some 500 in all, many of whom did not wish to serve. The "enlistees" were gathered at Hilton Head, South Carolina, and given regulation coats with red trousers. (Because the soldiers felt set apart from the white troops, they were issued blue trousers in February 1863.) The men performed manual labor, but it is unclear if Hunter ever completed them with firearms; they were afterward supplied with European rifle muskets. Morale plunged when it became evident that money for pay or equipage would not be forthcoming, and the unit was disbanded, save a single company stationed at St. Simon's Island.

Two other occurrences signified General Hunter's stand against slavery. On May 9, 1862, he took it upon himself to issue General Order Number 11, declaring "the persons in . . . Georgia, Florida and South Carolina, heretofore held as slaves, are therefore declared forever free." It took only ten days for President Abraham Lincoln to officially repudiate the order, but as with Major General John C. Frémont's August 1861 proclamation freeing the slaves in Missouri, Brigadier General Lane's efforts in Kansas, and Major General Benjamin Butler's June

Silver badge with inscription, "In Emancipation is National Unity." (Private Collection)

Two Civil War envelopes with "humorous" illustrations denigrating Black refugees known as contrabands. Many of those refugees eventually joined U.S. Colored regiments. (Private Collection)

Privately purchased silver 22nd Corps badge, worn by Ira Fields of the 100-man volunteer Virginia Colored Guards. Officially designated on September 28 as "Company A, United States Colored Troops, Unassigned," the unit was raised on an Arlington plantation in late summer 1864 to serve for one year. The company comprised both free and "contraband" Black men, commanded by two white officers. Their specific duty was to garrison the village of Accotink and guard the railroad bridge across the adjacent creek; during their term they had several clashes with Confederate raiders, including those commanded by Colonel John Mosby. One of the enlisted men was Douglas Syphax, Mary Custis Lee's (Robert E. Lee's wife) half-grand-nephew, "her father having sired Douglas's grandmother on Martha Washington's enslaved maid." (Information courtesy of Albert A. Nofi and Michael Schaffner)

1861 more impactful "contraband of war" decision, eventually codified in Federal legislation, all were stepping stones toward arming Black Americans and ending slavery.

In 1862 the Confederate War Department ordered that since Generals Hunter and John Phelps "have organized and armed negro slaves for military service against their masters," they were to be considered "outlaws" and if captured, "shall not be regarded as a prisoner of war, but held in close confinement for execution as a felon at such time and place as the President shall order." In April 1863 Hunter replied to Jefferson Davis:

> You say you are fighting for liberty. Yes you are fighting for liberty: liberty to keep four millions of your fellow-beings in ignorance and degradation; liberty to separate parents and children, husband and wife, brother and sister; liberty to steal the products of their labor, exacted with many a cruel lash and bitter tear. . . . This is the kind of liberty—the liberty to do wrong—which Satan . . . was contending for when he was cast into Hell.

It is fortunate Thomas Higginson, colonel from November 1862 until invalided out in October 1864, left an excellent account of the 1st South Carolina (A.D.)'s service in *Army Life in a Black Regiment*; published in 1869, it is still available. Higginson and his officers were aware that their men's performance would affect white Americans' opinions of Black soldiers' worth, and took great care in their training. Colonel Higginson later wrote: "We, their officers, did not go there to teach lessons, but to receive them. There were more than a hundred men in the ranks who had voluntarily met more dangers in their escape from slavery than any of my young captains had incurred in all their lives." In any event, the troops did not disappoint them, and while never participating in any large actions, they proved their competence on numerous small operations. As Higginson later noted, "Fighting with ropes around our necks . . . We had touched the pivot of the war. . . . Till the blacks were armed, there was no guaranty of their freedom . . . their demeanor under arms shamed the nation into recognizing them as men."[42]

Sources: Jack D. Foner, *Blacks and the Military in American History: A New Perspective* (New York and Washington: Praeger Publishers, 1974), 27; Thomas Wentworth Higginson, "Army Life in a Black Regiment," *Army Life in a Black Regiment and Other Writings* (originally published in 1870—New York: Penguin Books, 1997), 1, 206–7, 211–15, https://www.gutenberg.org/files/6764/6764-h/6764-h.htm (1st Native Guard, first muster September 27, 1862; 1st South Carolina, first muster November 1862; 1st Kansas (Colored), first action October 29, 1862, first muster January 1 or 13, 1863; 54th Massachusetts, first muster April 1863). William A. Dobak, *Freedom by the Sword: The U.S. Colored Troops, 1862–1867* (New York: Skyhorse Publishing, 2013), 3–4, 14, 30–44, 47–48, 59–61, 64–71, 69–70, 74–75, 80, 424, 470, 502–3 (1st Native Guard, 96–98; 1st Kansas Colored, 164–67); Noah Andre Trudeau, *Like Men of War: Black Troops in the Civil War, 1862–1865* (Boston, New York, and London: Little, Brown and Company, 1998), 15–16, 60–61, 63, 261 (33rd, 256–57, 257–62; 1st Native Guard, 15–16, 27, 28–29, 41–42, 396; 1st Kansas Colored, 3, 14, 19–20, 105); Don Troiani, Earl J. Coates, and James L. Kochan, *Don Troiani's Soldiers in America, 1754–1865* (Mechanicsburg, PA: Stackpole Books, 1998), 184–85; "General David Hunter, 'General Orders—No.11,' Hilton Head, S. C., May 9, 1862," https://www.americanantiquarian.org/Manuscripts/generalorders.html; "General Order No. 11. Declaring Order of General Hunter Emancipating Slaves Void, Etc.," https://www.loc.gov/resource/lprbscsm.scsm0579/?st=gallery; U.S. War Department, *The War of the Rebellion: A Compilation of the Official Records of the Union and Confederate Armies* (Washington, DC: Government Printing Office, 1885), Series 1, vol. 14, part 1, 599; "Commander of the Department of the South to the Confederate President," April 22, 1863, http://www.freedmen.umd.edu/Hunter2.html; William A. Gladstone, *United States Colored Troops, 1863–1867* (Gettysburg, PA: Thomas Publications, 1990), 103.

1863, Drummer, 54th Regiment Massachusetts Volunteers

The July 17, 1862, congressional amendment to the Militia Act, led the way for states' formation of and Federal recognition for Black military units. Sections 12 to 15 authorized "persons of African descent" to enter

the service of the United States, for the purpose of constructing entrenchments, or performing camp service, or any other labor, or any military or naval service for which they may be found competent . . . [they] shall be enrolled and organized under such regulations, not inconsistent with the Constitution and laws, as the President may prescribe.

Furthermore, "any man or boy of African descent" serving aforesaid and held in bondage by persons in armed rebellion against the United States, or those who gave such persons "aid and comfort . . . he, his mother and his wife and children, shall forever thereafter be free."

Section 15 was a point of contention until it was overridden by Congress in spring 1864; it directed "that persons of African descent, who under this law shall be employed, shall receive ten dollars per month and one ration, three dollars of which monthly pay may be in clothing." Thus, Black soldiers from 1862 to March 1865 were paid ten dollars monthly, minus a three-dollar clothing allowance; white soldiers received thirteen dollars with no deductions. Besides vociferous protests, many soldiers of color refused their pay, including those in the 54th and 55th Massachusetts regiments. The congressional rectification was signed by President Abraham Lincoln in June 1864; it went into effect retroactively in March the following year.

Massachusetts governor John Andrew received permission on January 26, 1863, to enlist three-year volunteers in regiments containing "persons of African descent, organized into separate corps." The 54th Regiment began recruiting at once. Officials soon found that not enough Massachusetts men were enlisting, so recruiters were sent throughout the North, "stripping some states of their most educated and patriotic black men." When completed, the regiment's personnel included 294 from Pennsylvania, 183 from New York, 155 from Ohio, and at least one Canadian; among them were activist Frederick Douglass's sons Lewis and Charles. The regiment's colonel was Robert Shaw, scion of a prominent Boston abolitionist family and veteran of the 1862 battles of First Winchester, Cedar Mountain, and Antietam.

On May 28, 1863, the 54th Massachusetts was aboard ship, bound for South Carolina. On July 10 Brigadier General George Strong landed six regiments on Morris Island, at the mouth of Charleston Harbor; the next day his force attacked and failed to capture Fort Wagner on the island's north end. On the 16th the 54th Massachusetts fought their first action against Confederate forces on James Island, Major General Alfred Terry commending their "steadiness and soldierly conduct."

Late in the afternoon of July 18 the 54th soldiers landed on Morris Island, reinforcing 4,000 Union troops already there. Tired and hungry, Colonel Shaw's regiment was chosen by Brigadier General Truman Seymour to lead an evening assault on Fort Wagner. Seymour's decision was likely because the 54th Massachusetts was his largest regiment, with 624 officers, and rank and file, but *New-York Tribune* reporter and

Brass drum inscribed to Thomas Baker, Company A, 55th Massachusetts Volunteers. Baker was born in Ohio and mustered in May 31, 1863. When he enlisted Drummer Baker was eighteen years old and five-feet-five-and-one-half inches tall. He served in that role until being discharged at Charleston, South Carolina, on August 29, 1865. (Private Collection)

Commission of Robert Gould Shaw as colonel, 54th Massachusetts Regiment, April 17, 1863 (Massachusetts State Archives)

eyewitness Nathaniel Paige testified before the American Freedmen's Inquiry Commission that he heard General Seymour say, "well, I guess we will . . . put those d---d niggers from Massachusetts in the advance; we may as well get rid of them, one time as another." Four months after the action Seymour stated, "the Fifty-fourth Massachusetts, a colored regiment of excellent character, well officered, with full ranks . . . was placed in front."

To get into position the 54th marched past already-formed brigades to the column's head, massed 150 soldiers wide. The attack began about 7:45 p.m.; General Seymour recalled, "our troops were to use the bayonet alone." The distance to Fort Wagner was about 1,600 yards; as the troops neared the fort, the island narrowed, compressing and mixing the advancing formations. Confederate fire, artillery and small arms, intensified; hit in the flanks as they paused by the watery ditch below the ramparts, 54th captain John Appleton recalled, "I could hear the rattle of the balls on the men & arms." He and his surviving soldiers moved forward:

> On my left the Colonel with the colors. . . . We . . . climbed up the parapet, our second battalion right with us. On the top of the work we met the Rebels, and by the flashes of their guns we looked down into the fort, apparently a sea of bayonets, some eight or ten feet below us. . . . The enemy were very brave and met us eagerly.

Colonel Shaw was killed on top of the works; after an hour the Federals were forced to retreat. Besides Shaw, thirty-three Massachusetts soldiers were killed, 146 wounded, and ninety-two missing; it was later learned that twenty-nine of the missing were prisoners, the rest dead. Sergeant Major Douglass wrote his parents: "The splendid 54th is cut to pieces." In May 1900, Sergeant William Carney of Company C was awarded a Medal of Honor for saving the regiment's flag at Fort Wagner.

The 54th Massachusetts Regiment went on to fight in the battles of Olustee and Honey Hill, and the smaller action at Boykin's Mill, the last on April 18, 1865. They were mustered out that August.

The pictured 54th drummer wears a short jacket with light blue cording on the front and carries a standard regulation eagle-painted drum.

Sources: "Militia Act, July 17, 1862," https://history.iowa.gov/history/education/educator-resources/primary-source-sets/african-americans-and-civil-war/militia-act#:~:text=Passed%20alongside%20the%20Second%20Confiscation,or%20any%20military%20or%20naval; William A. Dobak, *Freedom by the Sword: The U.S. Colored Troops, 1862–1867* (New York: Skyhorse Publishing, 2013), 21–22, 44–45, 49–54, 62–65, 68–69, 71, 73–74, 78–80, 85–87, 112, 305, 312, 473, 499 (55th Massachusetts, 55, 64, 71, 74–75, 78–79, 112, 312, 315, 320, 473, 481: Black soldiers' pay, 8, 56–57, 324, 333, 446, 504); Noah Andre Trudeau, *Like Men of War: Black Troops in the Civil War, 1862–1865* (Boston, New York, and London: Little, Brown and Company, 1998), 63, 71–86, 127–30, 137–51, 154, 252, 254, 256, 354, 357, 373, 375–95 (55th Massachusetts, 115, 135, 255, 256, 257, 258–63, 315–33, 354, 357, 374, 468: Black soldiers' pay, 91–93, 155, 252–55); U.S. War Department, *The War of the Rebellion: A Compilation of the Official Records of the Union and Confederate Armies* (Washington, DC: Government Printing Office, 1890), Series 1, vol. 28, part 1, 345–49; "The Colored Troops—History of Their Organization—Their Losses in Battle and by Disease," excerpted from William F. Fox, *Regimental Losses in the American Civil War, 1861–1865. A Treatise on the Extent and Nature of the Mortuary Losses in the Union Regiments, with Full and Exhaustive Statistics Compiled from the Official Records on File in the State Military Bureaus and at Washington* (Albany, NY: Albany Publishing Co., 1889), 54, https://www.nps.gov/rich/learn/historyculture/background.htm; "Roster of the 54th," http://54th-mass.org/about/roster/); "Fire and Thunder: Massachusetts Blacks in the Civil War," https://www.sec.state.ma.us/mus/pdfs/Fire-and-Thunder.pdf; "Written in Glory: Letters from the Soldiers and Officers of the 54th Massachusetts," http://54th-mass.org/.

September 20, 1863, Battle of Chickamauga, Enslaved Servant, 4th Tennessee Cavalry Regiment

One prevailing myth of the 1861–1865 American Civil War is the existence of Confederate Black soldiers; any "evidence" is based on the known presence of enslaved Black servants and laborers with Confederate forces, on campaign and in military camps. Southern forces hired or impressed slaves to build fortifications, drive wagons, and serve the military in other support missions. Enslaved servants accompanied officers and enlisted men into service; artilleryman Thomas Caffey told of slave-servants with troops on the march "some fifty yards in front of the band, whistling and singing, forming in regular or irregular files, commanded by some big black rogue who, with a stick and a loud voice, enforces discipline, among his heavy-heeled corps." British lieutenant colonel Arthur Fremantle accompanied General Robert E. Lee's Army of Northern Virginia during its 1863 invasion of Pennsylvania, observing that with "each regiment were from twenty to thirty negro slaves."

A propaganda piece in the May 7, 1862, *Nashville Daily Union* told of enslaved laborers pressed to work with the artillery, not enlisted soldiers.

> *Negros Uniformed and in Arms*
> *Two miles and a quarter below Yorktown are three rebel forts, on the West side of the Warwick river. . . . These forts have six guns. . . . In the centre one can be seen, every day, from two to three hundred negroes, with red coats, gray pants and slouch hats, strengthen[ing] the work with sand bags, digging ditches, etc. Whenever they dare to come out to fire their artillery, which is simply field artillery, these negroes ram home the [charges] with which white men fire at the hearts of our soldiers. Any one who doubts that the rebels are fighting side by side with their slaves, can be convinced at any hour of the day by going up to the edge of the woods, about twelve hundred yards in front of their works. With the aid of any ordinary glass, the matter can be put beyond room for a doubt.*

That account is accompanied by the misleading note, "let the Rebels of Tennessee who have been telling the people that the United States would arm slaves read this and blush."

In May 1861 the New Orleans-city-supported all-Black Planche Guards militia, later called the Regiment of Free Men of Color, was formed. Having 440 men in fourteen companies, that regiment and two Black companies on Isle Brevelle were refused any support from the Confederate government. After New Orleans was captured and occupied, those men were mustered into Federal service as the 1st Regiment Louisiana State Guards.

A postwar account tells of Black servants, likely enslaved, fighting in one action during the battle of Chickamauga, in the afternoon of September 20, 1863, on the Confederate right.

(*Hawkinsville* [GA] *Dispatch*, February 5, 1885)
Mr. J.B. Briggs of Briggsville, Ky. . . . is the only person who commanded colored troops on the Confederate side during the war. [He] was Captain and Assistant Quartermaster of the Fourth Regiment Tennessee Volunteer Cavalry, C.S.A. . . . At the battle of Chickamauga the Fourth Tennessee Cavalry was dismounted to fight as infantry, every fourth man being told off to hold horses. These horse-holders, and also all of the colored servants, were kept in the rear. The colored men numbered about 40, and having been in the service a long time, had gradually armed themselves . . . on successful . . . [actions] they could follow in the rear and pick up those things the soldiers had no time to secure. . . . Each [could] boast of one or two revolvers and a fine carbine or repeating rifle . . . as it became evident that a victory was to be won, Col. McLemore . . . ordered Captain Briggs to return to the horse-holders, and after placing the horses, teams, etc., under charge of the servants, to bring up . . . [that] quarter of the regiment . . . so that they might take part in the final triumph. Capt. Briggs, on reaching the horses, was surprised to find the colored men organized and equipped, under Daniel McLemore, colored (servant to the Colonel . . .), and demanding the right to go into the fight. After trying to dissuade them . . . Capt. Briggs led them up to the line of battle which was just preparing to assault Gen. [George] Thomas's position [the action was actually against mounted Federal cavalry]. Thinking they would be of service in caring for the wounded, Capt. Briggs held them close up [on] the line, but when the advance was ordered the negro company became enthused as well as the masters, and filled a portion of the line of advance as well as any company of the regiment.

While they had no guidon or muster roll, the burial after the battle of four of their number and the care of seven at the hospital, told the tale of how well they fought that day.

The first serious Southern plan to use Black men as soldiers came in January 1864 when Major General Patrick Cleburne proposed that slaves be enlisted in return for their manumission. His plan was suppressed by the government, not to be revealed until 1890. Ten months later President Jefferson Davis asked the Confederate Congress to enlist 40,000 enslaved men for noncombat roles, with the proviso they might in future be used as soldiers. In March 1865, only weeks from defeat, the Confederacy moved to emancipate some slaves that they may serve as soldiers, but the action was far too late.

Sources: Kevin M. Levin, *Searching for Black Confederates: The Civil War's Most Persistent Myth* (Chapel Hill: University of North Carolina Press, 2019), 12–35, 37–67, 57–60; Colin Edward Woodward, "Marching Masters: Slavery, Race, and the Confederate Army, 1861–1865," Dissertation, Louisiana State University, May 2005, 32–35, 105–13; *Noah Andre Trudeau, Like Men of War: Black Troops in the Civil War, 1862–1865* (Boston, New York, London: Little, Brown and Company, 1998), 19, 27; Charles Kelly Barrow, J. H. Segars, and R. B. Rosenburg, comp. and eds., *Forgotten Confederates: An Anthology About Black Southerners* (Atlanta: Southern Heritage Press, 1995), 128–29; Peter Cozzens, *This Terrible Sound: The Battle of Chickamauga* (Urbana and Chicago: University of Illinois Press, 1992), 463–66, 552.

1863–1864, 10th Regiment United States Colored Troops

In the *Weekly Anglo-African*, dateline "Norfolk, Va., Nov. 19, 1863," publisher Robert Hamilton wrote:

> The Tenth Regiment U.S. Colored Troops (Zouaves) is now encamped at Craney Island . . . about three miles from the city. Their dress is blue, trimmed with red, and white leggins, cap blue with green tassel. The colored people of this city follow them in large numbers about the streets. Their uniform is exceedingly becoming, and make them the finest-looking soldiers we ever saw. Our readers can imagine what the feelings of Jeff. Davis's friends must be in witnessing all this; and to crown all their misery, Judge Underwood is now here to confiscate their property, and has got much of it in his hands. Poor Secesh has a hard road to travel.

Federal Black soldiers were rarely stinted or given shoddy clothing and equipment, but what they were issued usually conformed with the regulation U.S. Army uniform. The men of the 10th were the only U.S.C.T. soldiers known to have worn the distinctive Zouave clothing, a uniform based on that of early-to-mid-nineteenth-century French North African troops, and worn by some thirty-five Union and Confederate volunteer regiments. The clothing issued the 10th U.S.C.T. matched that worn in 1863 by the 164th New York Volunteers, also called the (Irish) Corcoran Guard.

The 10th U.S.C.T. originated in Virginia and had a varied career. In November and December 1863, the regiment was at Craney Island, off Portsmouth, then in January 1864 moved to the now-defunct village of Drummondtown on Virginia's eastern shore. In mid-April 1864 a U.S.C.T. division, the 3rd, was added to the 18th Corps. The 3rd Division's commander was Brigadier General Edward Hinks, and his two newly formed brigades were commanded by Brigadier General Edward Wild (1st, 10th, and 22nd regiments) and Colonel Samuel Duncan (4th, 5th, and 6th). Almost immediately General Hinks objected to his soldiers' firearms; writing to Army of the James commander Benjamin Butler on April 29, Hinks referred to recent Confederate atrocities against Black troops at Fort Pillow in Tennessee:

> In view of the approaching campaign, and . . . on account of the recent inhumanities of the enemy perpetrated upon [United States Colored] troops . . . I deem it my duty to urge that these troops shall be more efficiently armed, to enable them to defend themselves and lessen their liability to capture. There certainly ought to be no objection to arming these troops with as effective a weapon as any that are placed in the hands of white soldiers, who are to go into battle with none of the peculiar disadvantages to which my men will be subject. The present arms of several regiments in the division are inferior in kind and manufacture. The Springfield rifled musket of the Bridesburg manufacture is an unreliable gun. The contract Enfield rifle is also unreliable, and one regiment is armed with the old Harper's Ferry smooth-bore. Now, these arms will, perhaps, answer for troops who will be well cared for if they fall into his hands, but to troops who cannot afford to be beaten, and will not be taken, the best arm should be given that the country can afford.

General Hinks seems to have some personal animus against Enfield and Bridesburg Springfield rifle muskets; the smooth-bore muskets he mentions were certainly obsolete.

As General Grant's Overland Campaign began, Hinks's division led 30,000 troops of Major General Butler's Army of the James, transported in some seventy-five ships moving up the James River toward Richmond. The 10th and 37th U.S.C.T. landed and occupied Fort Powhatan on the south bank, while the rest of Butler's army moved on to disembark at Bermuda Hundred. Meanwhile Hinks's regiments strengthened the fort and entrenched at Wilson's Wharf on the opposite side. On the afternoon of May 24, 1864, 2,000–3,000 Confederate troops under Major General Fitzhugh Lee attacked 1,100 soldiers of Wild's 1st and 10th Regiments at Wilson's Wharf. The Southerners fired into the Union trenches for about ninety minutes, before Lee summoned the fort; he offered fair treatment if they surrendered, but no promise for survival if they did not. The Confederates then assaulted the fort, but were repulsed with the assistance of a Federal gunboat offshore. About two dozen bodies remained in front of the fortifications when Lee's forces withdrew overnight.

The 10th U.S.C.T. took part in the June 15 Petersburg assault, in which General Hinks's division came close to taking the city. During the September 29 attacks on New Market Heights and at Chaffin's Farm, the 10th Regiment was left to garrison Deep Bottom. On December 3, 1865, the 25th Corps was created to contain all the army's Black regiments; the 10th was first assigned to the 3rd Brigade of Brigadier General

Blue Zouave fez with green tassel, the style issued to the 10th U.S. Colored Troops and 164th New York Volunteers (Smithsonian Institution)

Charles Paine's 1st Division; the
regiment remained in Virginia
*Near right: Pattern 1853 British
Enfield rifled musket, the firearm
issued to the 10th U.S. Colored
Troops. Despite Brigadier
General Edward Hinks's April
1864 comments, the Enfield,
widely used by both sides, was
considered an excellent weapon.
(Troiani Collection)*

while most of Paine's Division
participated in the January 1865
capture of Fort Fisher and Major
General William Sherman's
North Carolina campaign. In the
trenches before Richmond when
Southern forces evacuated, the
10th Regiment entered the city
on April 3 with the 1st Division;
Captain James Rickard of the
same division noted, "12 o clock
M[eridian] . . . in Richmond
. . . the negros flock around us
in thousands & are in Extacies
It is thought we may stay here
a while."

Beginning in June 1865 the
10th U.S.C.T. was stationed in
Texas with the 25th Corps. The
regiment was discharged on
May 17, 1866.

Sources: *Weekly Anglo-African*, December 12,
1863; "The Anglo-African," https://en.wikipedia
.org/wiki/The_Anglo-African; Frederick P. Todd
American Military Equipage, 1851–1872 (New
York: Charles Scribner's Sons, 1980), 45–50;
Roger Sturcke and Anthony Gero, "Zouave
Dress for the 10th United States Colored Troops.
1863–1864: A Probability," *Military Collector
& Historian*, vol. 49, no. 3 (Fall 1997), 132–33;
"10th United States Colored Troops," https://
civilwarintheeast.com/us-regiments-batteries/us
-colored-troops/10th-united-states-colored-troo
ps/; William A. Dobak, *Freedom by the Sword:
The U.S. Colored Troops, 1862–1867* (New York
Skyhorse Publishing, 2013), 317–18, 333, 337,
344, 347, 409, 444, 452; U.S. War Department,
*The War of the Rebellion: A Compilation of the
Official Records of the Union and Confederate
Armies* (Washington, DC: Government Printing
Office, 1891), Series 1, vol. 33, 957, 1020–21;
vol. 47, part 1, 46–57; Noah Andre Trudeau,
*Like Men of War: Black Troops in the Civil War,
1862–1865* (Boston, New York, and London: Lit
tle, Brown and Company, 1998), 215, 220n, 228.
286n, 359–64, 417–24 (Richmond occupation).

July 30, 1864, Battle of the Crater, Petersburg, Brigadier General Edward Ferrero's 9th Corps Division of U.S. Colored Troops

On the third day of the Battle of the Wilderness (May 5–7, 1864), Lieutenant General Ulysses Grant determined to shift his forces, but unlike earlier Union commanders in dire straits he moved them south, toward Richmond. One old soldier recalled: "Our spirits rose, we marched free. The men began to sing." But elation died as the war of attrition continued, with the May 8 to June 12 battles of Spotsylvania, North Anna, Bethesda Church, and Cold Harbor.

Brigadier General Edward Ferrero's division contained all the Army of the Potomac's Black regiments, tasked with guarding the army's wagon trains. Colonel Delevan Bates, 30th U.S.C.T., noted, "the colored troops stand everything well that we have had to go through. . . . How they will fight remains to be seen."

On June 15 the 18th Corps, with six U.S.C.T. regiments taking the lead, assaulted the Petersburg defenses; by the time support arrived from Grant's army, the best chance to capture the city in one stroke had been lost. The siege ensued. On June 25 9th Corps' soldiers began digging a mine ending under a section of Confederate trenches fronting Petersburg; completed and packed with gunpowder, the mine would be exploded to make way for a Federal assault.

Major General Ambrose Burnside chose Ferrero's 9th Corps division to lead the assault, including:

Late-nineteenth-century copy of flag designating the 4th Division, Ninth Army Corps. This division comprised eight Black regiments and participated in the July 30, 1864, Battle of the Crater, at Petersburg: First Brigade—27th, 30th, 39th, 43rd U.S.C.T. Regiments; Second Brigade—19th, 23rd, 29th, 31st U.S.C.T. Regiments. The motif is an anchor crossed by a single cannon, on a green background, the assigned divisional color. (Smithsonian Institution)

First Brigade U.S.C.T. (Lieutenant Colonel Sigfried):

27th, 30th, 39th, 43rd (seven companies) Regiments

Second Brigade U.S.C.T (Colonel Thomas):

19th (28th Regiment attached), 23rd, 29th, 31st Regiments

Ferrero's Black soldiers were inexperienced and short of officers, but 9th Corps' white troops were little better, comprising twenty-four depleted veteran regiments, plus seventeen with less than a year service. In the end, Ferrero's men were replaced by a white division; General Grant recalled:

General Meade said that if we put the colored troops in front . . . and it should prove a failure, it would then be said . . . we were shoving those people ahead to get killed because we did not care anything about them. But that could not be said if we put white troops in front.

Brigadier General James Ledlie's white regiments, the division assigned, did not receive notice of their role until the afternoon of the day before the attack.

On July 30, 1864, at 4:45 a.m., the mine was blown, tearing a hole in the Confederate line 250 feet long, fifty wide, and twenty-five to thirty feet deep. Moving forward, Ledlie's troops halted in the newly made crater and responded to Southern troops firing from the flanks. At one point Brigadier General Robert Potter received an order to leave the crater and charge the crest of the ridge; doing so, a few dozen men reached their objective, but were forced to retreat under heavy fire.

Ferrero's regiments advanced just after 8:00 a.m.; Colonel Sigfried told of "living, wounded, dead, and dying crowded so thickly that it was very difficult to make a passage way through [the crater]." Brigadier General John Hartranft noted of the Black troops, "[in] passing through the crater . . . their regimental and company organization was completely gone." The Black brigades made two charges; Sigfried's soldiers attempted to advance but were blocked by white troops in front; only the 43rd U.S.C.T. succeeded, clashing with the enemy, taking a Confederate battle flag and recapturing a 9th Corps color. The 43rd also took prisoners, despite just voicing the cry "Remember Fort Pillow!" Thomas's first try died aborning, with only fifty 30th U.S.C.I. men responding, "the fire was so hot that half the few who came out of the works were shot." He then attempted to reform soldiers of the 28th and 29th Regiments among the mass in the crater, when he received Ferrero's order to move forward. Some 150 men of the 23rd, 28th, and 29th Regiments advanced about fifty yards,

but meeting "a heavy charging column of the enemy and after a struggle [were] driven back." Colonel Thomas recalled, "at this moment panic commenced." Many fled to the apparent safety of the crater. Colonel Sigfried attempted to advance again, but

just as the troops in front were about to make a charge a white color-bearer . . . crossed the work in retreat. The troops gave way and sought shelter in the crater. . . . My brigade held its position until pushed back by the mass of troops, black and white, who rushed back upon it. . . . The enemy occupied the works to its left and the opposite side of the intrenchments, when, becoming exposed to a terrific flank fire, losing in numbers rapidly and in danger of being cut off, [my brigade] fell back.

Hundreds remained in the torn depression. Captain Theodore Gregg noted, "a major of one of the negro regiments placed his colors on the crest of the crater, and [his]. . . . Troops [likely one hundred men of the 19th] opened a heavy fire on the rebels." Southern reinforcements massed for a counterattack. Gregg stated it was 2:00 p.m. when he left the crater to rejoin the portion of his regiment left in support. Soon after, the Confederates charged in, killing or capturing all Federals still remaining.

General Ferrero's nine regiments lost 55 percent of their men, killed, wounded, and captured in this debacle. Colonel Thomas recalled that in the weeks leading up to July 30 his Black soldiers often sung the air "Like Men of War"; "After that defeat they sang it no more."

Sources: "Overland Campaign," https://en.wikipedia.org/wiki/Overland_Campaign; William A. Dobak, *Freedom by the Sword: The U.S. Colored Troops, 1862–1867* (New York: Skyhorse Publishing, 2013), 338–43, 353–68; Edwin S. Redkey. ed., *A Grand Army of Black Men: Letters from African-American Soldiers in the Union Army, 1861–1865* (Cambridge, UK: Cambridge University Press, 1992), 107–10; Ernest B. Furgurson, *Not War but Murder: Cold Harbor 1864* (New York: Vintage Books, 2000), 252–53; U.S. War Department, *The War of the Rebellion: A Compilation of the Official Records of the Union and Confederate Armies* (Washington, DC: Government Printing Office, 1892), Series 1, vol. 40, part 1, 136, 596–99; Noah Andre Trudeau, *Like Men of War: Black Troops in the Civil War, 1862–1865* (Boston, New York, and London: Little, Brown and Company, 1998), 229–51; John Cannan, *The Crater: Burnside's Assault on the Confederate Trenches, June 30, 1864* (Cambridge, MA: Da Capo Press, 2002); "The Colored Troops—History of Their Organization—Their Losses in Battle and by Disease," excerpted from William F. Fox, *Regimental Losses in the American Civil War, 1861–1865. A Treatise on the Extent and Nature of the Mortuary Losses in the Union Regiments, with Full and Exhaustive Statistics Compiled from the Official Records on File in State Military Bureaus and at Washington* (Albany, NY: Albany Publishing Co., 1889), https://www.nps.gov/rich/learn/historyculture/background.htm.

1864, 14th Rhode Island Heavy Artillery (8th U.S. Heavy Artillery; 11th U.S. Colored Heavy Artillery)

On July 19, 1863, Rhode Island governor James Smith received permission to form the state's only Civil War Black regiment. In a letter requesting the honor the governor had declared, "Rhode Island has a historic right to this regiment," and invoked the state's "colored regiment in the war of independence [which] gained for itself an enduring fame."

The new unit was initially called the 14th Rhode Island Heavy Artillery; renamed the 8th U.S. Heavy Artillery on April 4, 1864, a little over a month later it was finally designated the 11th Regiment U.S. Colored Heavy Artillery. There was such a surfeit of volunteers that the regiment eventually fielded almost 1,800 men in three four-company battalions. Black Rhode Islanders formed the bulk of Company A, but the remaining companies contained men from Massachusetts, Connecticut, New York, New Jersey, and even Canada. The initial regimental training site was at Camp Smith in Providence; by September 1863 elements of the 1st Battalion were moved to 102-acre Dutch Island, in Narragansett Bay, just off James Island's western shore; eventually the remainder of the battalion and regiment followed. A November article in the *Evening Press* noted:

> The members of the Fourteenth Rhode Island . . . have nearly completed a large earthwork fortification, commanding Dutch Island and the West Passage. Eight guns are already in position—seven of them sixty-four pounders, and one thirty-two pounder. . . . The erection of barracks will soon be commenced and comfortable winter quarters are anticipated.

In December 1863 the 14th Regiment's 1st battalion boarded the steamer *Cahawba* for passage to Union-occupied New Orleans, Louisiana; the 2nd Battalion followed in January. An outbreak of smallpox delayed the 3rd Battalion's departure until April 1864. Two months prior to leaving,

> in Railroad Hall [at Providence], a beautiful silk standard donated to the Third Battalion by the colored ladies of the city of New York, was formally presented to the battalion. Several of the commissioned and noncommissioned officers were present to receive it . . . Colonel [Nelson] Viall . . . delivered the flag to the sergeant appointed to receive it. . . . The flag was a very rich and costly one, presenting on one side the arms of the State, and on the other those of the United States.

During their service the regiment saw little action, spending most of their time in various garrisons. The men did their best to alleviate the tedium: the second battalion formed a string band and some men began to teach illiterate fellow soldiers; one account mentions a Washington's birthday celebration with greased pig contest, and sack and wheelbarrow races. Two soldiers, Sergeant Julius Hamblin and brother George, instigated *The Black Warrior*, a semimonthly newspaper published at Camp Parapet at Shrewsbury, Jefferson Parish. An early issue proclaimed, "owned, printed, and edited by the black warriors of the Fourteenth R.I.H.A."

Most 14th Rhode Island deaths were from illness, but there were exceptions. Before they left for Louisiana "Private Frederick C. Grames, of Company C, died Saturday, November 7th, from lockjaw, caused by having two fingers cut off while driving tent-pins a few weeks since." Eight months later Private Charles Cisco was shot and mortally wounded by a fellow soldier, who was executed for the crime. On August 5 the only enemy-caused deaths occurred when a detachment camped at Plaquemine, below Baton Rouge, was attacked by Confederate raiders; three 14th Regiment soldiers—Samuel Jefferson, Anthony King, and Samuel Mason—were taken prisoner and then executed by their captors.

Federal Black soldiers' service had been authorized under the 1862 Militia Act, which stipulated pay at ten dollars per month, minus a three-dollar clothing deduction. White soldiers were paid thirteen dollars with no deduction, causing unrest in all the Black regiments. Third Battalion Hospital wardmaster James Jones likely referred to this when he complained of being "betrayed and cheated by conniving recruiting officers . . . [and] being unfaithfully and unjustly dealt with by the general Government."

An August 1864 inspection report noted: "The Battalion . . . is a superior one. The men are almost all free, and not freed men. There is hardly a contraband [runaway] in the organization, and the majority of the command can read and write, and are usually well informed. Their superiority . . . is marked." Although heavy artillery, the 14th's soldiers wore light artillery jackets, and were also equipped with infantry accoutrements and rifle muskets. The soldier in the image has a "shod" or hand spike used for maneuvering heavy cannon into firing position.

The 1898 regimental history provides this fitting encomium:

> We may not boast the honor of inscribing on our banners a long list of battles, yet may we not point with pardonable pride to services faithfully performed on the picket line, and in the daily routine of camp and garrison duty. Let the many mounds in the lowlands of Louisiana, where we laid away the silent forms of our comrades in the untimely graves to which they had been borne, through the deadly effects of miasmatic swamps, testify to our contribution of noble souls who freely gave their lives for the preservation of this republic.

Add to this the reply a soldier of the 14th gave to the regimental commander when asked why he wished to serve when it might result in his death: "But my people will be free."

Artillery uniform jacket worn by Private J. Clark, Company A, 8th U.S. Colored Artillery. A blacksmith by trade, he mustered into Federal service at Paducah, Kentucky, on August 30, 1864. The 8th served in Kentucky, until transferred to Texas in early 1865. Clark died of scurvy on July 23, 1865, at the Corps d'Afrique United States General Hospital in New Orleans. (Dr. Michael Cunningham Collection)

Sources: "The Fourteenth Regiment Rhode Island Heavy Artillery (Colored) During the Civil War," http://smallstatebighistory.com/fourteenth-regiment-rhode-island-heavy-artillery-colored
-civil-war/; William H. Chenery, *The Fourteenth Regiment Rhode Island Heavy Artillery (Colored) in the War to Preserve the Union, 1861–1865* (Providence, RI: Snow & Farnham, 1898),
10–13, 32, 37–39, 61–62, 67–68, 74, 148, https://catalog.hathitrust.org/Record/009610907; "Soldiers of the 14th Rhode Island Heavy Artillery," https://w3.ric.edu/northburialground/tours
_civilwar-14regiment.html; William A. Dobak, *Freedom by the Sword: The U.S. Colored Troops, 1862–1867* (New York: Skyhorse Publishing, 2013), 135–37, 473, 479; Edwin S. Redkey.
ed., *A Grand Army of Black Men: Letters from African-American Soldiers in the Union Army, 1861–1865* (Cambridge, UK: Cambridge University Press, 1992), 141–46, 190–94, 226–27,
265–68; Don Troiani, Earl J. Coates, and James L. Kochan, *Don Troiani's Soldiers in America, 1754–1865* (Mechanicsburg, PA: Stackpole Books, 1998), 187–88; "11th Regiment, United
States Colored Heavy Artillery," https://www.nps.gov/civilwar/search-battle-units-detail.htm?battleUnitCode=UUS0011RAH0C; "The Fourteenth Regiment Rhode Island Heavy Artillery
(Colored) During the Civil War," http://smallstatebighistory.com/fourteenth-regiment-rhode-island-heavy-artillery-colored-civil-war/; Noah Andre Trudeau, *Like Men of War: Black Troops in
the Civil War, 1862–1865* (Boston, New York, and London: Little, Brown and Company, 1998), 91–93, 155, 252–55.

September 29, 1864, Third Battle of New Market Heights, 6th Regiment U.S. Colored Troops

Major General Benjamin Butler gained his rank for party rather than military prowess, and in service was a political lightning rod. Still, despite having voted for Jefferson Davis at the 1860 Democratic Convention, while commanding at Fortress Monroe in 1861 he originated the "Contraband Decision," allowing thousands of enslaved people to flee rebelling states for protection within Union lines. At New Orleans (where he gained the Southern sobriquet the "Beast"), in August 1862 Butler was instrumental in accepting the Native Guard, a free Black militia unit, into Federal service. Admittedly, this was after he denied Brigadier General John Phelps permission to enlist slaves, leading to Phelps's resignation, but "Beast Butler," one way or another, always managed to play some significant role in advancing the Black man's cause.

In 1863 General Butler was given command of the Department of Virginia and North Carolina, forming subordinate Federal units into the 18th Corps. In April 1864 the 10th Corps was transferred to Butler's command, and together the two corps formed the Army of the James. That army was tasked with moving west up the Virginia Peninsula to threaten Richmond. Disembarking on the James River on May 4 (the same day the Battle of the Wilderness began), sixteen days later Southern forces had them stalemated in the Bermuda Hundred fortifications.

In September 1864 Lieutenant General Ulysses Grant devised a two-pronged attack, one against the Southside Railroad, the other, commanded by Benjamin Butler, attempting another drive to Richmond. Butler's initial attack would be on Confederate entrenchments atop New Market Heights, north of Bermuda Hundred on the James River. For this operation Butler reconstituted the Army of the James, the 18th Corps components having been dispersed in various garrisons, while the 10th Corps was serving with Major General George Meade south of Petersburg.

The September 29, 1864, New Market Heights assault was the initial phase of what would become the larger Battle of Chaffin's Farm. The task of assaulting the Heights was given Major General David Birney's 10th Corps, plus Brigadier General Charles Paine's 3rd Division, 18th Corps, totaling approximately 14,000 men. The task force included some 4,500 Black soldiers in five 10th Corps regiments, plus nine regiments in Paine's 18th Corps Division.

Crossing to the James River's north bank on the 28th, the attack began before sunrise on September 29. Historian Richard Sommers notes, "the most inexperienced [brigade] of all seventeen divisions in Grant's army spearheaded [Birney's] columns." Colonel Samuel Duncan's 3rd Brigade of Paine's Division moved forward, "deployed in two lines of battle . . .

U.S. Colored Troops Medal (also known as the Butler Medal), bearing the phrase, Ferro iis libertas perveniet—*"freedom attained by the sword." Major General Benjamin Butler, commanding the Army of the James, awarded these medals to 200 African American soldiers for bravery at the New Market Heights action; the medals were paid for by Butler and privately made. After the war General Butler proclaimed, "I had the fullest reports made to me of the acts of individual bravery of colored men on that occasion, and I had done for the negro soldiers, by my own order, what the government has never done for its white soldiers—I had a medal struck of like size, weight, quality, fabrication, and intrinsic value with those which Queen Victoria gave with her own hand to her distinguished private soldiers of the Crimea. . . . These I gave with my own hand, save where the recipient was in a distant hospital wounded, and by the commander of the colored corps after it was removed from my command, and I record with pride that in that single action there were so many deserving that it called for a presentation of nearly two hundred." (Private Collection)*

the 4th U.S.C.T. in front, the 6th U.S.C.T. echeloned to the left rear." The rest of General Paine's division were to deploy to Duncan's left, but arrived too late. General Duncan's regiments then obliqued right to close the gap between themselves and Major General Alfred Terry's 10th Corps division. That move meant the 4th and 6th Regiments would have to cross a creek and advance up the marshy bank, then immediately assault the heights. Doing so, they became tangled in the Confederate abatis; in the struggle some Black soldiers made it through only to be killed or captured.

Terry's division had also failed to advance alongside Duncan's brigade, leaving them as the sole focus of enemy fire. Fourth U.S.C.T. sergeant major Christian Fleetwood noted of the assault, "charged with the 6th at daylight and got used up. Saved colors." Captain James Wickes of the 4th was more explicit:

> We were all cut to pieces. We got up to the second line of abatis . . . but by that time the line was so cut up that it was impossible to keep the men any longer in their places. . . . I tried to force my men to make a dash over the work, but there were [only] five left out of the twenty-five I started up with, and they gave way.

The 4th U.S.C.T. began the action with approximately 320 officers and men, and lost 178 killed, wounded, and missing. The 6th Regiment started with 367 soldiers and suffered losses of 57 percent; forty-one killed, 160 wounded, and eight missing.

The featured painting portrays the three 6th Regiment U.S.C.T. soldiers who were awarded the Medal of Honor. After three color bearers had been shot down, Lieutenant Nathan Edgerton took up the regimental banner, bearing the motto "Freedom for All," and moved forward, only to find that "my hand was covered in blood, and perfectly powerless, and the flag staff [was] lying in two pieces." Under heavy fire Sergeant Major Thomas Hawkins then assisted Edgerton in taking the flag off the field. According to his citation, First Sergeant Alexander Kelly "gallantly seized the [national] colors, which had fallen near the enemy's lines of abatis, raised them and rallied the men at a time of confusion and in a place of the greatest danger." Theirs were among fourteen Medals of Honor awarded Black enlisted men of General Paine's division for bravery that day. Major General Butler was awed by his soldiers' performance at New Market Heights and awarded about 200 of them a privately made medal bearing the phrase, *Ferro iis libertas perveniet*—"freedom attained by the sword."

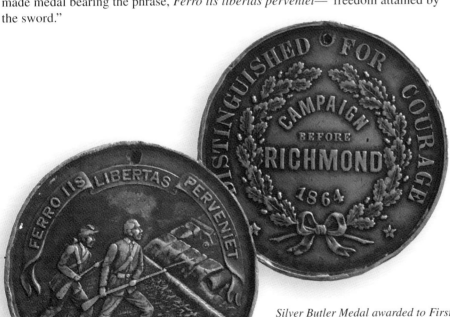

Silver Butler Medal awarded to First Sergeant Alexander Kelly, Company F, 6th U.S. Colored Troops, for his actions at the battle of New Market Heights Virginia, September 20, 1864. He also received the Medal of Honor for the same incident; the citation reads, Sergeant Kelly "seized the colors, which had fallen near the enemy's inner line . . . raised them, and rallied the men, at a time of confusion and [in] a place of the greatest possible danger." (Angelo Scarlato Collection)

Sources: Howard C. Westwood, "Benjamin Butler's Enlistment of Black Troops in New Orleans in 1862," *Louisiana History: The Journal of the Louisiana Historical Association*, vol. 26, no. 1 (Winter 1985), 5–22; Donald E. Everett, "Ben Butler and the Louisiana Native Guards, 1861–1862," *Journal of Southern History*, vol. 24, no. 2 (May 1958), 202–17; William A. Dobak, *Freedom by the Sword: The U.S. Colored Troops, 1862–1867* (New York: Skyhorse Publishing, 2013), 70–71, 333, 372–80; Richard J. Sommers, *Richmond Redeemed: The Siege at Petersburg* (Garden City, NY: Doubleday & Company, 1981), 4–38; "The Colored Troops—History of Their Organization—Their Losses in Battle and by Disease," excerpted from William F. Fox, *Regimental Losses in the American Civil War, 1861–1865. A Treatise on the Extent and Nature of the Mortuary Losses in the Union Regiments, with Full and Exhaustive Statistics Compiled from the Official Records on File in the State Military Bureaus and at Washington* (Albany, NY: Albany Publishing Co., 1889), https://www.nps.gov/rich/learn/historyculture/background.htm; "Listing of USCT Medal of Honor Recipients at New Market Heights," https://www.nps.gov/rich/learn/historyculture/mohrecip.htm.

1864–1865, Trooper and Bugler, 6th U.S. Colored Cavalry

The commonwealth of Kentucky lay in a central location, adjacent to two Confederate states (Tennessee and Virginia) and four Union (Illinois, Indiana, Missouri, and Ohio); early in his first presidential term Abraham Lincoln wrote, "I think to lose Kentucky is nearly the same as to lose the whole game."

Kentucky had a sizable contingent of Confederate regiments, but they were offset by white Union organizations: five light artillery batteries, thirty-four long-term volunteer infantry regiments plus two thirty-day units, ten mounted infantry regiments, and seventeen regiments and one battalion of cavalry. From 1863 to 1865 the state also raised four "Colored" artillery regiments, seventeen U.S.C.T. regiments, and two Black cavalry regiments. One source claims a state total of 23,706 Black soldiers, making 13 percent of the total African American Federal troops that served.

The Kentucky Black mounted units were the 5th and 6th Regiments U.S. Colored Cavalry, both formed at Camp Nelson, south of Lexington, in summer and autumn 1864; only seven Black cavalry units were formed during the war. Formation of the Kentucky and some other states' Black corps were facilitated by the February 24, 1864, Enrollment Act; an amendment to the 1863 conscription act, the 1864 legislation made enslaved men eligible to be drafted, including those belonging to loyal masters. Enactment was based on a state's failure to meet its quota of white troops. Virulent Kentucky opposition was overcome by the codicil that enslaved men could only enlist with their owner's permission, who would, in turn, receive $400 compensation.

Though not fully organized, the 5th U.S.C.C., with perhaps a small portion of the 6th, and a detachment of the 116th U.S.C.T. took part in Brigadier General Stephen G.

Burbridge's October 1864 Southwest Virginia raid. On the march out the white troops in Burbridge's contingent harassed the Black soldiers, "stealing their horses . . . [and catcalling] jeers and taunts that they would not fight." Nearing Saltville, the Black troopers showed their mettle. Mixed Confederate forces, including one soldier who noted that General Burbridge's African American soldiers "were the first we ever met," occupied a hillside fortification; the men of the 5th dismounted under fire, "rushed upon the works with a yell, and after a desperate struggle carried the entire line, killing and wounding a large number of the enemy and capturing some prisoners." They held the hill for two hours, when they withdrew, their ammunition being depleted; they carried many of their wounded away with them. According to Southern witnesses, all the captured injured Black soldiers were killed, some while in hospital.

Burbridge having not accomplished his objectives, Major General George Stoneman led a second expedition to Saltville (December 12–29, 1864), intending to destroy the saltworks and other facilities in the area. Now fully formed, the 5th and 6th U.S.C.C. regiments took part, along with the white soldiers of the 8th, 9th, and 13th Tennessee Cavalry regiments, 12th Ohio cavalry, and 1st Kentucky Light Artillery, 4,200 in all. Ammunition supply would not be a problem this time; besides ten days' rations, there were "100 rounds . . . [issued] per man, and, in addition, 150 rounds per man . . . taken in wagons."

Stoneman's December enterprise, with General Burbridge commanding a column, was an unmitigated success, as was the Black cavalry's performance. Following several days of besting Southern forces and destroying railroads, the expedition's largest action was fought against Confederate troops

Government-issue tin canteen with cloth cover and leather strap, marked to Company I, 15th U.S. Colored Troops. This regiment was organized at Chattanooga in January 1864 and served in Tennessee throughout the war. (Jan Gordon Collection)

under major general and Kentuckian John Breckinridge at Marion on December 17 and 18. Though outnumbered, Breckinridge's forces were strongly entrenched and resisted all efforts to oust them, until lack of ammunition forced them to withdraw on the morning of the 19th. During the two-day battle, the 6th U.S.C.C. distinguished itself in an encounter with Brigadier General Basil Duke's cavalry. Adjutant General Lorenzo Thomas wrote Secretary of War Edwin Stanton from Lexington on January 2:

> Major-General Burbridge, with his command, has just returned from a most successful expedition. Five hundred negroes accompanied his command and Gillem['s]. A battalion of the Sixth U.S. Colored Cavalry, 300 strong, attacked and whipped Duke's brigade, of 350—the last remnant of [Brigadier General John Hunt] Morgan's force. The rebels were driven half a mile, with a loss on their side of thirty men killed and wounded. They were on the crest of a hill at Marion, and the negroes charged over open ground, and did not fire a gun until within thirty yards of the rebels. This is the first time that any of these men were under fire.

Saltville, Virginia, was taken shortly thereafter and the salt manufactory destroyed.

The 5th and 6th Regiments returned to Kentucky; the former was transferred to Arkansas in autumn 1865, where it was mustered out on March 20, 1866. The 6th served in its home state until early January 1866, when it, too, moved to Arkansas. It was mustered out at Duvall's Bluff on April 15, 1866.

The accompanying images show a 6th Regiment U.S.C.C. trooper and bugler. They both wear regulation U.S. Army cavalry dress; the horn-player's uniform jacket has yellow worsted herringbone lace and his sky-blue kersey trousers' seat and inner legs are reinforced to prevent wear. He carries an M1860 light cavalry saber and a copper trumpet with brass trimmings and yellow cords.

Right: Regimental silk standard, 26th Regiment U.S. Colored Troops. This regiment was organized early in 1864 by New York City's Union League Club, and trained at Rikers Island. They were engaged at the battles of Johns Island, Honey Hill, and Tulifinny, South Carolina. (New York State Military Museum, New York State Division of Military Affairs)

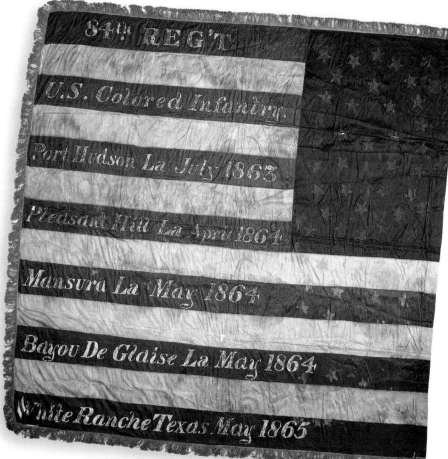

Left: Silk national flag of the 84th U.S. Colored Troops, painted with the names of the engagements they fought in. Organized in April 1864 from the 12th Corps d'Afrique, they served mostly in the Louisiana region. The regiment mustered out on March 14, 1866. (Smithsonian Institution)

Sources: William A. Dobak, *Freedom by the Sword: The U.S. Colored Troops, 1862–1867* (New York: Skyhorse Publishing, 2013), 381–88; "I think to lose Kentucky is nearly the same as to lose the whole game. Kentucky gone, we can not hold Missouri, nor, as I think, Maryland. These all against us, and the job on our hands is too large for us. We would as well consent to separation at once, including the surrender of this capitol," Abraham Lincoln to Orville H. Browning, September 22, 1861, in Roy P. Basler, ed., *The Collected Works of Abraham Lincoln*, nine vols. (New Brunswick: Rutgers University Press, 1953–55), vol. 4, 532 (courtesy of William Dale, November 26, 2019); "5th Regiment, United States Colored Cavalry," https://www.nps.gov/civilwar/search-battle-units-detail.htm?battleUnitCode=UUS0005RC00C; "6th Regiment, United States Colored Cavalry," https://www.nps.gov/civilwar/search-battle-units-detail.htm?battleUnitCode=UUS0006RC00C; "First Battle of Saltville," https://www.nps.gov/cane/battle-of-saltville-and-massacre.htm; "Southwest Virginia Raid," December 1864, https://www.nps.gov/cane/southwest-virginia-raid.htm#:~:text=The%20first%20engagement%20of%20Stoneman's,Rogersville%20and%20drove%20them%20away; U.S. War Department, *The War of the Rebellion: A Compilation of the Official Records of the Union and Confederate Armies* (Washington: Government Printing Office, 1894), Series 1, vol. 45, part 2, 494–95.

1864–1865, 4th Regiment U.S. Colored Troops

The 4th was the first U.S.C.T. regiment raised in Maryland. The state allowed for three classes of recruit: free Blacks, enslaved men enlisting with their owner's acquiescence, and those enslaved by disloyal masters, who could join without permission. Enslaved Marylanders became free upon enlistment, and loyal former owners received $300 in compensation.

By October 1863 the regiment was at Yorktown, Virginia. Soon after, they participated in a cross-river raid, after which their commander, Samuel Duncan, praised the "endurance, and *patience* of the men, uttering no complaints. . . . On the homeward trip, which was severer than marching out, the men were shouting and singing most of the way." The general commanding at Yorktown commented:

> The negro infantry . . . marched 30 miles a day without a straggler or a complaint. . . . Not a fence rail was burned or a chicken stolen by them. They seem to be well controlled and their discipline, obedience, and cheerfulness, for new troops, is surprising, and has dispelled many of my prejudices.

In late winter 1864 22nd U.S.C.I. assistant surgeon Charles Merrill tried to make sense of Colonel Duncan's brigade's uncharacteristic pillaging of "Disloyal" livestock during an operation on the north shore of the York River. He then saw something that helped explain their behavior.

> I found some of our boys hacking away at a sort of cross T set up in the ground, with two pegs projecting from the upper crossbeams. It was a whipping post & they were in a perfect fury as they cut it down. It seemed as though they were cutting at an inanimate enemy & revenging upon him the accumulated wrongs of two centuries. As fast as one tired, another took the axe & soon the infernal machine . . . came to the ground. . . . It was burned on the spot where it fell.

As part of Brigadier General Edward Hinks's 3rd Division, 18th Corps, Major General Benjamin Butler's Army of the James, Colonel Duncan's five regiments participated in the ill-fated May 1864 Bermuda Hundred campaign. The following month, as Lieutenant General Ulysses Grant's Army of the Potomac slowly made their way from Cold Harbor, Hinks's division, leading the 18th Corps, attacked the Petersburg defenses. General Hinks wrote in his after-action report,

> in the gallant and soldierly deportment of the troops engaged on the 15th . . . the celerity with which they moved to the charge, the steadiness and coolness exhibited by them under heavy and long continued fire, the impetuosity with which they sprang to the assault, the patient endurance of wounds,—we have a sufficient proof that colored men, when properly officered, instructed, and drilled, will make most excellent infantry of the line.

The June 15 offensive, and those over the three following days, were unsupported by Grant's forces, thus denying an early opportunity for taking Petersburg. After heavy fighting at New Market Heights in September, and hard labor on the Dutch Gap canal from August to October 1864, early in 1865 the 4th U.S.C.T. joined forces threatening Wilmington, North Carolina. In late March 1865 an anonymous 4th Regiment soldier wrote:

> February 20th [1865]—We had something of a skirmish with . . . General [Robert] Hoke['s Confederate forces]. . . . On the 21st, we built a line, and bivouacked for the night; being only four miles from the largest and oldest city in the State. We asked ourselves as well as others, "How would you like to march through Wilmington tomorrow, February 22d . . . the birthday of Washington?" The answer was, "It would be the proudest moment of my life!" . . . The 22d came, and a more lovely day I never saw. By half past six o'clock we were on the move, as General Hoke had evacuated during the night, and one hour's march brought us on the corporation line of Wilmington . . . We . . . entered the blockaded city of the Confederacy . . . the once [rising] city of the Confederacy; the place noted for its slave market! But now, alas! we march through these fine thoroughfares, where once the slave was forbid being out after nine P.M., or to puff a "regalia," [i.e., wear fine clothing] or to walk with a cane . . . Negro Soldiers! with banners floating! with their splendid brass bands and drum corps, discoursing the National airs and marches!—the colored division of the 25th army corps, commanded by General Charles J. Payne. . . . The colored people of Wilmington welcomed the Union troops—cheer after cheer they gave us—they had prayed long for their deliverance, and the 22d day of February, 1865, realized their earnest hopes. Were they not happy that day? Free, for evermore! The streets were crowded with them, old and young; they shook hands with the troops, and some exclaimed, "The chain is broken!" "Joy! Freedom today!" "Hurrah for Uncle Abe!" . . . We passed out of the town, and were soon on Hoke's track. We came up with at North East Bridge, or Station, nine miles from town—the 4th, 6th, and 30th U.S.C.T. Gen. [Samuel] Duncan's Brigade, gave him battle at this place, and during the night—as usual—Gen. Hoke retired.

The soldier pictured wears full winter marching kit, including knapsack and sky-blue overcoat. He is armed with an imported Enfield rifle musket. Following the April 1865 Confederate surrender, the 4th Regiment remained in North Carolina until being mustered out in May 1866.

Left: U.S. Navy sailor's wool cap worn by Charles Sharter. Seaman Sharter joined the West Gulf Squadron after being transported south from New York City (leaving September 15, 1864), aboard the U.S. steamers Vermont *and* Tallapoosa. *Sharter, promoted to steward, was honorably discharged November 19, 1866. (Dr. Michael Cunningham Collection)*

Dress coat worn by Assistant Surgeon Richard H. Green, U.S. Navy. Greene was the first African American to graduate from Yale University (1857). He served aboard the U.S. ships Ohio, State of Georgia, *and* Seneca, *from late 1863 until his resignation in May 1865. (Angelo Scarlato Collection)*

National flag of the 12th Regiment Infantry, Corps d'Afrique, U.S. Colored Volunteers. They were organized at Port Hudson, Louisiana, in September 1863. In April 1864, the regiment was designated the 84th Regiment, U.S. Colored Troops. (National Museum of the United States Army)

Sources: William A. Dobak, *Freedom by the Sword: The U.S. Colored Troops, 1862–1867* (New York: Skyhorse Publishing, 2013), 315–16, 317, 323–26, 328, 331–33, 335, 337, 345, 347–52, 375–76, 391, 394, 403–4, 409–11; Edwin S. Redkey. ed., *A Grand Army of Black Men: Letters from African-American Soldiers in the Union Army, 1861–1865* (Cambridge, UK: Cambridge University Press, 1992), 101–3, 127–28, 165–67; "United States Colored Troops 4th Regiment Infantry," https://nps.gov/rich/learn/historyculture/4thusct.htm; Petersburg attack, June 15, 1864: Gordon C. Rhea, "Cold Harbor and the Advance to Petersburg," https://www.essentialcivilwarcurriculum.com/cold-harbor-and-the-advance-to-petersburg.html; "United States Colored Troops in Opening Assaults," https://www.nps.gov/pete/learn/historyculture/united-states-colored-troops-in-opening-assaults.htm; William E. Furness, "The Negro as a Soldier," https://www.beyondthecrater.com/resources/mollus/il-mollus/mollus-il-v2-the-negro-as-a-soldier/; "The Colored Troops—History of Their Organization—Their Losses in Battle and by Disease," excerpted from William F. Fox, *Regimental Losses in the American Civil War, 1861–1865. A Treatise on the Extent and Nature of the Mortuary Losses in the Union Regiments, with Full and Exhaustive Statistics Compiled from the Official Records on File in the State Military Bureaus and at Washington* (Albany, NY: Albany Publishing Co., 1889), https://www.nps.gov/rich/learn/historyculture/background.htm.

1864–1865, 31st Regiment U.S. Colored Troops; Detachment 30th Connecticut (Colored)

By 1864 many state governors were happy to establish U.S. Colored regiments, as it gave them an opportunity to exercise political patronage in nominating each unit's thirty-nine officers. New York Democratic governor Horatio Seymour had no political interest in forming Black military units; even aiding the process would alienate his constituents. Thus, New York City's Union League Club took the initiative in forming the state's U.S.C.T. units, and Seymour did not object. His only response to the Club's recruiting committee was that "the organization of negro regiments . . . rests entirely with the War Department in Washington." After committee members wrote Secretary of War Edwin Stanton on the matter, informing him of the active interest and full commitment of their organization, "composed of over 500 of the [state's] wealthiest and most respected citizens," their offer was quickly accepted and recruiters went to work.

The 31st was the last of three New York U.S.C.T. regiments formed. The unit was organized on Hart Island (western end of Long Island Sound) in April 1864, while the 20th and 26th U.S.C.T. regiments had been formed on Rikers Island. In early May the 31st Regiment was in Annapolis, Maryland; it joined Brigadier General Edward Ferrero's U.S.C.T. division on or before May 18, when it was merged with the understrength four-company 30th Connecticut Regiment (Colored), at or near Salem Church, west of Fredericksburg. (As of April 30, 1864, Ferrero's division consisted of the 30th Connecticut detachment, and 19th, 27th, 30th, 39th, 43rd U.S.C.T. Regiments. The 23rd, 29th, and 31st regiments had yet to join.)

The 30th Connecticut formed when its brother regiment, the 29th, attracted too many recruits. On January 29, 1854, in camp at Fairhaven, both regiments were addressed by abolitionist Frederick Douglass:

You are pioneers of the liberty of your race. With the United States cap on your head, the United States eagle on your belt, the United States musket on your shoulder, not all the powers of darkness can prevent you from becoming American citizens. And not for yourselves alone are you marshaled—you are pioneers—on you depends the destiny of four millions of the colored race in this country. If you rise and flourish, we shall rise and flourish. If you win freedom and citizenship, we shall share your freedom and citizenship.

The newly augmented 31st Regiment missed three-quarters of General Grant's Overland Campaign, but joined the day before a substantial attack on the supply trains under Ferrero's division's protection. The action began about 5 p.m., and the general recorded, "we held the enemy in check until dark." A Pennsylvania soldier noted that the Black troops' "conduct was above criticism." Combat was not the only cause for casualties; prior to the 31st U.S.C.T.'s arrival, Ferrero's division had a number of men, stragglers and pickets, taken prisoner, many of whom were killed in cold blood. On May 8 a Virginia cavalryman wrote in his diary, "we captured three negro soldiers the first we had seen. They were taken out on the road side and shot, & their bodies left there."

Taking post before Petersburg with the rest of Major General Burnside's 9th Corps, Ferrero's first (27th, 30th, 39th, 43rd regiments) and second (19th, 23rd, 29th, 31st) U.S.C.T. brigades spent the last days of June and most of July digging trenches and performing other tasks required in siege warfare. On July 18, 31st U.S.C.T. soldier D. R. Brown corresponded with the New York weekly *Anglo African*: "We have seen the fruits of slavery, the desolation and despair of hundreds rushing into our lines, crying and praying for our protection." A Mr. Banks commented on Brown's letter: "We know, and the slave knows, that fighting for the Union is fighting against slavery." Twelve days later Brown and his comrades fought in the Battle of the Crater; the 31st Regiment suffered twenty-seven killed, forty-two wounded, and sixty-six missing.

The tedium and danger of trench warfare filled the men's days into autumn 1864. On October 27 Ferrero's division took part in the ill-fated Battle of Boydton Plank Road, an offensive intended to cut that thoroughfare and the Southside Railroad. The Black regiments attacked, then were ordered to hold their

Identity disc of Alexander Burns, 5th U.S. Colored Troops. Ohioan Burns, appointed sergeant on September 10, 1863, was reduced to the ranks in May 1865 for leaving his guard post. (Courtesy Heritage Auctions)

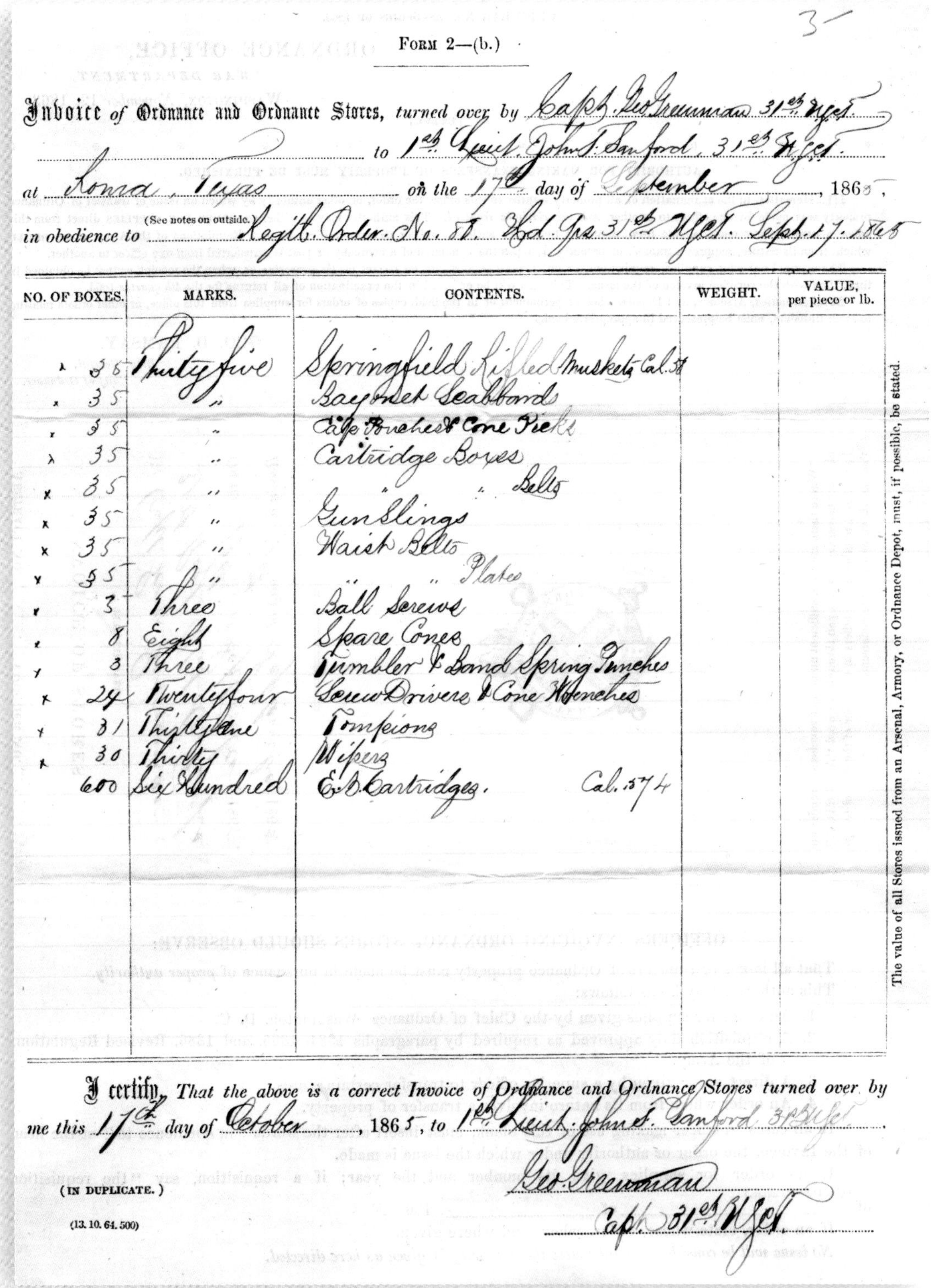

FORM 2—(b).

3

Invoice of Ordnance and Ordnance Stores, turned over by *Capt. Geo Greenman 31st Regt.*

to *1st Lieut John F. Sanford 31st Regt.*

at *Roma, Texas* on the *17* day of *September*, 186 5,

in obedience to *Regt'l Order No. 51 Hd Qrs 31st Regt. Sept. 17, 1865*

(See notes on outside.)

NO. OF BOXES.	MARKS.	CONTENTS.	WEIGHT.	VALUE, per piece or lb.
35	Thirty five	Springfield Rifled Muskets Cal. 58		
35	"	Bayonet Scabbard		
35	"	Wipe Brushes & Cone Picks		
35	"	Cartridge Boxes		
35	"	" Belts		
35	"	Gun Slings		
35	"	Waist Belts		
35	"	" " Plates		
3	Three	Ball Screws		
8	Eight	Spare Cones		
3	Three	Tumbler & Band Spring Punches		
24	Twenty four	Screw Drivers & Cone Wrenches		
31	Thirty one	Tompions		
30	Thirty	Wipers		
600	Six Hundred	E.B. Cartridges. Cal. 57/4		

I certify, That the above is a correct Invoice of Ordnance and Ordnance Stores turned over by me this *17* day of *October*, 186 5, to *1st Lieut. John F. Sanford 31st Regt.*

Geo Greenman

(IN DUPLICATE.)

(13. 10. 64. 500)

Capt. 31st Regt.

The value of all Stores issued from an Arsenal, Armory, or Ordnance Depot, must, if possible, be stated.

Return of arms and accoutrements, Company D, 31st U.S. Colored Troops, while in garrison at Roma, Texas, September 17, 1865. (Don Troiani Collection)

Silk flag of the 25th Army Corps. Created in December 1864 by combining the 10th and 18th Corps, the 25th became the first all-Black Union Army corps. Corps commander Major General Godfrey Weitzel said of his men, "there is no record which should give the colored race more pride than that left by the Twenty-Fifth Corps." The flags colors (red, white, and blue) represent the badge colors for each of the three divisions composing the Corps. (Courtesy Heritage Auctions)

position, losing seven killed, sixty-seven wounded, and six missing. They withdrew the next morning.

On December 3, 1864, General Ferrero's former division was broken up and assigned to the new all-Black 25th Corps, Army of the James. The 31st Regiment was assigned to the 3rd Brigade (29th, 31st, and 116th), Brigadier General William Birney's 2nd Division, one of three Black divisions in the new corps.

On March 27, Birney's Division, attached to 24th Corps, moved to join Grant's forces southwest of Petersburg. On April 5, Birney's seven regiments belatedly joined the pursuit of General Lee's forces; Sergeant William McCoslin of the

29th U.S.C.T. remarked, "our march was rapid and devious, being . . . through mud, rain, and stones." They also took part in the April 9 morning fighting near Appomattox Court House, advancing in support of the cavalry; 8th U.S.C.T. colonel Samuel Armstrong noted, "formed line of battle; arrested the progress of the enemy." Lee surrendered the Army of Northern Virginia that afternoon.

With the war's end, the 25th Corps was sent to occupy Texas and cover the Mexican border. The 31st Regiment was in the state on June 19, 1865, when Major General Gordon Granger issued his "Juneteenth" Special Order No. 3, announcing slavery's end.

Sources: William A. Dobak, *Freedom by the Sword: The U.S. Colored Troops, 1862–1867* (New York: Skyhorse Publishing, 2013), 309–10, 338, 362–65, 402, 413–18, 434–44 (30th Connecticut, 16, 332–33, 338). Noah Andre Trudeau, *Like Men of War: Black Troops in the Civil War, 1862–1865* (Boston, New York, and London: Little, Brown and Company, 1998), 206–14, 228–51, 301–4, 425–32; "30th Regiment, Connecticut Infantry," https://www.familysearch.org/en/wiki/30th_Regiment,_Connecticut_Infantry#:~:text=The%2030th%20Regiment%2C%20Connecticut%20Infantry,Regiment%20United%20States%20Colored%20Troops; William D. Matter, *If It Takes All Summer: The Battle of Spotsylvania* (Chapel Hill and London: University of North Carolina Press, 1988), 359; "Connecticut's Black Civil War Regiments," https://connecticuthistory.org/connecticuts-black-civil-war-regiment/; *The Connecticut War Record*, February 1864, 9; U.S. War Department, *The War of the Rebellion: A Compilation of the Official Records of the Union and Confederate Armies* (Washington, DC: Government Printing Office, 1891), Series 1, vol. 36, part 1, 987–93, vol. 33 (1891), 1045–46; Edwin S. Redkey, ed., *A Grand Army of Black Men: Letters from African-American Soldiers in the Union Army, 1861–1865* (Cambridge, UK: Cambridge University Press, 1992), 125–27; "The Colored Troops—History of Their Organization—Their Losses in Battle and by Disease," excerpted from William F. Fox, *Regimental Losses in the American Civil War, 1861–1865. A Treatise on the Extent and Nature of the Mortuary Losses in the Union Regiments, with Full and Exhaustive Statistics Compiled from the Official Records on File in the State Military Bureaus and at Washington* (Albany, NY: Albany Publishing Co., 1889), 55, 109–10; "Order of Battle—Appomattox Court House," https://www.nps.gov/apco/order-of-battle-appomattox-court-house.htm; National Archives Safeguards Original "Juneteenth" General Order, https://www.archives.gov/news/articles/juneteenth-original-document.

Afterword

"Will they fight?" Many white Americans during the 1860s war and since have asked that question, having forgotten or never known that free and enslaved Black men fighting in North America and elsewhere had long ago provided a positive answer as well as a soldierly role model.[1]

The story of Black soldiers serving in North America, and men of color in the U.S. and Canadian militaries, did not end in 1865, nor did their fight for human rights and the full benefits of citizenship. In the war's aftermath Union Black veterans living in the South suffered from harassment and reprisal, and while the brief Reconstruction era led to some political and societal advances for African Americans in the South, those benefits were soon erased with the advent of the Jim Crow era, lasting from 1877 to 1965. Military segregation continued in Canada through World War I, and for the United States through World War II. During that conflict, needing to replace high combat losses, the U.S. Army in Europe implemented the Volunteer Infantry Replacement Program, in which Black soldiers in noncombat roles could volunteer for combat service in white units. Despite President Harry Truman's July 26, 1948, Executive Order 9981 enacting integration and nondiscrimination in the U.S. military, during the 1950–1953 Korean War some Black units remained, including the 24th Infantry Regiment and the 503rd Artillery Battalion. In civilian society the struggle for Black equality continues to the present day.[2]

Acknowledgments

Special thanks to James L. Kochan.

Additional thanks to Andrew Bamford, John L. Bell, Joel Bohy, Maria Alessandra Bollettino, Todd W. Braisted, Christopher Bryant, René Chartrand, Dr. Michael Cunningham, Charles Fithian, Jan Gordon, Marvin-Alonzo Greer, Tom Grinslade, Don N. Hagist, John Hannigan, Jennifer Locke Jones, Matthew Keagle, Paul Loane, Bruce C. MacGunnigle, Aaron Mair, Phillip Mead, Jason Melius, Timothy Messer-Kruse, Tyler Mink, Paul Morando, Colonel J. Craig Nannos, Aimee Newall, Albert A. Nofi, Joshua Provan, Daniel Popek, Robert Selig, Brian Rollason, Jan Gordon, Marcus Rediker, C. Samuel Rees, Joseph P. Reidy, Steve Rogers, Angelo R. Scarlato, Adam Schenkman, Eric H. Schnitzer, Robert A. Selig, Matthew Skic, Michael Schaffner, R. Scott Stephenson, Garry W. Stone, Brendan Synomon, Jamie Synomon, James Taub, Mary Walsh, Lee White, Luzerne County Historical Society, Museum of the American Revolution, New York State Military Museum, Smithsonian Institution, U.S. Army Center for Military History, and West Point Museum.

Notes

PREFACE

1. James Forten to William Lloyd Garrison, February 23, 1831, Boston Public Library, Rare Books, Anti-Slavery Collection; Julie Winch, *A Gentleman of Color: The Life of James Forten* (Oxford and New York: Oxford University Press, 2002), 29–52.

2. Winch, *Gentleman of Color*, 29–52.

3. Winch, *Gentleman of Color*, 29–52.

4. Daniel M. Popek, *They ". . . fought bravely, but were unfortunate": The True Story of Rhode Island's "Black Regiment" and the Failure of Segregation in Rhode Island's Continental Line, 1777–1783* (Bloomington, IN: AuthorHouse, 2015).

5. Carole W. Troxler, "Re-enslavement of Black Loyalists: Mary Postell in South Carolina, East Florida, and Nova Scotia," *Acadiensis*, vol. 37, no. 2 (2008), 70–85.

6. Peter Linebaugh and Marcus Rediker, *The Many-Headed Hydra: Sailors, Slaves, Commoners, and the Hidden History of the Revolutionary Atlantic* (Boston: Beacon Press, 2013), 49; Charles Johnson and Patricia Smith, *Africans in America: America's Journey through Slavery* (San Diego: Harcourt & Brace, 1999), 37–43.

CHAPTER 1

1. Veteran Richard Rhodes (1st Rhode Island Regiment—segregated—February 1778 to June 1780) related in his July 1820 pension deposition: "he is a Mariner & has followed the sea ever since the war, but is unable to follow that business in consequence of age—that he is very much crippled in one arm in consequence of a wound received in the battle of Monmouth . . . he was born in Africa **brought to this country and sold as a slave** and enlisted in the black Regiment so called to obtain his freedom." National Archives & Records Administration (NARA), Revolutionary War Pension and Bounty-Land Warrant Application Files (Microfilm Publication M804), Records of the Department of Veterans Affairs, Record Group 15, Washington, DC, reel 2030, Richard Rhodes (W22060).

2. Michael Cohn and Michael K. H. Platzer, *Black Men of the Sea* (New York: Dodd, Mead, 1978), 24; Peter Linebaugh and Marcus Rediker, *The Many-Headed Hydra: Sailors, Slaves, Commoners, and the Hidden History of the Revolutionary Atlantic* (Boston: Beacon Press, 2013), 57, 104–35; Kenneth Morgan, *Slavery and the British Empire: From Africa to America* (Oxford, UK: Oxford University Press, 2007), 5–6, 8, 12, 15, 55–66.

3. "Annual Number of Slaves Transported from Africa to Mainland North America 1628–1860," June 21, 2022, https://tinyurl.com/Statista-NAmerica; "Slave Arrivals from Africa to the British Caribbean by Region and Century 1606–1842," June 21, 2022, https://tinyurl.com/Statista-Carib; Morgan, *Slavery and the British Empire*, 12; Darald D. Wax, "Preferences for Slaves in Colonial America," *Journal of Negro History*, vol. 58, no. 4 (October 1973), 374, 376–79, 389, 395; Darald D. Wax, "Black Immigrants: The Slave Trade in Colonial Maryland," *Maryland Historical Magazine*, vol. 73, no. 1 (Spring 1978), 37–38.

4. Morgan, *Slavery and the British Empire*, 16.

5. Seymour Drescher, *Abolition: A History of Slavery and Antislavery* (New York: Cambridge University Press, 2009), 118–19, 184;

"Estimated Population of Haiti by Ethnicity and Slave Status 1789," August 25, 2022, https://tinyurl.com/Statista-Haiti-1789.

6. Drescher, *Abolition*, 172, 184; Benjamin Quarles, *The Negro in the American Revolution* (New York, London: W.W. Norton & Company, 1973), 49–50; John U. Rees, *"They Were Good Soldiers": African Americans Serving in the Continental Army, 1775–1783* (Warwick, UK: Helion & Company, 2019), 166–68; "Law of 4 February 1794" (French), https://en.wikipedia.org/wiki/Law_of_4_February_1794; Sonia Phalnikar, "Remembering That Napoleon Reinstated Slavery," May 4, 2021, https://tinyurl.com/1802-Napoleon-slavery; "The Slave Trade Act of 1807" (Britain), https://en.wikipedia.org/wiki/Slave_Trade_Act_1807; "Act Prohibiting the Importation of Slaves" (United States), https://en.wikipedia.org/wiki/Act_Prohibiting_Importation_of_Slaves; Joel K. Bourne Jr., "Last American Slave Ship Is Discovered in Alabama," May 22, 2019, https://www.nationalgeographic.com/culture/article/clotilda-the-last-american-slave-ship-found-in-alabama.

7. Morgan, *Slavery and the British Empire*, 49, 191–92, 197–98, 392; "Emancipation" (No. 8), http://sainthelenaisland.info/slavery.htm; Chandima S. M. Wickramasinghe, "Coloured Slavery in Ceylon (Sri Lanka)," *Journal of the Royal Asiatic Society of Sri Lanka*, New Series, vol. 54 (2008), 170–71; James M. McPherson, *Battle Cry of Freedom: The Civil War Era* (New York: Ballantine Books, 1989), 557–59; "13th Amendment to the U.S. Constitution: Abolition of Slavery (1865)," https://www.archives.gov/milestone-documents/13th-amendment.

8. NARA, Pension, reel 2030, Richard Rhodes (W22060 – R.I.); reel 2168, Cezar Shelton (S19764 – Ct.); reel 1544, Richard Leet (S38908—Ct.); reel 1615, Peter Maguira (R6830—Ct.), deposition of Titus Thomas; reel 313, Jeffrey Brace (S41461—Ct.).

9. NARA, Pension, reel 111, Prince Bailey/Dunsick (W17230).

10. Linebaugh and Rediker, *Many-Headed Hydra*, 152, 184.

11. Linebaugh and Rediker, *Many-Headed Hydra*, 184–85.

12. Linebaugh and Rediker, *Many-Headed Hydra*, 185.

13. National Park Service. *Low Country Gullah Culture Special Resource Study and Final Environmental Impact Statement* (Atlanta: NPS Southeast Regional Office, 2005), 13; Marcus Rediker, *The Fearless Benjamin Lay: The Quaker Dwarf Who Became the First Revolutionary Abolitionist* (Boston: Beacon Press, 2017), 55; "West Africa, 1300–1800 CE," https://www.ncpedia.org/anchor/africans-atlantic-slave; Mechal Sobel, *The World They Made Together: Black and White Values in Eighteenth-Century Virginia* (Princeton, NJ: Princeton University Press, 1987), 5, 244–45 (Note 6); Kari J. Winter (ed.), *The Blind African Slave, or Memoirs of Boyrereau Brinch, Nick-Named Jeffrey Brace, as told to Benjamin F. Prentiss* (Madison: University of Wisconsin Press, 2004), 4. For a full discussion of the subject see Marcus Rediker, *The Slave Ship: A Human History* (New York: Penguin Books, 2007), chapter 3, "African Paths to the Middle Passage," 73–107. See also Gary Sellick, "Black Men, Red Coats: The Carolina Corps, Race, and Society in the Revolutionary British Atlantic," Dissertation, University of South Carolina, 2018, 76–83, https://scholarcommons.sc.edu/etd/4932.

14. "Senegal & Guinea" (No. 1), http://nationalhumanities center.org/pds/maai/freedom/text1/text1read.htm; Rediker, *Slave Ship*, 6.

CHAPTER 2

1. Olaudah Equiano was a former slave, seaman, veteran of the 1758 Louisbourg siege, abolitionist, and author of *The Interesting Narrative of the Life of Olaudah Equiano or Gustavus Vassa the African* (1794). Writing of the Battle of Lagos, August 18, 1759: "The engagement now commenced with great fury on both sides: the [French ship-of-the-line] *Ocean* immediately returned our fire, and we continued engaged with each other for some time; during which I was frequently stunned with **the thundering of the great guns**, whose dreadful contents hurried many of my companions into awful eternity." Olaudah Equiano, *The Interesting Narrative and Other Writings* (New York and London: Penguin Books, 2003), 83; "Battle of Lagos," https://en.wikipedia .org/wiki/Battle_of_Lagos.

2. Maria Alessandra Bollettino, "Slavery, War, and Britain's Atlantic Empire: Black Soldiers, Sailors, and Rebels in the Seven Years' War," Dissertation, University of Texas at Austin, December 2009, 34–37, https://repositories.lib.utexas.edu/handle/2152/ETD-UT-2009-12-543; John F. Hannigan, "King's Men and Continentals: War and Slavery in Eighteenth-Century Massachusetts," Dissertation, Brandeis University, August 2021, 13. For a discussion of Cuba's Black militia during the 1762 siege of Havana, see John U. Rees, "'Some of the best soldiers in the world': The Havana Battalions of Free Blacks and Mulattos, 1762–1781," https://www.academia.edu/105729245/_Some_of _the_best_soldiers_in_the_world_The_Havana_Battalions_of _Free_Blacks_and_Mulattos_1762_1781.

3. Robin W. Winks, *The Blacks in Canada: A History* (Montreal: McGill-Queen›s University Press, 1997); Kenneth Morgan, *Slavery and the British Empire: From Africa to America* (Oxford, UK: Oxford University Press, 2007), 16.

4. Bollettino, "Slavery, War, and Britain's Atlantic Empire," 54, 165–67; Equiano, *Interesting Narrative*, 68–94; Douglas R. Egerton, *Death or Liberty: African Americans and Revolutionary America* (Oxford and New York: Oxford University Press, 2009), 15–16; Kari J. Winter (ed.), *The Blind African Slave, or Memoirs of Boyrereau Brinch, Nick-Named Jeffrey Brace, as told to Benjamin F. Prentiss* (Madison: University of Wisconsin Press, 2004), 27–30.

5. David L. Preston, *Braddock's Defeat: The Battle of the Monongahela and the Road to Revolution* (Oxford and New York: Oxford University Press, 2015), 167, 338–40. For more on Black sailors see John U. Rees, "'They stripped to the waist & fought like devils': Black Sailors in British and American Sea Service (1754–1865)," https://www.academia.edu/113016514/_They _stripped_to_the_waist_and_fought_like_devils_British_and _American_Sea_Service_1754_1865_.

6. *Virginia Gazette*, February 28, 1755, no. 216, 4; Preston, *Braddock's Defeat*, 85.

7. Larry G. Bowman, "Virginia's Use of Blacks in the French and Indian War," *Western Pennsylvania Historical Magazine*, vol. 53 (1970), 58–59.

8. *Carlisle Gazette*, June 18, 1788, vol. 3, no. 150; Preston, *Braddock's Defeat*, 85.

9. "Provincial Troops in the French and Indian Wars," https:// tinyurl.com/7-Years-Provincial-troops; NARA, Founders Online, George Washington to Peter Hog, December 27, 1755, https:// founders.archives.gov/documents/Washington/02-02-02-0241; Bowman, "Virginia's Use of Blacks," 58–63; Murtie June Clark, *Colonial Soldiers of the South*, 1732–1774 (Baltimore: Genealogical Publishing Co., Inc., 1986), 390, 450, 451, 463, 473, 475, 487 (Courtesy of Jason Melius); "Land Bounty Certificates for Service in the French and Indian Wars" (Matthew Roberts), https://genealogytrails.com/vir/land_bounty_certificates. html?fbclid=IwAR3gunV1eHTVQ-lNcorO5RLy3H6l6ddjBXvo3 tD-k6U38C1rP2dEkf031sM (Courtesy of J. Melius).

10. Marcus Rediker, *The Fearless Benjamin Lay: The Quaker Dwarf Who Became the First Revolutionary Abolitionist* (Boston: Beacon Press, 2017), 55; Morgan, *Slavery and the British Empire*, 137, 139–41. Bollettino, "Slavery, War, and Britain's Atlantic Empire," 34–37.

11. "Provincial Troops in the French and Indian Wars"; Clark, *Colonial Soldiers of the South*, 708, 716, 718 (Courtesy of Jason Melius). See also, North Carolina State Archives, Military Collection, Colonial Period, Record Group 5864, Muster Roll, Craven County, Captain Abner Neale company, October 4, 1755, https://digital.ncdcr.gov/digital/collection/p16062coll26/ id/199; Muster Roll, Granville County, Colonel William Eaton's Regiment, 1, 3, https://digital.ncdcr.gov/digital/collection/ p16062coll26/id/134/rec/229.

12. Muster Roll, Granville County, Colonel William Eaton's Regiment, 37–38, 44; Robert Scott Stephenson, "An Extreme Bad Collection?: Signs of Professionalism in the Pennsylvania Regiment, 1757–1759," Thesis, University of Virginia, January 1990, 59–77, 110–13; Matthew C. Ward, "An Army of Servants: The Pennsylvania Regiment during the Seven Years' War," *Pennsylvania Magazine of History and Biography*, vol. 119, nos. 1/2 (January/April 1995), 82, 85–86, 89–92; Bollettino, "Slavery, War, and Britain's Atlantic Empire," 38.

13. Bollettino, "Slavery, War, and Britain's Atlantic Empire," 47–48.

14. Bollettino, "Slavery, War, and Britain's Atlantic Empire," 87.

15. John A. Munroe, *Colonial Delaware, A History* (Millwood, NY: KTO Press, 1978), 220, 223–26; "Provincial Troops in the French and Indian Wars". For more information on the Forbes Expedition see, "French and Indian War Journal Documents the Brutality of War," https://tinyurl.com/1758-JournalForbesExp; *Public Archives Commission of Delaware, Delaware Archives, Military* (Wilmington: Mercantile Printing Company, 1911), vol. I, 11–13, 19–20; John B. Linn and William H. Egle, eds., *Pennsylvania Archives*, Series 2, vol. 10 (Harrisburg: Clarence M. Busch, State Printer, 1896), 527–29; Thomas Lynch Montgomery, ed., *Pennsylvania Archives*, Series 5, vol. 1 (Harrisburg: Harrisburg Publishing Company, State Printer, 1906), 254, 300–301, 354 (Courtesy of Charles Fithian).

16. Scott Padeni, "The Role of Blacks in New York's Northern Campaigns of the Seven Years' War," *Bulletin of the Fort Ticonderoga Museum*, vol. 16 (1999), 156; "An Act to Encourage the Enlisting of Five Hundred Free-men or Well Affected Indians in the Colony of New-Jersey, for His Majesty's Service in the Present Expedition, in Conjunction with the Forces of New-England and New-York, for Erecting a Strong Fortress near Crown-Point . . . ," passed April 22, 1755, Samuel Allinson, *Acts of the General Assembly of New-Jersey from . . .* (April 17, 1702–January 14, 1776 (Burlington: Isaac Collins, Printer, 1776), 204.

17. Edward H. Knoblauch, "Mobilizing Provincials for War: The Social Composition of New York Forces in 1760," *New York History*, vol. 78, no. 2, 1997, 147–48, 151.

18. Knoblauch, "Mobilizing Provincials for War," 162.

19. "Muster Rolls of the New York Provincial Troops, 1755–1764," *Collections of the New-York Historical Society for the Year 1891*, vol. 24 (New York: Printed for the Society, 1892), 60–61, 66–73, 123–32, 154–55, 178–79, 194–207, 234–35,

294–95, 306–7 (with thanks to Mark Turdo). See also Bollettino, "Slavery, War, and Britain's Atlantic Empire," 72–75.

20. Knoblauch, "Mobilizing Provincials for War," 163; Thomas Agostini, "'Deserted His Majesty's Service': Military Runaways, the British-American Press, and the Problem of Desertion during the Seven Years' War," *Journal of Social History*, vol. 40, no. 4 (Summer 2007), 960; *New-York Mercury*, November 24, 1760.

21. Fred Anderson, *The Crucible of War: The Seven Years' War and the Fate of Empire in British North America, 1754–1766* (New York: Alfred A. Knopf, 2000), 118–21; "Letter from a Gunner to His Cousin," Edmund B. O'Callaghan, ed., *Documents Relative to the Colonial History of the State of New York*, vol. 6 (Albany, NY: Weed, Parsons and Company, 1855), 1006.

22. Anderson, *Crucible of War*, 499–501; Howard M. Chapin, *Rhode Island in the Colonial Wars: A List of Rhode Island Soldiers & Sailors in the Old French & Indian War, 1755–1762*, 1918 (reprint, Baltimore: Genealogical Publishing Co., Inc., 1994), 28, 29, 36, 37, 38, 45, 71, 74, 85, 95, 97, 100, 104, 111, 116, 133, 140, 146.

23. Ian K. Steele, *Betrayals: Fort William Henry & the "Massacre"* (New York and Oxford: Oxford University Press, 1990), 140, 196. Bollettino, "Slavery, War, and Britain's Atlantic Empire," 92–93.

24. Harold E. Selesky, *War and Society in Colonial Connecticut* (New Haven and London: Yale University Press, 1990), 174.

25. Bollettino, "Slavery, War, and Britain's Atlantic Empire," 92; Glenn F. Williams, *Year of the Hangman: George Washington's Campaign Against the Iroquois* (Yardley, PA: Westholme Publishing, 2005), 121–31.

26. Williams, *Year of the Hangman*, 168. John U. Rees, *"They Were Good Soldiers": African Americans Serving in the Continental Army, 1775–1783* (Warwick, UK: Helion & Company, 2019), 37.

27. "Provincial Troops in the French and Indian Wars."

28. Anderson, *Crucible of War*, 190–98; Bollettino, "Slavery, War, and Britain's Atlantic Empire," 84–87; Steele, *Betrayals*, 140, 187–99; Edward P. Hamilton, ed., *Adventure in the Wilderness: The American Journals of Louis Antoine De Bougainville, 1756–1760* (Norman: University of Oklahoma Press, 1990), 175; Charles W. Thayer and Melinde Lutz Sanborn, "John Bush of Shrewsbury, Massachusetts: Master Horn Carver," *National Genealogical Society Quarterly*, vol. 95, no. 2 (June 2007), 89, 91, 98–100; Padeni, "The Role of Blacks in New York's Northern Campaigns," 158–63.

29. Padeni, "Role of Blacks in New York's Northern Campaigns," frontispiece.

30. Thayer and Sanborn, "John Bush," 98.

CHAPTER 3

1. Declaration of Independence, July 4, 1776 (Preamble): "We hold these truths to be self-evident, that all men are created equal, that they are endowed by their Creator with certain unalienable Rights, that among these are **Life, Liberty and the pursuit of Happiness**," https://tinyurl.com/Dec-of-Indep.

2. "full Security," Sir Henry Clinton, "Philipsburg proclamation," June 30, 1779; John U. Rees, *"They Were Good Soldiers": African Americans Serving in the Continental Army, 1775–1783* (Warwick, UK: Helion & Company, 2019), 19; "Whig": *The Compact Edition of the Oxford English Dictionary*, two vols. (Glasgow, New York, Toronto: Oxford University Press, 1971), vol. 2, 3757; *The American Heritage Dictionary of the English Language*, 3rd ed. (Boston, New York, and London: Houghton Mifflin Co., 1992), 2033.

3. Robert K. Wright Jr., *The Continental Army* (Washington, DC: Government Printing Office, 1984), 23–24.

4. NARA, Founders Online, John Thomas to Adams, October 24, 1775, https://founders.archives.gov/documents/Adams/06-03-02-0123.

5. Jesse J. Johnson, ed., *The Black Soldier (Documented, 1619–1815): Missing Pages in United States History* (Hampton, VA: Hampton Institute, 1969), 32 (cited as "Proceedings of the Committee of Safety of Massachusetts Bay. Cambridge, 20th May, 1775," Mass. Ms Archives, vol. 138, 67); Benjamin Quarles, *The Negro in the American Revolution* (New York, London: W.W. Norton & Company, 1973), 15; Library of Congress, George Washington Papers, General Correspondence, 1697–1799, Presidential Papers Microfilm (Washington, DC: Library of Congress, 1961), Series 4, Continental Army War Council, October 8, 1775, Proceedings at Cambridge, Massachusetts; with Copy General Orders, November 12, 1775; John C. Fitzpatrick, ed., *The Writings of George Washington from the Original Manuscript Sources 1745–1799,* vol. 4 (Washington, DC: Government Printing Office, 1936), 292.

6. "Diary of Richard Smith in the Continental Congress, 1775–1776," *American Historical Review*, vol. 1, no. 2 (January 1896), 292.

7. Todd W. Braisted, "The Black Pioneers and Others: The Military Role of Black Loyalists in the American War for Independence," in John W. Pulis (ed.), *Moving On: Black Loyalists in the Afro-Atlantic World* (New York and London: Garland Publishing, Inc., 1999), 8–11; General Orders, December 30, 1775, Fitzpatrick, *Writings of George Washington.*, vol. 4 (1936), 194; Worthington Chauncey Ford, ed., *Journals of the Continental Congress 1774–1789*, vol. 4, 1906 (Washington, DC: Government Printing Office, 1914), 60.

8. John Hannigan, "How Many Men of Color Served on April 19, and from Which Towns? Were They Slaves or Free Men?," *Patriots of Color*, Paper 4, https://www.nps.gov/mima/upload/PoC-Paper-4-SoC-on-April-19-Final-for-Web.pdf; Hannigan, "Soldiers of Color on April 19, 1775," *Patriots of Color*, Appendix, https://www.nps.gov/mima/upload/PoC-Appendix-FINALfor-WEB.pdf; Data gleaned from George Quintal Jr., *"A Peculiar Beauty and Merit": African Americans and American Indians at Battle Road & Bunker Hill* (Boston: Government Printing Office, 2004) and *Massachusetts Soldiers & Sailors of the Revolutionary War*, 17 vols. (Boston: Wright & Potter Printers, 1896–1904).

9. Quintal, *"A Peculiar Beauty and Merit": Bunker Hill*, 201; Charles Parker, *Town of Arlington, Past and Present: A Narrative of Larger Events and Important Changes in the Village Precinct and Town from 1637 to 1907* (Arlington, MA: C. S. Parker & Son, Publishers, 1907), 197.

10. Frederick Mackenzie, *A British Fusilier in Revolutionary Boston*, Allen French, ed. (Cambridge: Harvard University Press, 1926), 58.

11. Quintal, *"A Peculiar Beauty and Merit": Bunker Hill*, 26, 34, 39–41.

12. Quintal, *"A Peculiar Beauty and Merit": Bunker Hill*, 201; Samuel Swett, *History of Bunker Hill Battle: With a Plan* (Boston: Monroe and Francis, 1826), 24.

13. Quintal, *"A Peculiar Beauty and Merit": Bunker Hill*, 159.

14. Quintal, *"A Peculiar Beauty and Merit": Bunker Hill*, 153–56, 159–61. For other New England soldiers see, Rees, *"They Were Good Soldiers,"* 48–81.

15. NARA, Founders Online, William Heath to John Adams, October 23, 1775, https://founders.archives.gov/documents/Adams/06-03-02-0118.

16. Norman Fuss, *Billy Flora at the Battle of Great Bridge*, October 14, 2014, https://allthingsliberty.com/2014/10/billy-flora -at-the-battle-of-great-bridge/); Will Graves and C. Leon Harris, Southern Campaign Revolutionary War Pension Statements & Rosters, Nathan Fry (S39545), http://www.southerncampaign .org/pen/; see original copies of depositions and related materials in NARA Microfilm Publication M804 (2,670 reels).

17. Graves and Harris, Southern Campaign, Nathan Fry (S39545).

18. Graves and Harris, Southern Campaign Pension, Andrew Pebbles (S38297); NARA, Compiled Service Records of Soldiers who Served in the American Army During the Revolutionary War (Microfilm Publication M881), Record Group 93 (Virginia), Andrew Pebbles. For other Southern soldiers see Rees, *"They Were Good Soldiers,"* 108–53.

19. NARA, Pension, reel 2265, William Stacey (40688); Mark Edward Lender and Garry Wheeler Stone, *Fatal Sunday: George Washington, the Monmouth Campaign, and the Politics of Battle* (Norman: University of Oklahoma Press, 2016), 342–47.

20. NARA, Pension, reel 2265, William Stacey (40688).

21. John B. B. Trussell Jr., *The Pennsylvania Line: Regimental Organization and Operations, 1776–1783* (Harrisburg: Pennsylvania Museum and Historical Commission, 1977), 9–20, 85–91; John U. Rees, "'Almost all old soldiers, and well disciplined . . .': Brigadier General Anthony Wayne's 1781 Pennsylvania Provisional Battalions": A. "I fear it is now too late . . .": The Pennsylvania Line Mutiny, January 1781, http://revwar75.com/ library/rees/pdfs/PA-A.pdf); B. "Our Regiments are yet but very small . . .": Settling with the Troops and Rebuilding the Line, http://revwar75.com/library/rees/pdfs/PA-B.pdf); C. "The whole Line . . . behaved in a most orderly manner.": "Reorganizing the Pennsylvania Provisional Battalions and Service in the 1781 Campaign," http://revwar75.com/library/rees/pdfs/PA-C.pdf, *Brigade Dispatch*, vol. XXXVII, no. 2 (Summer 2007), 2–19; vol. XXXVII, no. 4 (Winter 2007), 2–15; vol. XXXVIII, no. 1 (Spring 2008), 2–21.

22. (Pennsylvania) Record Group 33, Records of the Supreme Court Eastern District Revolutionary War Soldiers Claims, 1781–1789, images 216–222, https:// digitalarchives.powerlibrary.org/psa/islandora/object/ psa%3A1795845?overlay_query=RELS_EXT_isMemberOf Collection_uri_ms%3A%22info%3Afedora%2Fpsa%3Arwscrp 1786%22&fbclid=IwAR0FZ9L09mk12kuV90XqbEIdzuWHJ5 _8S_XY4tsjthCHqbwi4U0-nuF6v68).

23. (Pennsylvania) Record Group 33, image 221.

24. Michael A. McDonnell, "'Fit for Common Service?': Class, Race, and Recruitment in Revolutionary Virginia," in John Resch and Walter Sargent, eds., *War & Society in the American Revolution: Mobilization and Home Fronts* (DeKalb: Northern Illinois University Press, 2007), 108. See also, Michael A. McDonnell, *The Politics of War: Race, Class, & Conflict in Revolutionary Virginia* (Chapel Hill: University of North Carolina Press, 2007), 261, 282, 338, 417–18, and Hannigan, "Massachusetts Laws Concerning the Enlistment of Men of Color in the Military" (including emancipation of slaves in return for service, and owners use of enslaved men as substitutes in military service), *Patriots of Color*, Paper 3 (National Park Service, 2014), 8, https://www.nps.gov/mima/upload/PoC-Paper-3-Enslaved -Enlistment-FINAL-for-web.pdf.

25. Hannigan, "Massachusetts Laws Concerning the Enlistment of Men of Color, 6; Richard Hobby, *Massachusetts Soldiers & Sailors*, vol. 8 (1901), 21; Library of Congress, George Washington Papers, Series 4, "Proceedings of a Court of Inquiry,"

February 3, 1783; George Washington Papers, Series 4, David Humphreys to Jonathan Hobby, Newburgh, February 7, 1783.

26. Christopher Ward, *The War of the Revolution*, two vols., vol. 2 (New York: Macmillan, 1952), 671–78; Carl P. Borick, *A Gallant Defense: The Siege of Charleston, 1780* (Columbia: University of South Carolina Press, 2012), 87, 118, 145, 198.

27. Ray W. Pettengill, ed. and trans., *Letters from America 1776–1779: Being Letters of Brunswick, Hessian, and Waldeck Officers with the British Armies during the Revolution* (Port Washington, NY: Kennikat Press, 1964), 119.

28. Evelyn M. Acomb, ed., *The Revolutionary Journal of Baron Ludwig von Closen, 1780–1783* (Chapel Hill: University of North Carolina Press, 1958), 90–92, 102.

29. Acomb, *Journal of Baron Ludwig Von Closen*, xxii–xxvii.

30. Judith L. Van Buskirk, *Standing in Their Own Light: African American Patriots in the American Revolution* (Norman: University of Oklahoma Press, 2017), 68; John U. Rees, "'The pleasure of their number': 1778, Crisis, Conscription, and Revolutionary Soldiers' Recollections," Part I. "'Filling the Regiments by drafts from the Militia.': The 1778 Recruiting Acts," *ALHFAM Bulletin*, vol. XXXIII, no. 3 (Fall 2003), 23–34; no. 4 (Winter 2004), 23–34, https://tinyurl.com/Levies-One.

31. Rees, *"They Were Good Soldiers,"* 20–25. John U. Rees, "'Being a coloured man he was taken as a waiter': Overview of African Americans as Officers' Servants," https://tinyurl.com/ black-waiters. Sampson Coburn (1775) and Thomas Carney (1778) were corporals for a short time. Quintal, *"A Peculiar Beauty and Merit,"* 45, 78; John U. Rees, "Nineteenth Century Remembrances of Black Revolutionary Veterans: Thomas Carney, Maryland Continental Soldier," *Journal of the American Revolution* (online), February 4, 2021, https://allthingsliberty .com/2021/02/nineteenth-century-remembrances-of-black -revolutionary-veterans-thomas-carney-maryland-continent al-soldier/.

32. Hard numbers for Black population in the American colonies, circa 1775–1780, are difficult, but a number of sources give a good idea. Perhaps the most recent is Ray Raphael's *A People's History of the American Revolution: How Common People Shaped the Fight for Independence* (New York: Perennial, 2002; 311, 355) which gives the following totals: slaves, about 430,000 in the Southern colonies, approximately 50,000 in the North. Numbers of free Blacks is even harder to obtain, with a low of 17,900 given by Ray Raphael, to a high of 30,000 postulated by Donald Wright; my decision was to settle on a number between the two. By 1790 there were 59,150 free Blacks and 694,280 enslaved. We do know that during and after the war numbers of free African Americans grew and kept growing, as did numbers of the enslaved. See also table of "Whites, Free Blacks, and Slaves, 1790–1800," based on the 1790 and 1800 censuses inDouglas R. Egerton, *Death or Liberty: African Americans and Revolutionary America* (Oxford and New York: Oxford University Press, 2009), 173. For the total population (white and Black) figure in all the British American colonies of 2.5 million, see Robert L. Middlekauff, *The Glorious Cause— The American Revolution, 1763–1789* (New York and Oxford: Oxford University Press, 1982), 28, 32, and Donald R. Wright, *African Americans in the Early Republic* (Wheeling, IL: Harlan Davidson Inc., 1993), 126. For a discussion of the estimate of 5,000 Black men in Whig forces see Van Buskirk, *Standing in Their Own Light*, 243, note 19. For more on Black seamen see John U. Rees, "They stripped to the waist & fought like devils," https://www.academia.edu/113016514/_They_stripped_to_the _waist_and_fought_like_devils_British_and_American_Sea _Service_1754_1865_.

33. George Washington Papers, Series 4, "Return of the Negroes in the Army," August 24, 1778. This return is transcribed incorrectly in a number of books, one of the most recent being Alan Gilbert's *Black Patriots and Loyalists* (Chicago: University of Chicago Press, 2013), 97 (see 2nd Pennsylvania brigade numbers); an older, but seminal work, Trussell's *Pennsylvania Line* (1977), does not reproduce the return, but also mistakenly notes that the 2nd Pennsylvania brigade contained thirty-five Black soldiers, when, in fact, the number was zero. Rank-and-file numbers found in Charles H. Lesser, *Sinews of Independence: Monthly Strength Reports of the Continental Army* (Chicago and London: University of Chicago Press, 1976), 80–81.

34. Popek, *They ". . . fought bravely,"* 1778 1st Regiment company listings, 211–12.

35. Braisted, "Black Pioneers and Others," 4.

36. David F. Hemmings, "Butler's Rangers (Those Butler's Rangers who also served in, or lived through, the War of 1812)," Compiled for the Niagara Historical Society, Niagara-on-the-Lake, Ontario, Canada, 2012; "Richard Pierpoint National Historic Person (c.1744–c.1838)," https://parks.canada.ca/culture/designation/personnage-person/richard-pierpoint); Frank Mackey, *Done with Slavery: The Black Fact in Montreal, 1760–1840* (Montreal: McGill-Queen's University Press, 2010), 143–44.

37. Don N. Hagist, "Black Drummers in a Redcoat Regiment," *Journal of the American Revolution* (online), February 22, 2022, https://allthingsliberty.com/2022/02/black-drummers-in-a-redcoat-regiment/); Mackey, *Done with Slavery*, 142, 144; Steven M. Baule with Stephen Gilbert, *British Army Officers Who Served in the American Revolution, 1775–1783* (Westminster, MD: Heritage Books, 2004), 153.

38. Todd W. Braisted, "Bernard Griffiths: Trumpeter Barney of the Queen's Rangers, Chelsea Pensioner, and Freed Slave," *Journal of the American Revolution* (online), February 21, 2019, https://allthingsliberty.com/2019/02/bernard-e-griffiths-trumpeter-barney-of-the-queens-rangers/.

39. Braisted, "Bernard Griffiths."

40. "Book of Negroes," Guy Carleton, 1st Baron Dorchester: Papers, The National Archives, Kew (PRO 30/55/100), 10427, https://blackloyalist.com/cdc/documents/official/book_of_negroes.htm; Daniel Green, Discharge Certificate, 38th Regiment of Foot, April 24, 1801 (courtesy of Todd W. Braisted).

41. James W. St. G. Walker, "Myth, History and Revisionism: The Black Loyalists Revisited," *Acadiensis*, vol. 29, no. 1 (1999), 91–92, https://journals.lib.unb.ca/index.php/Acadiensis/article/download/10802/11589?inline=1; Philip R. N. Katcher, *Encyclopedia of British, Provincial, and German Army Units, 1775–1783* (Harrisburg, PA: Stackpole Books, 1973), 31–32.

42. Braisted, "Black Pioneers and Others," 23–27; Michael S. Adler, *The American Revolution in Monmouth County: The Theatre of Spoil and Destruction* (Charleston and London: The History Press, 2010), 84–95.

43. *New York Gazette*, July 21, 1779; Braisted, "Black Pioneers and Others," 16; Quarles, *Negro in the American Revolution*, 112.

44. Lord Dunmore's Proclamation, The Gilder Lehrman Institute of American History, https://www.gilderlehrman.org/sites/default/files/inline-pdfs/01706_fps_1.pdf). In June 1780 Commander in Chief Clinton informed Lord Cornwallis at Charleston that, "'those Negroes who belong to Rebels . . . after serving [the Crown] faithfully during the War are entitled to their Freedom.' Yet, 'while it lasts' Clinton placed them in a kind of ward status as neither slaves nor subjects. They 'belong to the public,' but nevertheless received wages for their 'work in the Departments.'" Sir Henry Clinton, "Philipsburg proclamation," June 30, 1779, Rees, *They Were Good Soldiers,"* 19; Sean Gallagher, "Black

45. Refugees and the Legal Fiction of Military Manumission in the American Revolution," *Slavery & Abolition*, vol. 43, no. 1 (2022), 145.

46. Samuel Johnson, "Taxation No Tyranny: An Answer to the Resolutions and Address of the American Congress," Jean Hagstrum and James Gray, eds., *The Works of Samuel Johnson* (Troy, NY: Pafraets & Company, 1913), vol. 14, 93–144.

46. Gary Sellick, "Black Men, Red Coats: The Carolina Corps, Race, and Society in the Revolutionary British Atlantic," Dissertation, University of South Carolina, 2018, 76–83, https://scholarcommons.sc.edu/etd/4932, 16–17, 33–35, 38–49, 58–59, 71–73, 85, 94.

47. "Book of Negroes" ; "The Importance of the Book of Negroes," February 1, 2017, https://loyalist.lib.unb.ca/atlantic-loyalist-connections/importance-book-negroes). Note, the essay on this website states that the BlackLoyalist.com copy is the British Public Record Office version; Gilbert, *Black Patriots and Loyalists*, 305–6 (note 97). See also, NARA, "Inspection Roll of Negroes Book No. 1," https://catalog.archives.gov/id/17337716); "Inspection Roll of Negroes Book No. 2," https://catalog.archives.gov/id/5890797.

48. Michael Anthony White, "Liberty to Slaves: The Black Loyalist Controversy," Thesis, University of Maine, May 2019, 1–2, https://digitalcommons.library.umaine.edu/cgi/viewcontent.cgi?article=4122&context=etd. White's analysis is based on Graham Russell Hodges, *The Black Loyalist Directory: African Americans in Exile After the American Revolution* (New York: Garland Publishing, 1996), compiled from Tables 1–9, 217–23.

49. "Black Loyalists in the Evacuation of New York City, 1783" (November 15, 2023), https://www.gothamcenter.org/blog/black-loyalists-evacualtion-zy4la); Cassandra Pybus, "Jefferson's Faulty Math: The Question of Slave Defections in the American Revolution," *William and Mary Quarterly*, Third Series, vol. 62, no. 2 (April 2005), 243, 258–63; Sellick, "Black Men, Red Coats," 64 (note 107), 92, 123.

50. Pybus, "Jefferson's Faulty Math," 264.

51. Sellick, "Black Men, Red Coats," 64 (note 106).

52. John W. Pulis, "Bridging Troubled Waters: Moses Baker, George Liele, and the African Diaspora to Jamaica"; Pulis, *Moving On*, xx, 185–86.

53. Sellick, "Black Men, Red Coats," 23.

54. "Return of People Embarked from South Carolina, 13th & 14th Dec., 1782," George Smith McCowen, Jr., *The British Occupation of Charleston, 1780–82* (Columbia: University of South Carolina Press, 1972), 149 (note 72).

55. Boston King, "Memoirs of the Life of Boston King a Black Preacher. Written by Himself, during His Residence at Kingswood School," *Methodist Magazine* (March 1798), 105–10; (April 1798), 157–61; (May 1798), 210–13; (June 1798), 261–65. "Book of Negroes," vol. 1; Katcher, *Encyclopedia*, 93–94.

56. King, "Memoirs," 157.

CHAPTER 4

1. (National Archives) Records of the Office of the Secretary of War, 1791–1947 (Record Group 107, M221), reel 61, William Duane, U.S. Army Adjutant General to Secretary of War John Armstrong, July 12, 1814; Armstrong to Duane, July 15, 1814, "Selections from the Duane Papers," *Historical Magazine*, vol. IV, Second Series (Morrisania, NY: Henry B. Dawson, 1868), 63. Concerning the creation of an all-Black battalion of the U.S. 26th Regiment, and Black soldiers in general, Duane noted, "there are many thousands of free people of color in this state [Pennsylvania] who would make as good soldiers as any in the world." Receiving the letter three days later, Armstrong quickly sent a

reply, stating that raising African American troops en masse "has been much under my consideration, and I have been attempting to sound the depths and shoals of southern prejudice in relation to it. How long shall even history and experience go for nothing! No service in Europe rejects black or coloured men. The nations of Asia and Africa are all such. Our Navy has no scruples of this kind, and yet *we* are more squeamish and stand on the complexion of our rank and file, meagre as it is. We must get over this nonsense, and much more than this, **if we mean to be what we ought to be**."

2. John D. Ellis, "A Revolutionary Activist in His Own Cause: William Afflick of the 10th Hussars," *Westminster History Review 5* (City of Westminster Archives Centre: London, 2007), 25, https://www.academia.edu/40349077/_A_Revolutionary_Activist_in_his_own_cause_William_Afflick_of_the_10th_Hussars_.

3. Pierre Branda and Thierry Lentz, "Napoleon, Slavery, and the Colonies," *Napoleonica, the Journal*, vol. 1, no. 1 (2022), 24–25, 28–31, https://www.cairn-int.info/journal-napoleonica-the-journal-2022-1-page-7.htm.

4. "Decree of the National Convention of 4 February 1794, Abolishing Slavery in All the Colonies," https://revolution.chnm.org/d/291.

5. Branda and Lentz, "Napoleon, Slavery, and the Colonies," 85–96.

6. Roger Norman Buckley, *Slaves in Red Coats: The British West India Regiments, 1795–1815* (New Haven and London: Yale University Press, 1979), 3, 9–12, https://archive.org/details/slavesinredcoats0000buck/page/15/mode/1up?view=theater.

7. Buckley, *Slaves in Red Coats*, 12.

8. Buckley, *Slaves in Red Coats*, 6, 12–13, 55–56; David Lambert, "'Mere Cloak for their Proud Contempt and Antipathy towards the African Race': Imagining Britain's West India Regiments in the Caribbean, 1795–1838," *Journal of Imperial and Commonwealth History*, vol. 46, no. 4 (2018), 629–30; Roger N. Buckley, "Slave or Freedmen: The Question of the Legal Status of the British West India Soldier, 1795–1807," *Caribbean Studies*, vol. 17, nos. 3/4 (1977), 91–92, 107–10; Philip D. Morgan and Andrew O'Shaughnessy, "Arming Slaves in the American Revolution," in Christopher Leslie Brown and Philip D. Morgan, eds., *Arming Slaves, from Classical Times to the Modern Age* (New Haven and London: Yale University Press, 2006), 180; Timothy Lockley, "Creating the West India Regiments," The British Library, UK (November 16, 2017), https://www.bl.uk/west-india-regiment/articles/creating-the-west-india-regiments.

9. John D. Ellis, "George Rose—An Exemplary Soldier, 73rd and 42nd Foot, 1809–1837," https://www.historycalroots.com/george-rose-an-exemplary-soldier/.

10. John D. Ellis, "From Nova-Scotia to Liverpool, via the Battlefields of the Napoleonic War: The Travels and Travails of Drummer George Wise of the 29th (Worcestershire) Regiment of Foot," https://www.historycalroots.com/george-wise-from-nova-scotia-to-liverpool-via-the-battlefields-of-the-napoleonic-wars/.

11. Ellis, "From Nova-Scotia to Liverpool; "Battle of Hampden," https://en.wikipedia.org/wiki/Battle_of_Hampden.

12. John D. Ellis, "'No Longer Concealed': The Career of Private Edward Baptist, a Black Bandsman in the 44th (East Essex) Regiment of Foot," https://www.academia.edu/37837565/_No_Longer_Concealed_The_Career_of_Private_Edward_Baptist_a_Black_bandsman_in_the_44th_East_Essex_Regiment_of_Foot).

13. Frank Mackey, *Done with Slavery: The Black Fact in Montreal, 1760–1840* (Montreal: McGill-Queen's University Press, 2010), 205–6.

14. Mackey, *Done with Slavery*, 203–5.

15. Wayne Edward Kelly. "Race and Segregation in the Upper Canada Militia," *Journal of the Society for Army Historical Research*, vol. 78, no. 316 (2000), 266–67; Gareth Newfield, "The Coloured Corps: Black Canadians and the War of 1812," https://www.thecanadianencyclopedia.ca/en/article/the-coloured-corps-african-canadians-and-the-war-of-1812.

16. Mackey, *Done with Slavery*, 194–95, 206, 206–8.

17. George F. G. Stanley, *The War of 1812: Land Operations* (Toronto: Macmillan of Canada, 1983), 4.

18. "Militia Act of 1792," https://www.mountvernon.org/education/primary-source-collections/primary-source-collections/article/militia-act-of-1792/. Subsumed by the February 28, 1795 "Act to provide for calling forth the militia to execute the laws of the Union, suppress insurrections, and repel invasions and to repeal the act now in force for those purposes," https://www.loc.gov/resource/rbpe.22201300/?st=gallery.

19. New York State Library, Cherry Hill Collection, doc. AHC04, Henry Knox, "Recruiting Instructions for Captain Jedediah Rodgers," May 7, 1792, https://wardepartmentpapers.org/s/home/item/78279); Filson Club, Louisville, KY, Manuscript Dept., Preston Family Papers—Joyes Collection, doc. CSB05, James McHenry, "Recruiting Instructions for Captain William Preston of the 4th Sub Legion at Lynchburg Virginia," July 18, 1796, https://wardepartmentpapers.org/s/home/item/54330; James McHenry (secretary of war), *Rules and Regulations Respecting the Recruiting Service, By John Adams, President of the United States* (1798), 4; NARA, Founders Online, William Bentley to Alexander Hamilton, September 19, 1799, https://founders.archives.gov/documents/Hamilton/01-23-02-0410; A. R. Hetzel, comp., *Military Laws of the United States; Including Those Relating to the Army, Marine Corps, Volunteers, Militia, and to Bounty Lands and Pensions*, 3rd ed. (Washington, DC: Published by George Templeman, 1846), 41–42 ("An act for regulating the Military Establishment of the United States," April 30, 1790), 57–58 ("An act for continuing and regulating the Military Establishment of the United States, and for repealing sundry acts heretofore passed on that subject," March 3, 1795), 62–63 ("An act to ascertain and fix the military establishment of the United States," May 30, 1796), 99, 102 ("An act fixing the military peace establishment of the United States," March 16, 1802), 156–57 ("An act supplementary to the act, entitled: An act for the more perfect organization of the army of the United States," January 30, 1813), 178 ("An act making further provisions for filling the ranks of the army of the United States," December 10, 1814), 183–84 ("An act fixing the military peace establishment of the United States," March 3, 1815), 295 ("An act more effectually to provide for the national defence, by establishing an uniform militia throughout the United States," May 8, 1792).

20. Anthony Gero, *Black Soldiers of New York State: A Proud Legacy* (Albany: State University of New York Press, 2009), 12.

21. Gene Allen Smith, *The Slaves' Gamble: Choosing Sides in the War of 1812* (New York: Palgrave Macmillan, 2013), 137.

22. NARA, Records of the Adjutant General's Office, 1780s–1917 (RG 94), War of 1812 Service Record Index, 1812–1815 (M602), Africa Peterson; NARA (RG 94), Army Register of Enlistments, 1798–1914 (M233), "Records of Men Enlisted in the U.S. Army Prior to the Peace Establishment, May 17, 1815," George Graves, Fortune Howland, John Lyndes, https://www.fold3.com/publication/891/us-army-register-of-enlistments-1798-1914. Gene Allen Smith names six possible Black soldiers in the 11th, 30th, 31st, and 34th regiments. None are specifically noted as men of color, but all are listed as having a black complexion, most with black eyes and hair, as well. Smith, *Slaves' Gamble*, 139.

23. NARA, "Records of Men Enlisted in the U.S. Army Prior to the Peace Establishment, May 17, 1815," Jacob Dexter, William Lynes/Lines; John U. Rees, "'She had gone to the Army . . . to her husband': Judith Lines' Unremarked Life," in Don N. Hagist, ed., *Journal of the American Revolution, Annual Volume 2022* (Yardley, PA: Westholme Publishing, 2022), 232–43, https://allthingsliberty.com/2021/04/she-had-gone-to-the-army-to-her-husband-judith-liness-unremarked-life/.

24. NARA, "Records of Men Enlisted in the U.S. Army Prior to the Peace Establishment, May 17, 1815," William Lynes/Lines.

25. Anon., *Official Correspondence with the Department of War, Relative to the Military Operations of the American Army Under the Command of Major General Izard of the Northern Frontier of the United States, in the Years 1814 and 1815* (Philadelphia: William Fry, Printer, 1816), 45–47.

26. Smith, *Slaves' Gamble*, 139, 237 (note 41).

27. NARA, "Records of Men Enlisted in the U.S. Army Prior to the Peace Establishment, May 17, 1815," Richard Boyington.

28. "Greeting the African American War of 1812 Veterans, New Orleans, April 18, 1825," https://sites.lafayette.edu/slavery/farewell-tour/farewell-tour-documents/.

29. "Greeting the African American War."

CHAPTER 5

1. Sgt. John Collins, 54th Massachusetts, South Carolina, January 24, 1865, "As I write it rains quite hard, and has done so for some days. The mud is quite deep, and our shelter very poor, and it is very hard living at this time. We are all destitute of clothes, and some of us have not as much as a shoe upon our feet, but when we look at the suffering condition of the poor slaves, we can stand all: only give us our liberty and freedom, and we will give our lives for liberty, for we love that well-known sound." Edwin S. Redkey. ed., *A Grand Army of Black Men: Letters from African-American Soldiers in the Union Army, 1861–1865* (Cambridge, UK: Cambridge University Press, 1992), 69–71.

2. Frederick Douglass, "If there is no struggle, there is no progress," 1857, https://www.blackpast.org/african-american-history/1857-frederick-douglass-if-there-no-struggle-there-no-progress/.

3. Douglass, "If there is no struggle."

4. "The Missouri Compromise," https://billofrightsinstitute.org/essays/the-missouri-compromise; Ibram X. Kendi, *Stamped from the Beginning: The Definitive History of Racist Ideas in America* (New York: Bold Type Books, 2016), 172–73; James M. McPherson, *Battle Cry of Freedom: The Civil War Era* (New York: Ballantine Books, 1989), 154–69.

5. McPherson, *Battle Cry of Freedom*, 205–13, 221–33, 264–75.

6. NARA, "Records of Men Enlisted in the U.S. Army Prior to the Peace Establishment, May 17, 1815," Richard Boyington; "John C. Calhoun (March 18, 1782–March 31, 1850)," https://www.clemson.edu/about/history/bios/john-c-calhoun.html; Anon., *Official Correspondence with the Department of War, Relative to the Military Operations of the American Army Under the Command of Major General Izard of the Northern Frontier of the United States, in the Years 1814 and 1815* (Philadelphia: William Fry, Printer, 1816), 45–47.

7. Andrew Jackson Papers, February 18, 1820 (document courtesy of Matthew C. White); Jack D. Foner, *Blacks and the Military in American History: A New Perspective* (New York and Washington: Praeger Publishers, 1974), 27.

8. Foner, *Blacks and the Military in American History*, 27 ; Winfield Scott, *General regulations for the Army, or, Military Institutes* (Philadelphia: M. Carey and Sons, 1821), 312 ("All free white male persons, above eighteen and under thirty-five years, who are able bodied, active, and free from disease, may be enlisted"); Robert E. May, "Invisible Men: Blacks and the U.S. Army in the Mexican War," *Historian*, vol. 49, no. 4 (1987), 463–77. A very small number of Black men did serve in state volunteer units, most notably Jacob Dodson, with a company of the California Battalion under John C. Fremont.

9. "An act to provide for calling forth the militia to execute the laws of the Union, suppress insurrections, and repel invasions and to repeal the act now in force for those purposes," February 28, 1795, https://www.loc.gov/resource/rbpe.22201300/?st=gallery. Reference is made to the 1795 militia act in, "Militia Act, July 17, 1862," https://history.iowa.gov/history/education/educator-resources/primary-source-sets/african-americans-and-civil-war/militia-act; Noah Andre Trudeau, *Like Men of War: Black Troops in the Civil War, 1862–1865* (Boston, New York, London: Little, Brown and Company, 1998), 7–8.

10. Trudeau, *Like Men of War*, 7, 11–12; "H. Ford Douglass," https://coloredconventions.org/black-illinois-organizing/delegates/ford-douglas/#:~:text=He%20was%20mustered%20into%20the,of%20the%20time%20in%20Louisiana; "Guide to African American Resources at the Pennsylvania State Archives," https://www.phmc.state.pa.us/bah/aaGuide/AA-RG-19.html); Redkey, *Grand Army of Black Men*, 9–25. See also Juanita Patience Moss, *Forgotten Black Soldiers Who Served in White Regiments during the Civil War* (Westminster, MD: Heritage Books, Inc., 2008).

11. Redkey, *Grand Army of Black Men*, 266–68.

12. Trudeau, *Like Men of War*, 8.

13. Confederate Vice-President Alexander Stephens, 1861, "The new Constitution has put at rest forever all the agitating questions relating to our peculiar institutions—African slavery as it exists among us—the proper status of the negro in our form of civilization," Frank Moore, ed., *Rebellion Record: A Diary of American Events, with Documents, Narratives, Illustrative Incidents, Poetry, etc.*, vol. I, (New York: G.P. Putnam, 1861), following page 108, "Documents and Narratives," 44–46; "Constitution of the Confederate States; March 11, 1861," Art. 1, Sec. 9; Art. 4, Sec. 2, https://avalon.law.yale.edu/19th_century/csa_csa.asp; Michael P. Johnson, ed., *Abraham Lincoln, Slavery, and the Civil War: Selected Speeches and Writings* (Boston: Bedford/St. Martin's, 2001), 63; McPherson, *Battle Cry of Freedom*, 769.

14. William A. Dobak, *Freedom by the Sword: The U.S. Colored Troops, 1862–1867* (New York: Skyhorse Publishing, 2013), 30–47, 164; John Paul Ringquist, "Color No Longer a Sign of Bondage: Race, Identity and the First Kansas Colored Volunteer Infantry Regiment (1862–1865)," Dissertation, University of Kansas, 2011, 30.

15. "Militia Act, July 17, 1862," sections 12–15.

16. Dobak, *Freedom by the Sword*, 164–67; Ringquist, "Color No Longer a Sign of Bondage," 41.

17. Ira Berlin, Joseph P. Reidy, Leslie S. Rowland, eds., *Freedom's Soldiers: The Black Military Experience in the Civil War* (Cambridge, New York, and Melbourne: Cambridge University Press, 1998), 91–92, 124–25, 126–28; "Militia Act, July 17, 1862," section 15; Ira Berlin, ed. (Joseph P. Reidy, Leslie S. Rowland, assoc. eds.), *Freedom: A Documentary History of Emancipation, 1861–1867* (Cambridge, London, and New York: Cambridge University Press, 1982), 362–68 (see also note 8).

18. War Department to Lorenzo Thomas, March 25, 1863, U.S. War Department, *The War of the Rebellion: A Compilation of the Official Records of the Union and Confederate Armies* (Washington, DC: Government Printing Office, 1902), Series 3, vol. 3, 100–103.

19. Dobak, *Freedom by the Sword*, 167–71, 179.

20. "War Department General Order 143: Creation of the U.S. Colored Troops (1863)," https://www.archives.gov/milestone-documents/war-department-general-order-143; Dobak, *Freedom by the Sword*, 312, 384; Edward W. Duffy, "Come and Join Us Brothers: the Legacy of Camp William Penn," June 16, 2023, https://hiddencityphila.org/2023/06/come-and-join-us-brothers-the-legacy-of-camp-william-penn/; "Camp Casey," February 26, 2015, https://rpwrhs.org/w/index.php?title=Camp_Casey.

21. Dobak, *Freedom by the Sword*, 21–22, 447, 499–500; Joseph T. Glatthaar, *Forged in Battle: The Civil War Alliance of Black Soldiers and White Officers* (New York: The Free Press, 1990), 81–84.

22. Redkey, *Grand Army of Black Men*, 261–62.

23. Dobak, *Freedom by the Sword*, 100–101.

24. Dobak, *Freedom by the Sword*, 101.

25. Dobak, *Freedom by the Sword*, 102; Glatthaar, *Forged in Battle*, 176–82, 279–80; Berlin, Reidy, and Rowland, *Freedom: A Documentary History*, 310–11.

26. Dobak, *Freedom by the Sword*, 194, 196, 504–5.

27. Dobak, *Freedom by the Sword*, 67–68; "Letter from Lt. Oliver Norton, 8th United States Colored Troops," February 29, 1864, https://battleofolustee.org/letters/onorton.html.

28. Thomas Wentworth Higginson, "Army Life in a Black Regiment," *Army Life in a Black Regiment and Other Writings* (originally published in 1870—New York: Penguin Books, 1997), 206, https://www.gutenberg.org/files/6764/6764-h/6764-h.htm; Trudeau, *Like Men of War*, 214; Dobak, *Freedom by the Sword*, 205, 209.

29. Dobak, *Freedom by the Sword*, 208

30. Dobak, *Freedom by the Sword*, 186.

31. Berlin, Reidy, and Rowland, *Freedom: A Documentary History*, 585.

32. Berlin, Reidy, and Rowland, *Freedom: A Documentary History*, 585.

33. Berlin, Reidy, and Rowland, *Freedom: A Documentary History*, 185–86, 187–88, 244–45, 444.

34. Berlin, Reidy, and Rowland, *Freedom: A Documentary History*, 244–45.

35. Kevin M. Levin, *Searching for Black Confederates: The Civil War's Most Persistent Myth* (Chapel Hill: University of North Carolina Press, 2019), 12–35, 37–67, 57–60; Colin Edward Woodward, "Marching Masters: Slavery, Race, and the Confederate Army, 1861–1865," Dissertation, Louisiana State University, May 2005, 32–35, 105–113. See also "Arming the Enslaved? March 13, 1865," https://www.nps.gov/rich/arming-the-enslaved.htm.

36. Dobak, *Freedom by the Sword*, 91–92; "1st Louisiana Native Guard (Confederate)," https://en.wikipedia.org/wiki/1st_Louisiana_Native_Guard_(Confederate); Krewasky A. Salter, *The Story of Black Military Officers, 1861–1948* (New York: Routledge, 2014), see chapter 1; John V. Quarstein, "Capture of New Orleans: Farragut's Rise to Fame," https://www.marinersmuseum.org/2020/07/capture-of-new-orleans-farraguts-rise-to-fame/.

37. Howard C. Westwood, "Benjamin Butler's Enlistment of Black Troops in New Orleans in 1862," *Louisiana History: The Journal of the Louisiana Historical Association*, vol. 26, no. 1 (Winter 1985), 5–22; Dobak, *Freedom by the Sword*, 94, 96, 99–102, 104–9, 213 (note 7); Trudeau, *Like Men of War*, 23–46; Donald E. Everett, "Ben Butler and the Louisiana Native Guards, 1861–1862," *Journal of Southern History*, vol. 24, no. 2 (May 1958), 202–17; "An address substantially as delivered before the Young Men's Christian Commission at Boston, October 30, 1864; and at Charlestown, Mass., November 1, 1864," Nathaniel P. Banks, *Emancipated Labor in Louisiana* (New York, 1864-1865), 34–35.

38. Dobak, *Freedom by the Sword*, 10–11, 549–52.

39. Berlin, Reidy, and Rowland, *Freedom: A Documentary History*, 12, 14–15.

40. Rees, "They stripped to the waist & fought like devils," https://www.academia.edu/113016514/_They_stripped_to_the_waist_and_fought_like_devils_British_and_American_Sea_Service_1754_1865_.

41. Dobak, *Freedom by the Sword*, 22–23.

42. Higginson, "Army Life in a Black Regiment," 206.

AFTERWORD

1. Higginson, "Army Life in a Black Regiment," 505; Trudeau, *Like Men of War*, 37.

2. Eric Foner notes, "Perhaps the remarkable thing about Reconstruction was not that it failed, but that it was attempted at all and survived as long as it did." Eric Foner, *Reconstruction: America's Unfinished Revolution, 1863–1877* (New York: Harper & Row, 1988), 603; NARA, "Executive Order 9981: Desegregation of the Armed Forces (1948)," https://www.archives.gov/milestone-documents/executive-order-9981; "African-Americans in the Korean War," https://koreanwarlegacy.org/chapters/african-americans-in-the-korean-war/.

Suggested Further Reading

The appended resources continue the story of American Black soldiers up to and including the 1965–1975 Vietnam War. Only one work used as a source for the narrative is included below; for deeper reading on the period covered by this work, please refer to the books and monographs cited in the endnotes.

United States

CIVIL WAR

Dobak, William A. *Freedom by the Sword: The U.S. Colored Troops, 1862–1867*. New York: Skyhorse Publishing, 2013, https://history.army.mil/html/books/030/30-24/cmh_pub_30-24.pdf.

Urwin, Gregory J. W. *Black Flag Over Dixie: Racial Atrocities and Reprisals in the Civil War*. Carbondale: Southern Illinois University Press, 2004.

RECONSTRUCTION AND POST–CIVIL WAR

Foner, Eric. *Reconstruction Updated Edition: America's Unfinished Revolution, 1863–1877*. New York: Harper & Row, 1988; also available in a 2015 abridged edition.

Shaffer, Donald R. *After the Glory: The Struggles of Black Civil War Veterans*. Lawrence: University Press of Kansas, 2004.

POST–CIVIL WAR TO PHILIPPINE INSURRECTION

Dobak, William A., and Thomas D. Phillips. *The Black Regulars, 1866–1898*. Norman: University of Oklahoma Press, 2001.

Gatewood, Willard B., Jr. *"Smoked Yankees" and the Struggle for Empire: Letters from Negro Soldiers, 1898–1902*. Fayetteville: University of Arkansas Press, 1987.

FIRST WORLD WAR

Slotkin, Richard. *Lost Battalions: The Great War and the Crisis of American Nationality*. New York: Henry Holt and Company, 2005.

SECOND WORLD WAR

Barksdale, Sarah Ayako. "Stationed in the Borderlands: A Study of Black World War II Soldiers in Combat Arms." Thesis: University of North Carolina at Chapel Hill, 2009, https://cdr.lib.unc.edu/concern/dissertations/ns064698c.

Delmont, Matthew F. *Half American: The Epic Story of African Americans Fighting World War II at Home and Abroad*. New York: Viking Books, 2022.

Lee, Ulysses. *The Employment of Negro Troops*. Washington, DC: Government Printing Office, 2001; discussion of the 1945 Black Volunteer Infantry Replacements, 688–705, https://history.army.mil/html/books/011/11-4/CMH_Pub_11-4-1.pdf.

Motley, Mary P. *The Invisible Soldier: The Experience of the Black Soldier, World War II*. Detroit: Wayne State University Press, 1987.

KOREAN WAR

Cline, David P. *Twice Forgotten: African Americans and the Korean War, an Oral History*. Chapel Hill: University of North Carolina Press, 2021.

VIETNAM WAR

Terry, Wallace. *Bloods: Black Veterans of the Vietnam War, An Oral History*. Novato, CA: Presidio Press, 1985.

Canada, 1861–1945

Prince, Bryan. *My Brother's Keeper: African Canadians and the American Civil War*. Toronto: Dundurn Press, 2015.

Reid, Richard M. *African Canadians in Union Blue: Volunteering for the Cause in America's Civil War*. Vancouver: University of British Columbia Press, 2014.

Ruck, Calvin W. *The Black Battalion, 1916–1920: Canada's Best Kept Military Secret*. Halifax, NS: Nimbus Publishing, Ltd., 1987.

Shaw, Melissa N. "'Most Anxious to Serve their King and Country': Black Canadians' Fight to Enlist in WWI and Emerging Race Consciousness in Ontario, 1914–1919." *Histoire Sociale/Social History*, vol. XLIX, no. 100 (November 2016), 543–80.

Theobald, Simon James. "A False Sense of Equality: The Black Canadian Experience of the Second World War." Thesis: University of Ottawa, 2008, https://ruor.uottawa.ca/bitstream/10393/27791/1/MR48629.PDF.